M000280819

COCKTAIL INFOGRAPHICS

A visual guide to creating 200 of the world's best cocktails

PUBLISHER'S NOTE: In this book, one measure is equal to one jigger. For more infornation on jiggers, please see p.28.

THIS IS A CARLTON BOOK

This edition first published in Great Britain in 2016 by Carlton Books
An imprint of the Carlton Publishing Group
20 Mortimer Street
London W1T 3JW

A CIP catalogue for this book is available from the British Library.

Project editor: Charlotte Selby
Design manager: Lucy Palmer
Layout: Gemma Wilson
Production: Maria Petalidou

ISBN 978-1-78097-815-4

Printed in China

The text in this book previously appeared in
The Complete Cocktail Guide 2003

10 9 8 7 6 5 4 3 2 1

COCKTAIL INFOGRAPHICS

A visual guide to creating 200 of the world's best cocktails

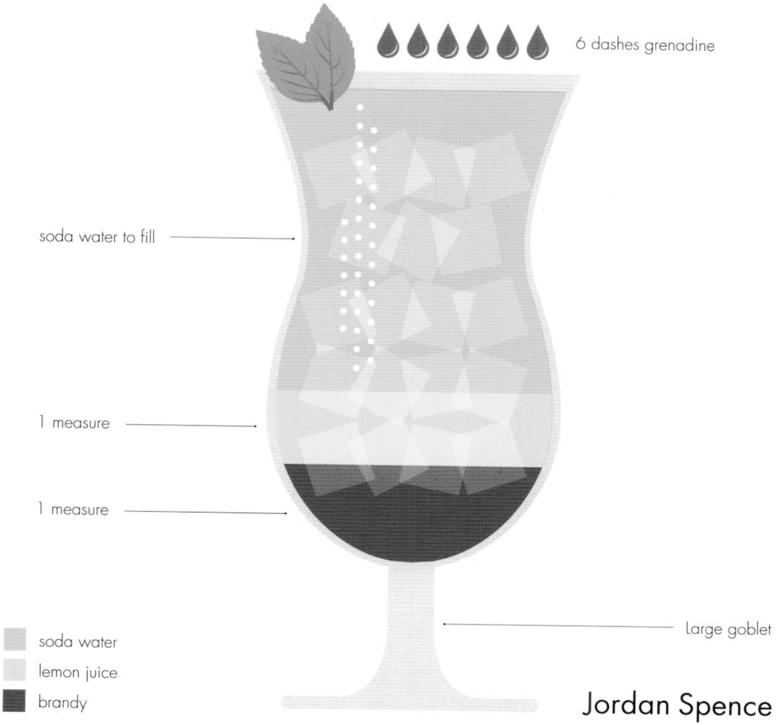

6 dashes grenadine

soda water to fill

1 measure

1 measure

Large goblet

soda water
lemon juice
brandy

Jordan Spence

CARLTON
BOOKS

CONTENTS

INTRODUCTION

Cocktails are cool once again. The very word "cocktail" conjures up an image of a glass with an elegant stem, chilled to the perfect temperature and filled with a shimmering pale-coloured liquid. It is a timeless work of art when created with the skill of a genuine bartender, not a mixologist.

Cocktails come from a world of cursory glances, social chit-chat, cocktail party LBDs worn with *Sex and the City* stilettos, shining with diamanté clips, waiters in white jackets proferring trays of fancy finger food, instantly at your beck and call – a world apart from the everyday! The cocktail encapsulates all of these fantasies.

Having stepped out of the speakeasy culture into the mainstream around the 1950s, cocktails cruised along through the 1980s and 1990s, and shook themselves into the twenty-first century with classics such as the Sidecar still in demand. As for the Martini, it has been reinvented countless times in recent years, and one begins to wonder when a Martini is not a Martini! Certainly the discussions as to what makes the prefect dry Martini still fill the cigar smoke-filled air in bars around the world.

When created thoughtfully, a cocktail can bring a range of taste sensations to your palate; it can stimulate taste memories of a flavour savoured long ago, bringing a lump to the throat. Open a bottle of vintage champagne and all the aromas of a far-flung foreign field fill the nose as you sniff the contents. Open a bottle of pure vodka made by a boutique company such as Ketel One or Grey Goose, and a host of flavours will waft by. Like a fine wine, a balanced cocktail satisfies the senses: taste, aroma, colour and sight, each discovered sip by sip.

Drink wisely. And remember, there is no cure for a hangover. Cheers!

A–Z OF COCKTAILS

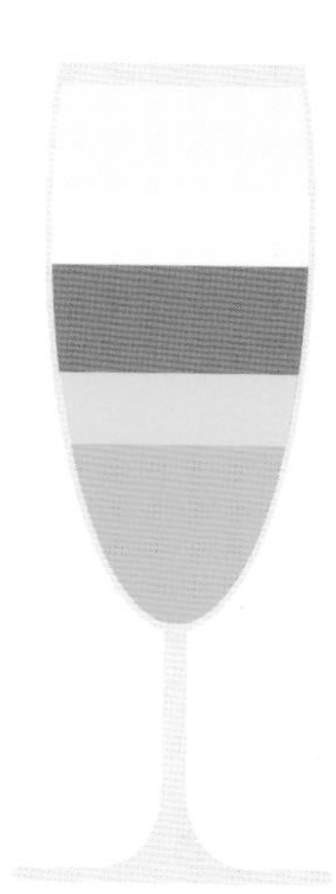

THE WELL-STOCKED BAR

Every professional or home bar requires a basic collection of spirits before interesting mixed drinks and cocktails can be made. Always buy the best quality brands to be assured of the purest taste. As with most things, good quality can be found at reasonable prices.

Ice

Ice cools the spirit as it is poured into a glass. All ice must be fresh. Only filtered, or even bottled, water should be used to make ice. There are four types of ice used in cocktails: crushed, shaved, cracked or cubed. Ice can be used in a blender, a shaker, a mixing glass or directly in a glass, but cubes should not be served in a cocktail glass. Cracked and shaved ice are more watery than cubes and they dilute the spirit more quickly than cubes. Use cubes in a shaker and crushed ice in a blender. Don't put ice from a blender into the glass.

Bar necessities

Spirits

Bourbon

Brandy

Gin

Pimm's No. 1 Cup

Rum, light and dark

Tequila, white (silver) and gold

Vodka

Whisky

Liqueurs

Amaretto

Baileys Irish Cream

Cointreau

Crème de menthe (white and green)

Crème de cacao (white and brown)

Curaçao, blue

Grand Marnier

Wines

Champagne (or sparkling wine)

Vermouths, dry and sweet

Wine, red and white

Extras

- Coconut cream
- Cream, double
- Egg-white powder*
- Tabasco sauce
- Worcestershire sauce
- Pepper
- Salt
- Sugar, caster

* Use instead of fresh egg white if preferred

Syrups

 Gomme syrup

 Grenadine

Bitters

 Angostura

Spoiling yourself
At home your cocktail menu can be as adventurous or conservative as you like

Whisky

How do you like your whisky? Scotch, American, Canadian or Irish? With a few pretenders in between, there is an incredible choice of types, blended or malts. Each method of distillation is just different enough to ensure that the taste experience is always varied.

Scotch whisky is brewed in the northern, eastern, western and central Highlands regions of Scotland, in Speyside (a premier malt whisky region on its own) and on the islands off the mainland, including Islay, Mull, Jura and the Orkneys. The Lowlands and Campbeltown also produce whisky. In the U.S., it centres on the Southern states of Kentucky and Tennessee.

Deer friend:
The Glenfiddich stag is one of the best-known Scotch whisky labels

Whisky is made from grain, water and yeast. The difference in taste and colour come from the distillation methods employed by the producer. Some of the variations are: pot still or patent still; types of yeast; the kinds of wood used for ageing, and the size of the barrel; how long the spirit is in the barrel; the source of the pure water; the type of cereal grains used (barley, corn, wheat, rye or oats). Flavour and its amber colour are added during the maturation process when the liquid is placed in wood (usually oak) vats or casks.

Scotch must be aged a minimum of three years. In the U.S., federal law states that bourbon must be aged for at least two years.

What do you look for in a whisky? Purity. Colour ranges from light amber to honey and a deeper chestnut brown. Malts are paler versions, whereas bourbons are darker, almost reddish. Kentucky bourbons and Tennessee whiskies are generally sweeter than Scotch; Irish whiskeys are like a light Scotch; and Canadian types, produced in Ottawa and Montreal, are easy-drinking, probably because the majority of the grain is corn. Japan is also a big producer of whisky, but mainly for domestic consumption.

Rum

The light rum industry is almost as large as, if not equal to, the vodka industry. Rum is a great mixer, the taste behind great cocktails filled with fresh fruit juices. Without rum we would have no Daiquiri, Piña Colada or Rum Punch, and the world would be an even sadder place than it is.

Rum is, along with tourism, a major industry in the Caribbean. This time-honoured nectar is made from sugarcane, and it has been a favourite drink of sailors for centuries. Islands in the Caribbean are dotted with vast plantations growing sugarcane to meet the demands of distilleries. Rum is produced from molasses, and is the byproduct of manufacturing raw sugar from sugarcane. The molasses is turned into alcohol by the process of fermentation. The alcohol is then distilled and becomes clear and colourless.

The spirit is aged in small oak barrels, whether the resulting rum is white or dark. Wood is porous and lets the rum spirit breathe, and with each breath, oxidation takes place. Light rum is matured in pale ash-wood barrels for one year only and then it is transferred to steel vats where it is left to age longer. Dark rum types are in the barrel for three years and longer (some for up to 20 years), after which, distillers believe, they start to lose flavour.

Rum Types

White
Also known as silver or light, it is clear and light, and has a dry flavour.

Gold
Also oro or ambré, it is sweeter, with the colour gained from the oak cask or sometimes from the addition of caramel colouring.

Dark
Also black, this type has been aged in a charred barrel.

Premium Aged/Añejo/ Rhum Vieux
Valued by connoisseurs, these are the pick-of-the-crop mature rums.

Flavoured and Spiced
These types are served with fruit juice or a mixer.

Overproof
The white types are used for blending.

Single Marks
These are rare, unblended rums produced by individual distilleries and are sought after. You don't often see them on top shelves.

Most rums are blended from a selection of aged rums and from different styles of rum. How much caramel and flavouring, and which spices are to be added, are up to the blender. Once the mix has been ordained, it is diluted with water to the required bottling strength.

Rum is made all over the world. But it should not be confused with cachaça. This is a spirit distilled in Brazil, made from molasses, sugarcane juice, or a combination of both. Cachaça is probably best known as the spirit underlying the delicious Caipirinha (see p. 37).

Ready for a caning
Molasses and raw sugar come from the cane, and from molasses comes rum

Gin

Gin, known as "Mother's Ruin" in England, has been produced since the 1600s, when the Dutch first produced this full-flavoured spirit. Then it was a distilled grain spirit flavoured with juniper berries, which were thought to have beneficial effects on problems with the kidney and the bladder.

Early gins, such as Old Tom, were more like sweet cordial-type spirits. But, in Britain, over many decades it lost its sweetness to become London Dry in style. Gin was introduced to Britain when British soldiers returned from the series of wars on the European mainland.

In the seventeenth and eighteenth centuries gin was so popular that the government was forced to take control of its production by legislation – the streets and public houses were full of too many gin-soaked people. In 1736 the distilleries were taxed; they, in turn, raised the price for drinkers; 20 years later the distillation of corn was outlawed, and a series of riots ensued. It took until 1760 for the laws to be repealed. Gin was not a respectable drink at that time, and it took decades for it to gain respectability in high society. It's a different matter these days.

The best gin is recognized as that made from a grain spirit – preferably corn – and contains very few impurities. Any gin made with a molasses spirit will taste slightly sweeter. Most gin is made in a continuous still to produce the 96 per cent alcohol by volume ratio required. Once this is achieved, the spirit is redistilled. The second distillation involves the spirit being distilled along with natural botanicals to produce a subtle premium gin.

When you pour a measure of gin, you get a whiff of the aroma instantly. Gin has a neutral-grain base and it is the addition of botanicals that gives gin its character. Each of the contemporary brands is blended to produce an individual taste.

If you have a refined palate, you might taste some of the following herbs in the gin: aniseed, angelica, coriander seeds, juniper berries, ginger, almonds, orange rind, cardamom, cinnamon or liquorice root. For example, extra-dry gins usually contain more angelica or liquorice, whereas gins with a dominant citrus flavour have more orange or lemon peel. The gin is then reduced to bottling strength, 75 proof in America and 35 per cent alcohol by volume (ABV) in Europe.

Many of the best-known classic cocktails are made with gin: the original Martini, Gibson, Pink Gin, Singapore Sling and White Lady.

Basically, there are four types of gin: Dry gin (unsweetened), London Dry gin (unsweetened), Old Tom gin (slightly sweetened), and Plymouth gin (slightly sweetened). Although you may have to search off-licences for Old Tom gin, the other types are generally available.

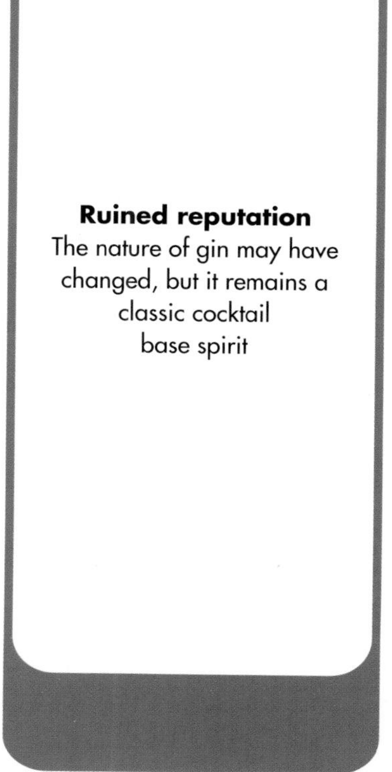

Ruined reputation
The nature of gin may have changed, but it remains a classic cocktail base spirit

Vodka

According to Pablo Picasso in 1950, "The three most astonishing things in the past half-century have been the blues, cubism and Polish vodka." He may well have been right. Vodka, Polish or otherwise, is the perfect base spirit for a cocktail because it is colourless, tasteless and odourless.

Pass someone an orange drink and they'd never know that underneath this colourful exterior might lie the world's "most drunk" spirit. Nearly everybody in the world of drinking age has had a sip of vodka and many of today's drinkers are brand loyal, preferring the flavour and style of one vodka over any other.

Vodka first came into America's consciousness after World War II when Heublein began to distribute Smirnoff vodka. Its advertising played up vodka's very tastelessness and, before you knew it, the classic Martini kissed gin goodbye and became a vodka-based cocktail. We have Ian Fleming's charismatic character, James Bond, to thank for that. Yet, the Bloody Mary (with or without the celery) was born using vodka, just like the ubiquitous Harvey Wallbanger and the Screwdriver.

The name "vodka" derives from the Russian word for water, voda. There is a long history associated with this spirit, allegedly born in Russia. Or was it? Scandinavians and Poles claim vodka was made as early as, or even earlier than, the era claimed by the Russians – the fourteenth century.

Note
Vodka should be served chilled, between 2 and 6°C (35–43°F), never higher than 10°C (50°F). Because the aroma of vodka is not perceptible when chilled, distillers put the greatest emphasis on taste.

As a general rule, spirit production uses starchy materials (potatoes and grains such as rye, wheat, barley, millet or corn) and sugary materials (molasses, sugar beets, fruit). However, vodka made in America is pure grain neutral spirit distilled from fermented corn, rye or wheat, which is distilled in a continuous still. Charcoal filtration results in a clear and clean-tasting product. In Europe rye grain is traditionally the main ingredient.

New vodkas, aimed at the connoisseur in the same way as Armagnac, Cognac and whisky, are distilled up to three times, and then a trace of a separately distilled, lower-strength spirit may be added for character. These types are best taken from a shot glass.

Flavoured vodkas are also creating an interest. Blackcurrant, cherry, pineapple, lemon, orange, peach and pepper are just some of the flavours on offer. Flavouring spirit can be a very simple process and distillers are secretive about the processes they use. In Poland, flavourings such as fruit and herbs are generally prepared in two ways, using either the classic maceration or the circulation method. With the classic method, ingredients are macerated in spirit which varies in strength (usually 40–60 per cent ABV), according to the type and ripeness of the ingredients.

After the first four weeks, the spirit is drained (and reserved), with another batch of spirit added for a further three-week maceration. These two liquids are blended, together with a residual liquid pressed from the macerated ingredients. Prior to bottling, all three "spirits" are then adjusted to ensure a standard alcoholic strength.

The circulation method uses ingredients such as bison grass spread across a sieve inside a stainless steel vat. The alcohol circulating in the tank passes through the sieve twice every eight hours, usually over a period of four to seven days, according to the ripeness and type of ingredients.

Vodka producers have jumped on the health bandwagon with products such as Poland's Korzen Zycia. It is the world's newest version of an ancient ginseng vodka produced by Lancut Distillery, which has mastered the secrets of its production and has obtained access to genuine red ginseng. Lancut is the only maker of red ginseng spirit outside of Asia. It is produced in the time-honoured Korean way, with red ginseng extract and a red ginseng root in every bottle.

Brandy

The category "brandy" encompasses perhaps the widest selection in the spirit world. The choice of flavours, textures, aromas and appearances is unique in the world of distilled spirits. At the top of the range, there is probably no more exclusive a drink than Cognac.

There is French brandy, including Armagnac and Cognac, and brandies made in other parts of France; there is Spanish brandy (Brandy de Jérez); Italian types, including grappa; South African, Mexican and American; and pisco from South America. Then there are eaux-de-vie and liqueur brandies. Statistics reveal that two-thirds of the brandy for the American market comes from California, centre of the nation's wine industry.

So, what are you buying when you ask for a drink? "Brandy" is a generic term for a spirit distilled from the fermented juice of fruit. The name itself, brandy, is from the Dutch word *brandewijn* – literally "burnt wine" – and from the perspective of history, the creation of brandy was due almost entirely to Dutch traders who travelled the coastal ports of France and Spain in search of wine for their sailors.

The Dutch demand eventually forced the French to change the way they shipped wine to Holland, where it was used as a raw material in *wijnbranders* ("wineburners"). Distilled spirit was cheaper than wine to ship (it was less bulk), so the French began to use the technique and equipment, introduced by the Dutch for distillation, particularly in the Charente region.

In the modern world, brandy is made from the grapes that have been distilled in either a small copper-pot still (called an alembic), or a continuous still, then transferred to age in oak barrels. After this period of maturation they are allowed to age further in glass jars.

South American brandy is called pisco and hails from Peru and Chile. Made from Muscat grapes, distilled and then aged in oak or in clay jars, pisco is the base spirit of a famous Pisco Sour cocktail.

What should brandy taste like?

You should be able to taste several layers, with sweet, woody and fruity flavours on the tongue. If it burns your throat, try another type. A brandy should make your throat feel warm, but it should not feel harsh and raw.

Cognac

Grapes from vineyards of the Charente–Maritime area in France are used to make cognac. Ugni Blanc, Folle Blanche and Colombard grapes are distilled and matured in oak casks from the Limousin or Troncais forests.

All cognac is a blend of cognacs from different houses and vintages, as is most whisky. Any details on a bottle's label refer to the number of years the youngest cognac in the blend has been in the cask. Three Star/V.S. is the youngest at three years; V.S.O.P., V.O. (Very Old), Very Special (or Superior) Old Pale has a four-and-a-half-year-old as the youngest; and XO, Extra, Napoleon, Vieille Réserve has, as its youngest, a six-year-old. The actual ageing is generally longer. When it is aged between 40 and 60 years old, it is considered excellent quality.

Armagnac is the second French region that comes to mind when brandy is mentioned. It is a relatively small player on the scene, and rivalry between the two regions is great, each claiming the benefits of its style of brandy. Armagnaçais producers claim single distillation gives their brandy the edge whereas the Cognaçais dismiss talk of vintages for distilled wines.

Centuries prior to cognac's production, grapes were being distilled by Spaniards in Andalucia, who had learnt distillation from the Moors who occupied Spain for over seven centuries. Generally, these are robust, perhaps sweeter (they are aged in former sherry casks) and simple brandies. Now, no country produces more brandy than Spain.

Tequila

To write of tequila is to write about the true spirit of Mexico, and to recall those nights when the moon shone brightly as you licked the salt, sipped the tequila shot and bit the lemon. The moon shone brighter after that. Oh, by the way, it's the spirit base of a Margarita. But you probably knew that.

Tequila is an unusual distilled spirit produced from the fermented juice of the swollen stem of the blue agave, a flowering succulent plant found all over Mexico. Tequila is a specific mezcal and is not to be confused with the drink with the worm in it. This is mezcal made from a different variety of the agave.

By law, tequila can be produced only in Mexico (in the same way that cognac can come only from Cognac) and is produced in designated regions, mostly in Jalisco, but also in designated villages within four states: Guanajuato, Nayarit, and Tamaulipas.

Types of Tequila

There are two basic types of tequila: 100 per cent agave and tequila mixed with other sugars (mixto). Read the label. If it does not say 100 per cent agave, it is mixto.

Tequila and cocktails go together like sex and the city. Well-known tequila cocktails include Margarita, Tequila Sunrise and Tequila Mockingbird. Each of these exotic names reminds the drinker of holidays in the sun, of lazy days and haunting evenings.

Seasoned drinkers claim it's harder to get a hangover from drinking a 100 per cent agave than with a mixto. Purity excels! At the

Tequila types

Blanco or plata (white or silver)
Clear in colour, and bottled immediately after distillation. Can be left for no longer than 60 days in stainless steel tanks before bottling. It may be 100 per cent agave or mixto.

Reposado (rested)
Aged for not less than two months in wooden vats or oak barrels. Can be 100 per cent agave or mixto.

Anejo (aged)
Produced from 100 per cent agave and must be left for a year or more in wooden barrels. Either 100 per cent agave or mixto. The very best are seldom left in the barrel for more than four years.

Joven abocado (often called gold)
Unaged tequila with the characteristics of an aged tequila, but the golden colour is produced by an additive such as caramel. A mixto variety, it can taste more mellow than the usual mixto.

bar, if you're set for an evening of tequila, it is preferable to ask for a blanco, a pure agave tequila, regardless of what you mix it with. At least the spirit remains untouched by added chemicals.

Before the Spanish conquest in 1521, Mexico was home to ancient American cultures that regarded the agave as a "gift of the gods" because it was useful in a variety of ways. (Aztecs painted many of their writings on agave fibre.) According to Bob Emmons in his fascinating account, *The Book of Tequila*, the alcoholic properties of the plant were discovered before the rise of the Aztecs. The discovery of the liquid known as *pulque* supplied a means of relaxation. The Aztecs also consumed it as a narcotic during the rather less palatable rites of human sacrifice.

In 1792 Ferdinand IV lifted the ban on spirit production in Mexico and in 1795 he granted a licence to one Jose Maria Guadalupe Cuervo, a Spaniard who set up a distillery in Tequila, Mexico, using cultivated, as opposed to wild, agave to produce the spirit. Now there are over 65 distilleries producing tequila for consumption at home and abroad. And, by the way, the U.S. consumes more tequila than the rest of the world.

What should tequila taste like? Connoisseurs speak of fine tequilas in much the same way as experts in cognac and fine wine drinkers describe their favourite drinks. For instance, of a Tequila Herradura blanco, one expert waxed lyrical with, "Dry complexity to the nose with floral overtones, good herbaceousness and smooth alcohol."

That's before you suck the lemon.

Liqueurs

It's all sweetness or creaminess in the liqueur business. Coffee, banana, chocolate, strawberry and raspberry flavours abound in delicious mixtures that swirl into the glass in an appealing way. And the colours can be as vivid as an artist's palette or as muted as a warm summer's evening.

Let's get this straight. A liqueur is not a cordial; we're talking true distilled liqueur. The word "liqueur" comes from the Latin *liquefacere*, to melt or dissolve. Centuries ago, liqueurs were distilled from recipes by monks and apothecaries whose main task was to cure ailments.

Dutchman Lucas Bols is responsible for the start of the modern liqueur industry in the sixteenth century. Knowing that caraway was good for the digestion, he created kummel. Benedictine has been made since 1510, and Chartreuse had been made for the brothers at an abbey in France long before it became available in 1848.

Spirits including brandy, Cognac, whisky and rum are used as the base for liqueurs. Fruits, plants, fruit skins and/or roots are steeped in alcohol in a still, heated, and the vapours are condensed to produce the spirit. Maceration is used only for fruit with pulp – raspberries, blackcurrants and aromatic plants, such as tea. The picked fruit is put into vats with alcohol and an infusion occurs.

A crème, such as crème de menthe, is a sweet and thick liqueur with 28 per cent sugar content. A cream, such as Baileys Irish Cream, is a combination of alcohol and dairy cream.

If you are serving a liqueur straight, do so at room temperature and in a small liqueur glass. It should be sipped and savoured, not gulped down, like a shot, in a single swallow. Liqueurs are usually served after a meal, without ice, to get the full flavour without it being diluted.

Patience is a virtue
Monks have been making Chartreuse for centuries; the recipe remains a secret

Champagne

Ask any champagne producer when is the best time to drink champagne and he will tell you "any time of the day or night." There is a magic about sipping champagne before lunch to which it never quite aspires in the late afternoon or evening. Champagne is also possibly the best apéritif.

The famous British wartime leader Winston Churchill, a great champagne drinker (mainly Pol Roger), called for it as he settled into his seat for a Clipper flight to America, much to the consternation of a colleague.

Many people who have been swilling champagne for a lifetime don't know it is made predominantly from the juice of red grapes. The proportion of juice from white grapes is usually around one-third. Another interesting fact is that a bottle of the best champagne may contain the juice from 15 different vineyards; some superb champagnes have juice from more than 30 vineyards.

Champagne is produced in an appellation controllée region in France. Only wine from this region can be labelled "champagne". Wine labelled "Méthode Champenoise" is made by a similar method, outside the Champagne region.

Champagne styles

Brut A tiny amount of sweetening is added.

Demi-sec Sweet champagne.

Extra Sec Dry champagne.

Non-vintage any champagne made using grapes from different years. A non-vintage champagne (NV) is not necessarily of lesser quality.

Rosé Made with some of the still red wine of the Champagne region with white wine.

Sec Medium-sweet champagne.

Vintage A "vintage year" is declared by the authorities when weather conditions have been superb. A bottle of vintage champagne is one for which all the grapes were harvested in the same year.

Mixers and Garnishes

Not every ingredient in a cocktail contains alcohol. Indeed there is probably no more refreshing a drink than a St. Clement's, made with fresh orange juice and bitter lemon. And without grapefruit and cranberry juice a Sea Breeze becomes a straight vodka.

Mixers

- Ginger ale (punches)
- Lemon-lime soda
- Soda water
- Spring water, still and sparkling
- Tonic water

Juices

- Cranberry
- Grapefruit, white and pink
- Orange
- Pineapple
- Tomato

Garnishes

Garnishes provide the finishing touch to a cocktail. To choose the right garnish, think about the dominant flavour and colour of the cocktail and choose a fruit or leaf that will go with it. Add a piece of fruit that's in proportion to the glass. Don't add a garish touch.

Strawberries are versatile as a garnish added to the drink, particularly in a champagne cocktail, or placed on the rim. Cut out the green stem, make a slit in the bottom of the strawberry and place it over the rim.

Bar craft

Citrus fruit spiral

Press a zester firmly into the rind of a lemon/lime/orange, starting from the top. Carefully cut around the fruit, making a long spiral as you go. Add it to the cocktail.

Twist

Cut a 1- to 2-inch (2.5–5-cm) wide piece of rind from a lemon or orange. Place it on a cutting board, pith down. With a sharp knife, trim a thin strip, about 2 inches (5 cm) long, from the wider piece. Hold it over the glass and twist the ends so that the juice from the rind falls into the drink.

Fruit

blackberries (nonalcoholic drinks)
mint, fresh
celery sticks (optional for Bloody Mary)
green olives (for a Martini)
cherries, maraschino (cocktail cherries)
pineapples
raspberries
cucumber peel (for punches, Pimm's)
strawberries (for champagne and punches)
oranges
lemons
limes

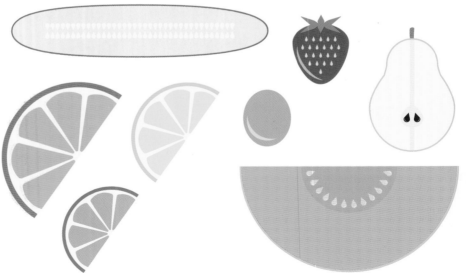

Shakers

The shaker is the most important tool for making great cocktails. As a rule, any recipe with a spirit, a juice and cream is shaken. The shaker used in most bars differs from the types you would find in a normal drinks shop; the professionals' Boston shake is a two-piece unit: one metal, the other clear glass.

Pour the ingredients into the glass section, and add the ice. Place the metal part over the glass, sealing the two sections. Turn the shaker upside down. Shake the drink and let it settle before separating the sections. To serve, pour the cocktail through a bar strainer into a glass.

The shaker most widely available consists of a base, a small lid with a fitted strainer, and a solid cap. When shaking, always hold the lid down firmly. If it becomes stuck, ease the lid up with two thumbs to loosen the vacuum. There's nothing worse than a lid coming loose and having the precious cocktail go everywhere but into the glass.

Cocktail shakers have also become collector's items and can sell at auction for considerable sums. One of the most popular antique shakers is the Penguin, dated circa 1936. It has a hinged beak that lifts to reveal a spout for pouring.

A search of the U.S. Patent Office files disclosed that applications for "an apparatus to mix drinks" were filed in the 1870s. By the late nineteenth century novelty cocktail shakers were all the rage. They included a lighthouse, buoy, skyscraper, golf bag and even a teapot!

Early shakers were made of silver, and as technology progressed, more were made of chrome-plated stainless steel. Today, most shakers are made of plated metal and are relatively inexpensive, but the crystal glass company William Yeoward has released a very expensive, colourful version called Lulu which, at one look, sparkles and seduces the mixer into creating the most fabulous cocktails.

Mr Bond would approve

A Martini with a shaker, not a stirrer

Glasses

Clear glasses are ideal for cocktails. Since the beginning of the cocktail craze, each type of drink has had a shape specifically for it. For example, a Martini is served in a Martini cocktail glass. Common sense dictates a liqueur should be sipped from a small glass because it is so sweet.

Main Glass Types and Sizes

Most glasses come in regular sizes as an industry standard, but there are some different shaped and sized glasses, particularly double cocktail glasses. This list should provide a useful guide. It should give an indication of the amount of drink required for a party. Smaller glasses mean less drink is consumed … unless the guests are very thirsty.

Glass cleaning

Clean the glass with a lint-free towel before pouring a drink. Do not wash with soapy liquids because these can leave a residue on the glass.

Glass type	Capacity	Characteristics
Cocktail	4 oz. (12 cl)	Popular for any cocktail served without ice
Flute	6–8 oz. (18–24 cl)	For champagne and champagne cocktails
Highball	10 oz. (30 cl)	Ideal for long drinks filled with ice cubes
Liqueur	2–3 oz. (6–9 cl)	A tiny glass for sipping after-dinner cocktails or a straight liqueur
Old-Fashioned	5–6 oz. (15–18 cl)	A short glass with a heavy base
Saucer	5–7 oz. (15–21 cl)	By legend the shape was modelled on the bust of Empress Josephine, but champagne goes flatter more quickly than in a flute
Shot	2–3 oz. (6–9 cl)	Small glass to hold a measure of spirit that will be thrown down the throat
Wine	4–9 oz. (12–27 cl)	For a drink not suited to a cocktail glass but too small for a highball

Other Equipment

A basic cocktail tool kit consists of a few small but important items, listed below. Most can be found in a household goods shop or in the kitchen or bar accessories department of major stores. As with all things, the cheapest is unlikely to be the best, but functional is more important than flashy.

- Bar knife must be very sharp, to slice fruit
- Barspoon mixes and stirs cocktail ingredients in a mixing glass or a shaker
- Blender blends spirits, juice, fruit and crushed ice, especially for frozen cocktails
- Champagne stopper keeps the champagne bubbly once opened
- Chopping board provides a hard, flat surface on which to chop mint, dice garnishes, slice fruit
- Cocktail sticks spear bits of fruit and cherries as garnish
- Corkscrew opens wine bottles; the best is a waiter's friend
- Dash pourer adds drops and dashes of other spirits and liqueurs
- Ice bucket saves regular trips to the freezer
- Ice crusher takes cubes and crushes them
- Ice scoop for adding ice to a shaker or blender
- Ice tongs for picking up ice cubes, which hasten the melting process
- Jigger obtains the correct spirit and liqueur measures for a cocktail. In the United States, one measure is 1 oz., and jiggers for single and double measures are also calibrated to measure common proportions: the quarter, third, half and three-quarters. In the United Kingdom the law defines one measure as either 25ml or 35ml, with jiggers calibrated for single and double measures. Premises may sell in multiples of 25ml or 35ml but not both
- Juicer for making fruit lemon and lime juices
- Mixing glass to mix two or more ingredients
- Muddler pestle that mashes or pulps mint or fruit berries
- Shaker for shaking cocktails
- Stirrers and straws. Long cocktails should be drunk through a straw
- Tea towel wipes up spills
- Zester peels lemon, orange and lime rinds to make garnishes

Bartending Techniques

Cocktails came back into fashion in the late 1980s and 1990s, as the bar – as opposed to the club or pub – returned to prominence. For a while the job of bartender ranked as one of the most glamorous. But, for all the show, the art of making cocktails should not be taken lightly.

Shaking

It might look simple when the guy behind the bar starts with his act, but for a beginner who has yet to hold a shaker ... Firstly, it's very cold, wet and slippery on the outside and that makes it hard to handle. Grip it firmly in both hands, with one hand under the base and the other firmly holding the top while, simultaneously, you splay the fingers around the sides.

Now here's the groovy bit. Move only the wrists, not the arms and shoulders. Flick it with finesse, hard, not half-heartedly. The aim is to combine the ingredients inside and chill them as they are swished back and forth over the ice. After about 20 attempts, a personal style will develop. Good bartenders have a personal rhythm to their shake and this is what novices should aspire to.

Using a mixing glass

Cocktails with ingredients that need mixing, and are served chilled, are mixed in a mixing glass, then poured through a bar strainer into an Old-Fashioned glass or a cocktail glass. Place the ice cubes into the mixing glass and stir the ice around with a barspoon so that it chills the glass. Add the spirits and stir, then strain into a glass. Use a tall glass with a solid base – or a large medicine beaker – if a proper mixing glass isn't available.

Shake it
Develop your own rhythm when using a cocktail shaker

Muddling

Muddling is an action that requires a bit of strength in the wrist. And it requires a muddler. Some barspoons have a section on the end that can act as a muddler, but usually they are made of fine wood or marble (as in a pestle and mortar).

Many younger bartenders use muddling to great effect in their new cocktails. The item is placed in the bottom of a shaker/Old-Fashioned glass/mixing glass/highball and mashed to release its colour, juice and flavour. A Mint Julep is made with mint muddled in the bottom of a glass. It is imperative to use a glass with a heavy base.

Layering/Floating

Layered drinks look superb. They're impressive, and everyone wonders how it is done. In fact, it's easy. Each spirit in a recipe weighs more or less than the others. Start with the heaviest, then add the second heaviest, and work up to the top until the lightest is floated as a finishing touch.

Usually, layered drinks are made in small glasses such as a shot or liqueur glass. A steady hand is needed, although a barspoon or a small teaspoon may be used to float each liquid over the one already in the glass.

If there are five ingredients in a recipe, begin with the first ingredient in the recipe, because it ought to be the heaviest. To pour, place the spoon on the edge of the first layer in the glass, with the back of the barspoon facing you. Pour the next spirit slowly over the spoon, and watch as it creates a second layer. Repeat the action until each ingredient in the recipe has been used.

Blending

Blended cocktails have a smooth, fruity texture and are a delicious summer drink. It's an unwritten rule that cocktails whose ingredients contain cream, fruit and crushed ice should be blended. With blended drinks, it is possible to make two or three drinks at a time, which is especially useful if there are a few people around for a pool party.

Wash any pieces of fruit before adding them to the blender. Follow instructions for dicing, too. If there isn't enough liquid in the blender when the fruit has been put in, add a teaspoon of water to aid the blades. For a really smooth result, pour the blended mixture through a strainer, and mash the mixture thoroughly, forcing the liquid through into the glass below.

Make this type of drink immediately and serve in a suitable glass, such as a wine goblet, a colada glass or even a margarita glass. Here's a tip: add the ice at the last minute and blend again to chill the drink.

Chilling a glass

Professional bartenders always chill cocktail glasses and champagne flutes before pouring in any liquid. The opaque glass effect makes a drink look mysterious and as it fades, the drinker is left watching the cocktail itself emerge. Alternatively, place a few glasses in the freezer compartment for about half an hour before guests arrive. If that is impractical, the same effect can be achieved by putting crushed ice in the glass while the cocktail is being shaken or mixed. Remove the ice before pouring in the drink.

Crusting a rim

For many drinkers, licking the rim of a Margarita, before sipping the drink, is the most pleasurable part of the whole experience. Many classic cocktails were born with a crusting and have remained that way ever since. Crusting a glass is a very simple task.

Rub a wedge of lime around the rim of a glass. Then turn the glass upside down and, holding it by the stem, twirl the rim around a saucer filled with fine salt. Make sure the salt sticks to the rim. If a more crusty effect is required, use slightly crushed sea salt. And, for a very special effect, salt only one half of the glass.

If the recipe requires a sugared rim, the method is exactly the same. Different and colourful effects can also be achieved by using chocolate or cocoa powder or a food colouring in sugar to give an exotic alternative.

CLASSICS

Bellini

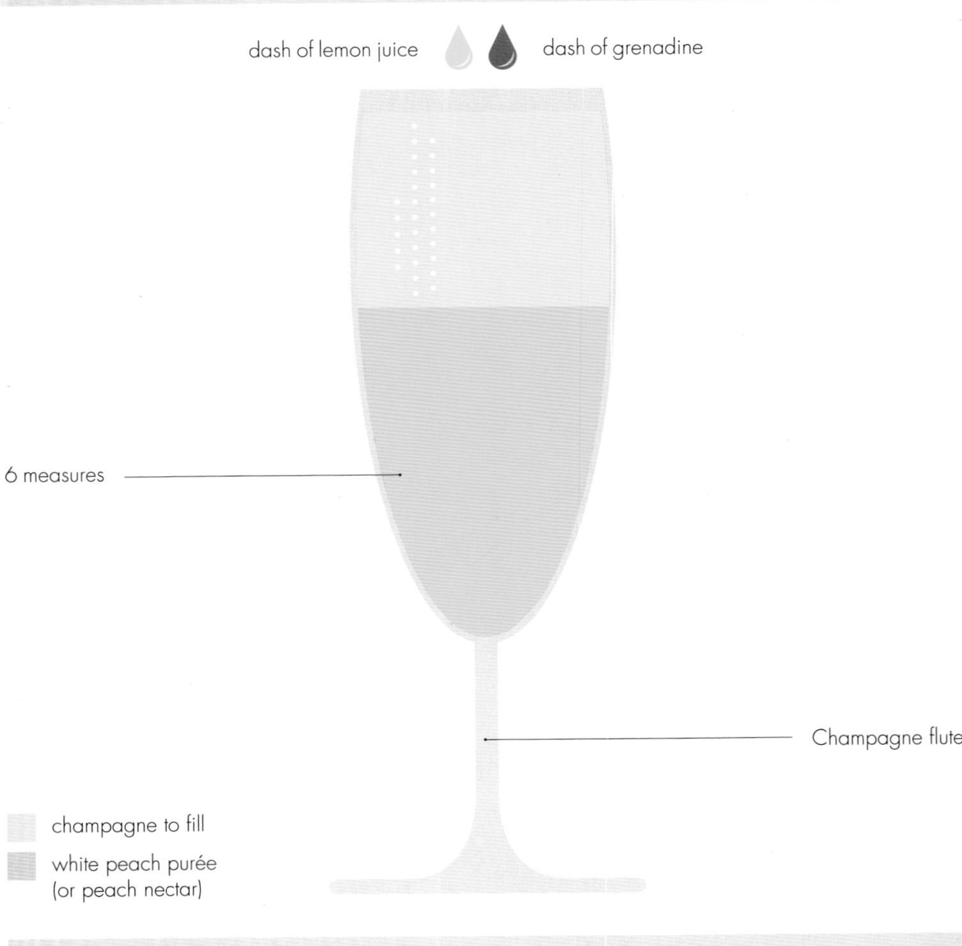

dash of lemon juice
dash of grenadine
6 measures
Champagne flute
champagne to fill
white peach purée
(or peach nectar)

Instructions

1 Mix the peach purée, grenadine, and lemon juice together in a champagne flute. **2** Then top up with champagne and serve.

Bloody Mary

pinch celery salt
ground black pepper
2–3 dashes Tabasco
2–3 dashes Worcestershire Sauce
celery stick (optional)

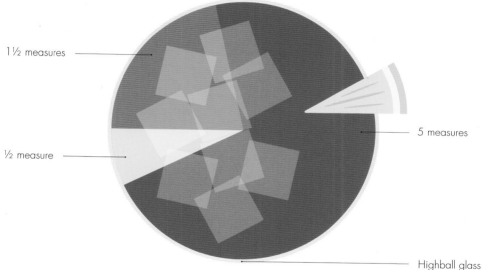

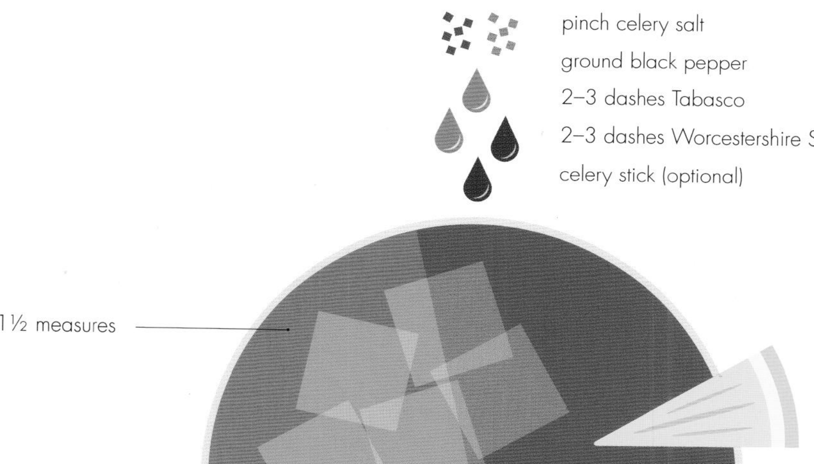
1½ measures
½ measure
5 measures
Highball glass

- fresh lemon juice
- tomato juice
- vodka

Instructions

1 Fill a highball with ice, then pour in the tomato and lemon juices. **2** Add the vodka. **3** Add the spices. Stir. **4** Add black pepper. **5** Garnish with a lemon wedge, a stirrer and a celery stick if requested.

Brandy Alexander

1 measure
1 measure
1 measure
Cocktail glass
double cream
brown crème de cacao
cognac

Instructions

1 Mix all the ingredients together in a shaker, then strain into a cocktail glass and serve.

Caipirinha

1 tsp caster sugar

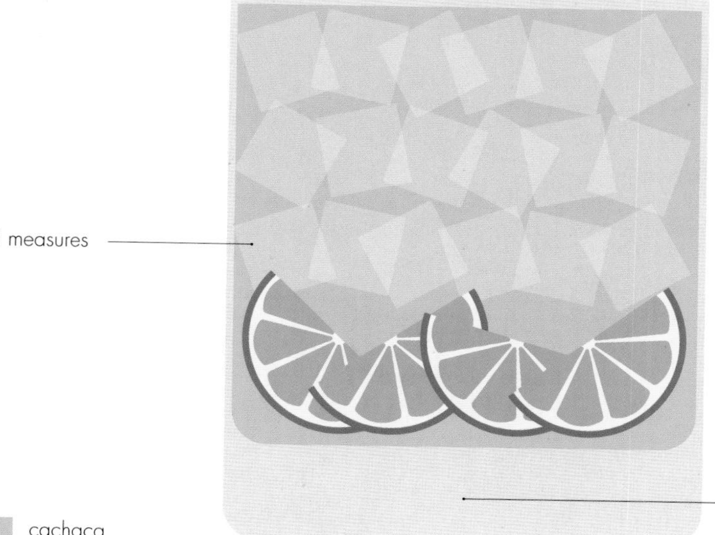
2 measures
Old-Fashioned glass
cachaça

Instructions

1 Cut the lime into quarters vertically and place them in the base of a chilled Old-Fashioned. 2 Add the sugar and crush the lime pieces until the sugar is dissolved. 3 Add the cachaça, then ice cubes, and stir.

Cosmopolitan

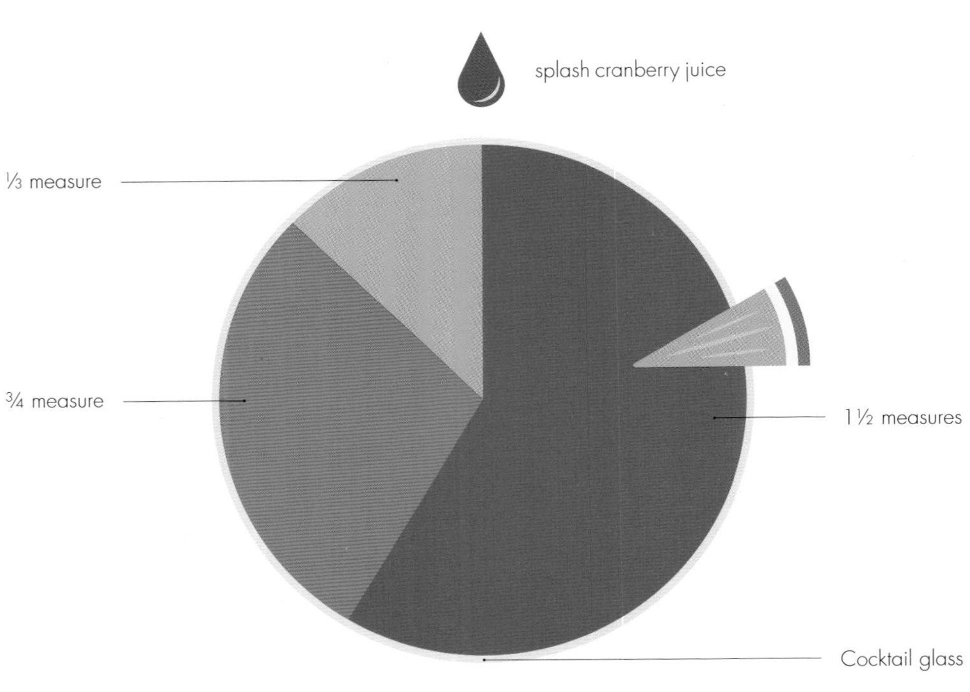

splash cranberry juice
⅓ measure
¾ measure
1 ½ measures
Cocktail glass

fresh lime juice

Cointreau

vodka

Instructions

1 Shake all ingredients with ice. 2 Strain into a cocktail glass. 3 Garnish with a lime wedge.

Daiquiri

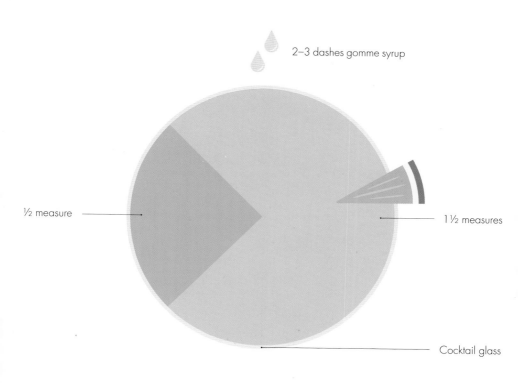

2–3 dashes gomme syrup

½ measure

1 ½ measures

Cocktail glass

lime juice
white rum

Instructions

1 Pour the ingredients into a shaker with cracked ice. 2 Strain into a chilled cocktail glass and garnish with a lime wedge in the glass.

Gimlet

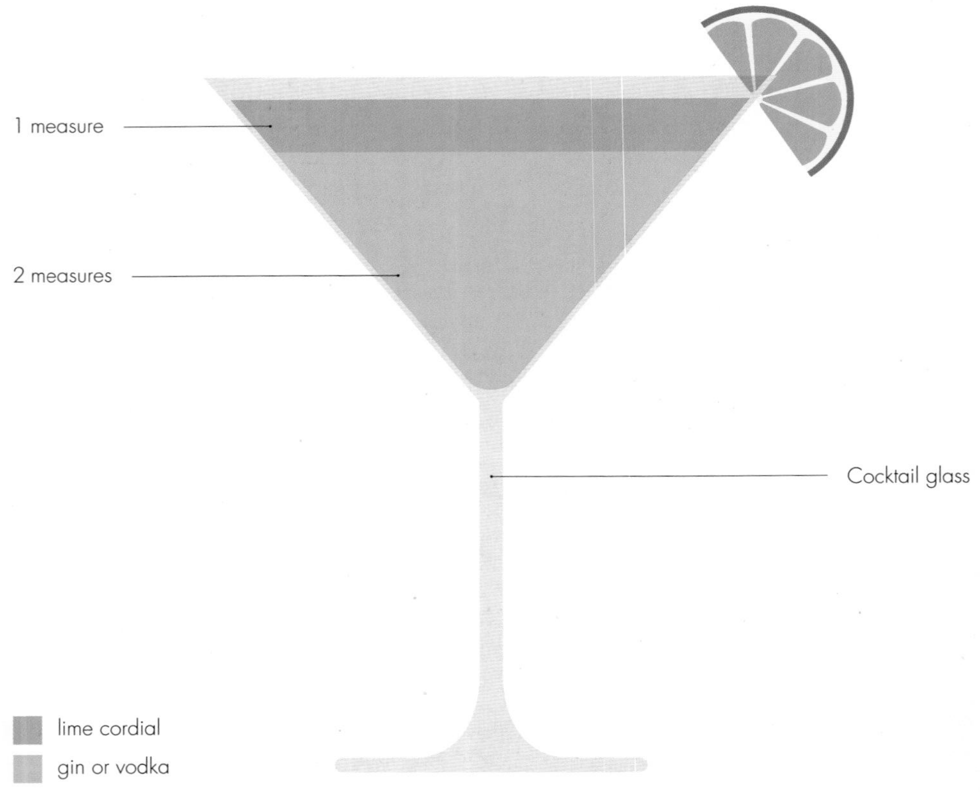
1 measure
2 measures
Cocktail glass
lime cordial
gin or vodka

Instructions

1 Over ice, pour the gin or vodka and lime cordial into a cocktail glass and serve with the lime wedge.

Manhattan

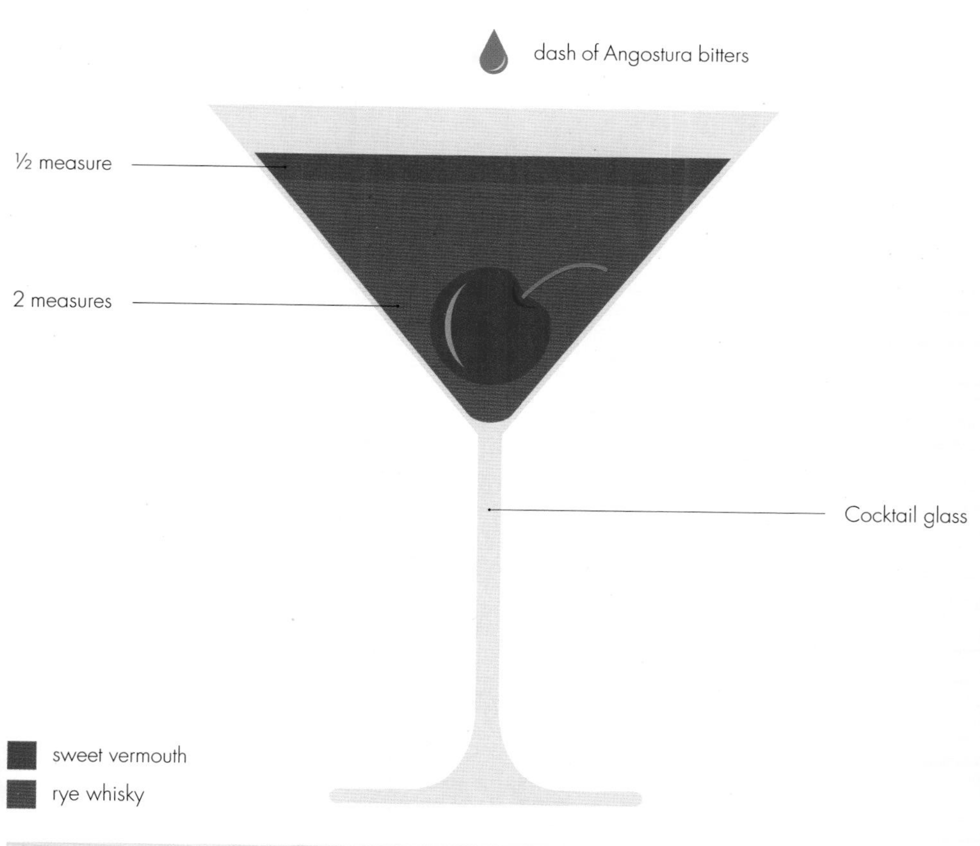
dash of Angostura bitters
½ measure
2 measures
Cocktail glass
sweet vermouth
rye whisky

Instructions

1 Pour all the ingredients into a mixing glass and stir. 2 Strain into a cocktail glass. 3 Drop a maraschino cherry in and watch it settle.

Long Island Iced Tea

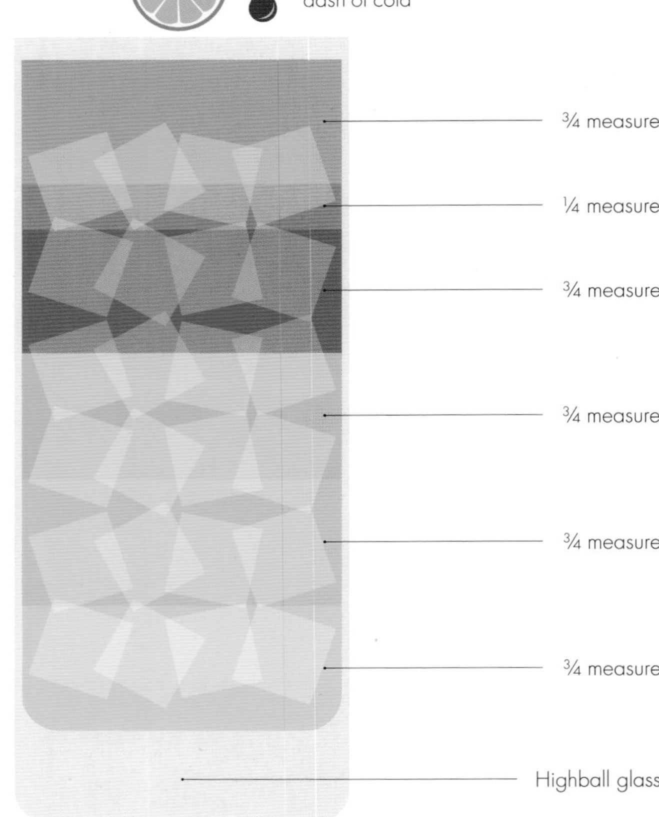

½ lime, freshly squeezed
dash of cola
¾ measure
¼ measure
¾ measure
¾ measure
¾ measure
¾ measure
Highball glass

orange juice
triple sec
tequila
gin
vodka
light rum

Instructions

1 Squeeze lime into a Collins glass, add ice cubes, spirits, triple sec and orange juice. **2** Stir and top up with cola.

Mai Tai No. 1

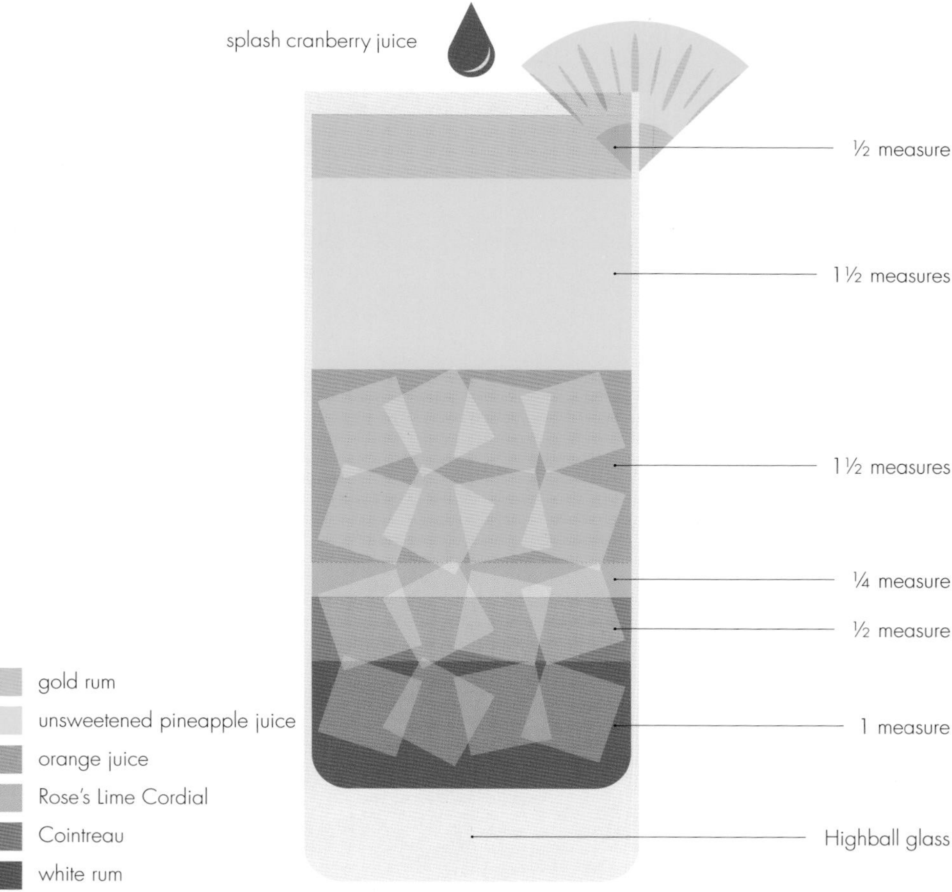

splash cranberry juice
½ measure
1 ½ measures
1 ½ measures
¼ measure
½ measure
1 measure
Highball glass
gold rum
unsweetened pineapple juice
orange juice
Rose's Lime Cordial
Cointreau
white rum

Instructions

1 Shake and strain the white rum, Cointreau, Lime Cordial and the juices into a Collins glass half-filled with ice. **2** Add the grenadine and gold rum and garnish with a pineapple wedge.

Margarita

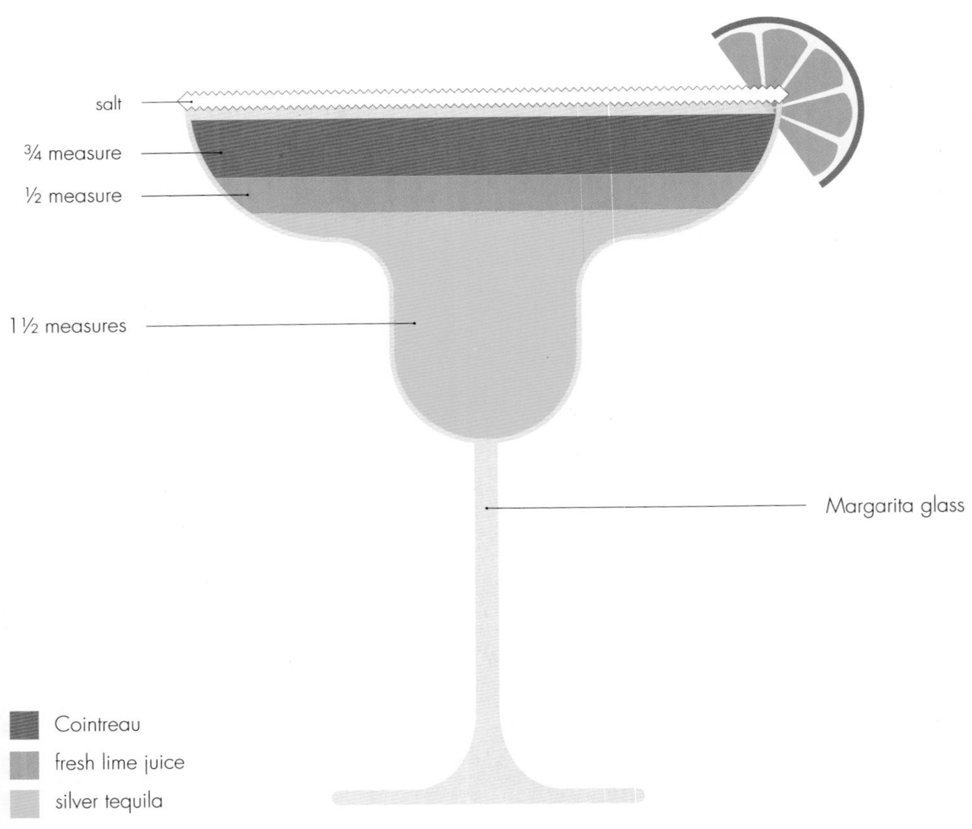
salt
¾ measure
½ measure
1 ½ measures
Margarita glass
Cointreau
fresh lime juice
silver tequila

Instructions

1 Rub a wedge of lime around the rim of a margarita glass and dip the glass into a saucer of salt to create a salt-crusted rim. **2** Pour all the ingredients into a shaker containing cracked ice and shake. **3** Strain into the glass. **4** Garnish with a lime slice.

Martini

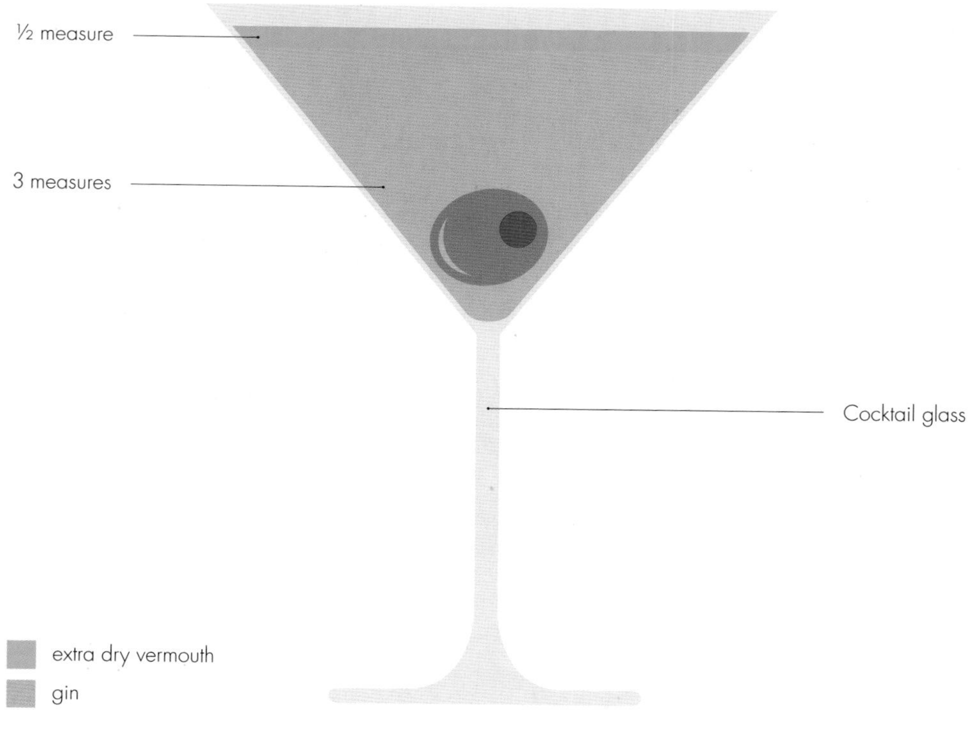

½ measure
3 measures
Cocktail glass
extra dry vermouth
gin

Instructions

1 Pour the dry vermouth into a mixing glass filled with the coldest ice imaginable. **2** Let it dribble down the ice and then strain it from the mixing glass. **3** Add the chilled gin and stir quickly with a barspoon. **4** Strain onto a chilled cocktail glass. **5** Add a thin twist of lemon or an olive before serving.

Mint Julep

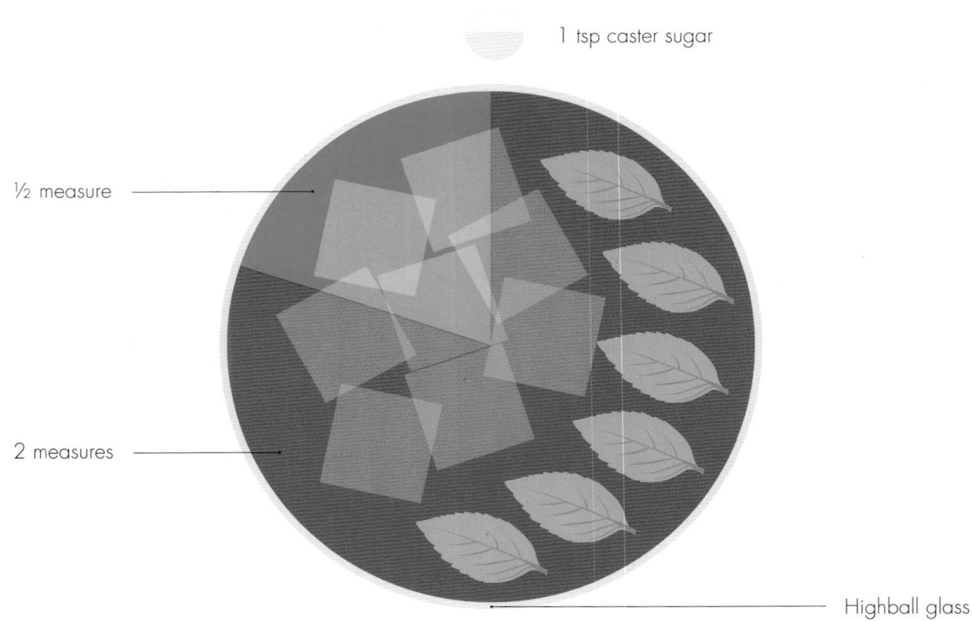
1 tsp caster sugar
½ measure
2 measures
Highball glass

cold spring water

bourbon

Instructions

1 Place the mint in a highball glass and then add the sugar and water. 2 Muddle the mint for about a minute. 3 Add the bourbon. 4 Fill the glass with crushed ice. Stir. 5 Add a sprig of mint as a garnish. 6 Serve with a straw and a stirrer.

Negroni

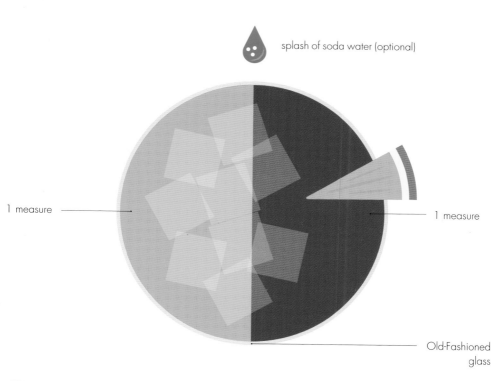

splash of soda water (optional)

1 measure

1 measure

Old-Fashioned glass

sweet vermouth

Campari

Instructions

1 Pour the Campari and sweet vermouth into an ice-filled Old-Fashioned glass and stir. **2** Add the soda, if using, then garnish with the orange slice and serve.

Old-Fashioned

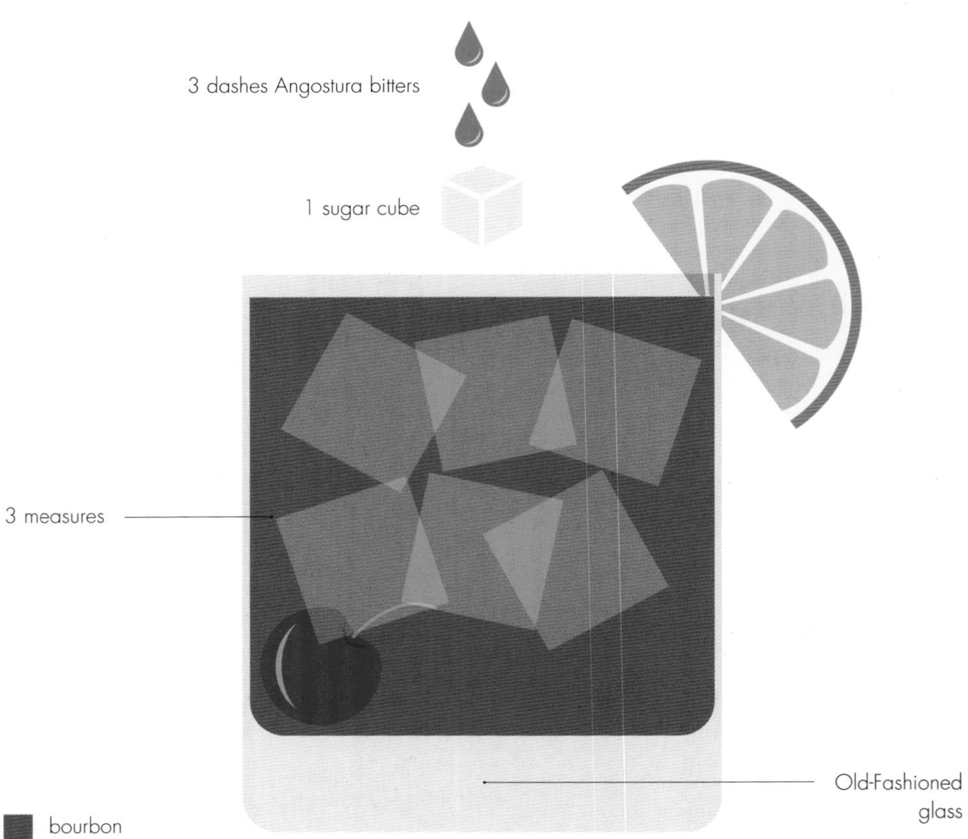
3 dashes Angostura bitters
1 sugar cube
3 measures
Old-Fashioned glass
bourbon

Instructions

1 Put the bitters, sugar cube, and a dash of the bourbon into an Old-Fashioned glass and muddle together. **2** Add 2 ice cubes and 1 measure of the bourbon and stir. **3** Squeeze some of the juice from the orange slice into the glass, then add 2 more ice cubes and 1 measure bourbon and stir again. **4** Finally add 2 more ice cubes, the remaining bourbon, the orange slice and cherry, then serve.

Pisco Sour

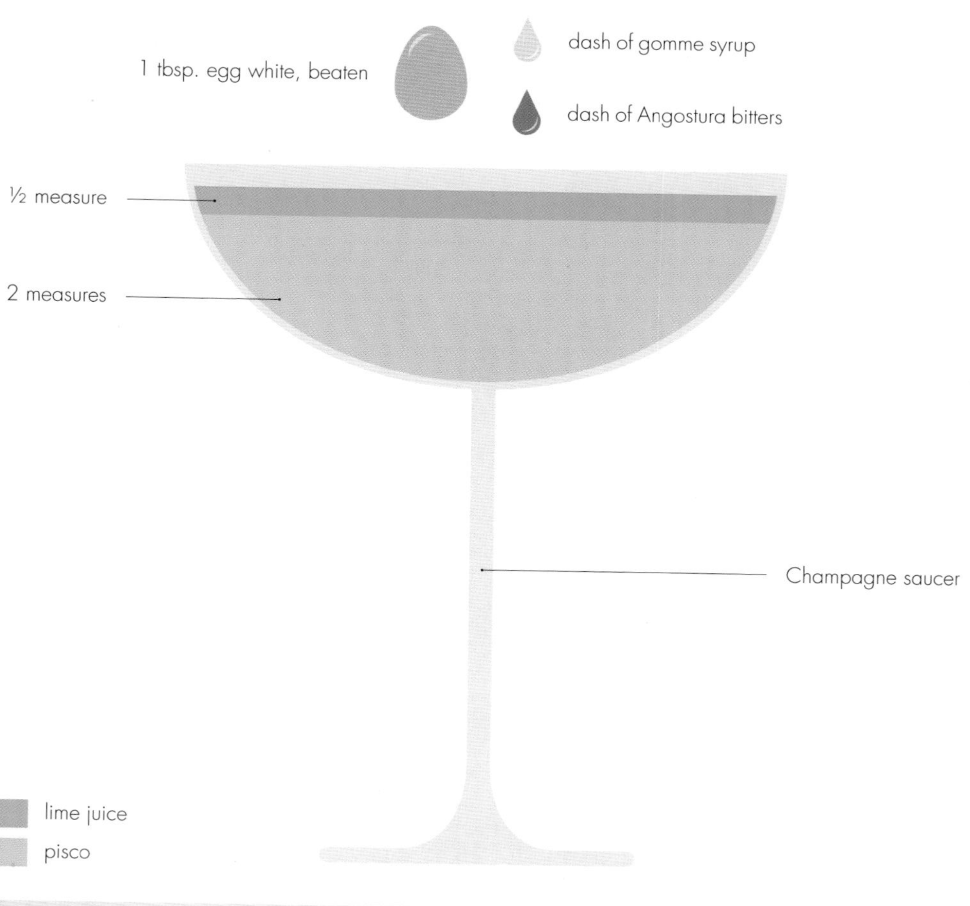
1 tbsp. egg white, beaten
dash of gomme syrup
dash of Angostura bitters
½ measure
2 measures
Champagne saucer
lime juice
pisco

Instructions

1 Pour all ingredients into a shaker with ice. Shake. **2** Strain into a white wine glass or a champagne saucer.

Sidecar

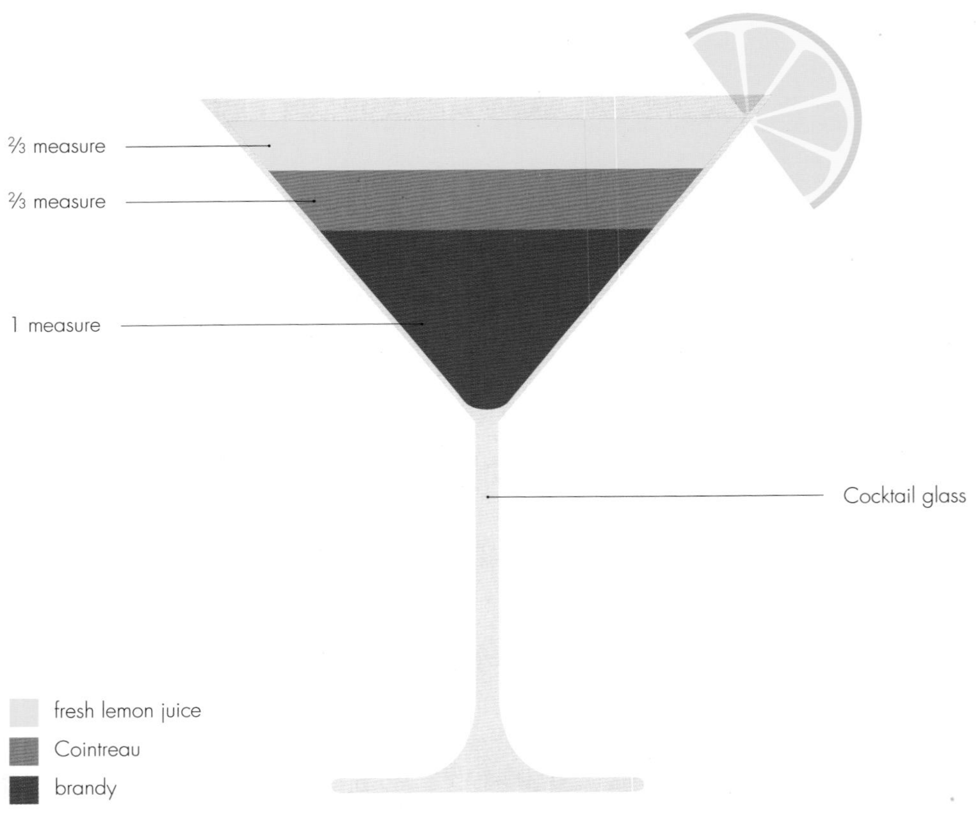

⅔ measure
⅔ measure
1 measure
Cocktail glass
fresh lemon juice
Cointreau
brandy

Instructions

1 Pour the ingredients into a shaker with cracked ice. **2** Shake and strain into an ice-cold cocktail glass. **3** Garnish with a discreet lemon wedge.

Singapore Sling

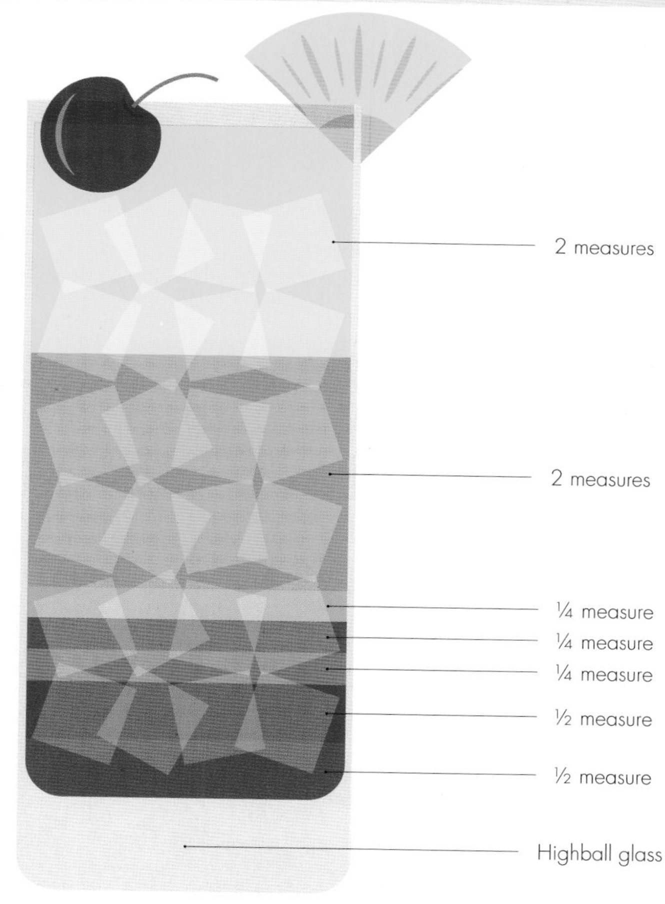

2 measures
2 measures
¼ measure
¼ measure
¼ measure
½ measure
½ measure
Highball glass

pineapple juice
orange juice
lime juice
Benedictine
Cointreau
cherry brandy
gin

Instructions

1 Pour the ingredients into a shaker with ice. **2** Shake and strain into a highball with ice. **3** Garnish with a pineapple slice and a maraschino cherry and serve with a straw and a stirrer.

Tom Collins

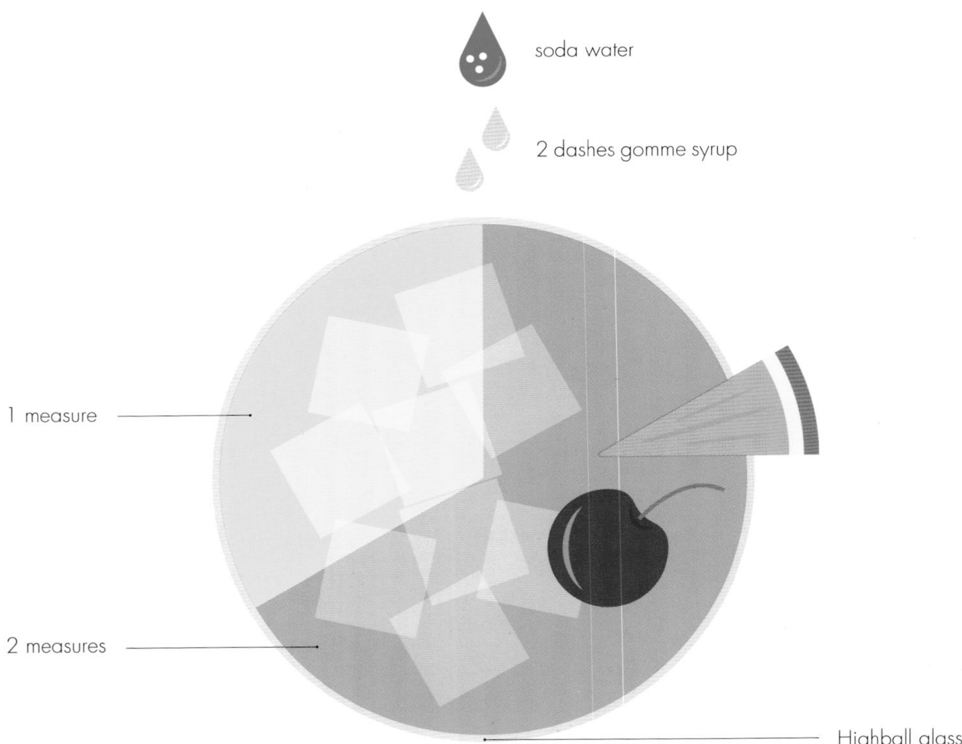
soda water
2 dashes gomme syrup
1 measure
2 measures
Highball glass

fresh lemon juice

London Dry gin

Instructions

1 Add the gin, lemon juice and syrup to a Collins or highball glass filled with lots of ice. **2** Top up with soda. **3** Add a slice of orange and a maraschino cherry, or a cherry and a slice of lime. Serve with a stirrer.

Whisky Sour

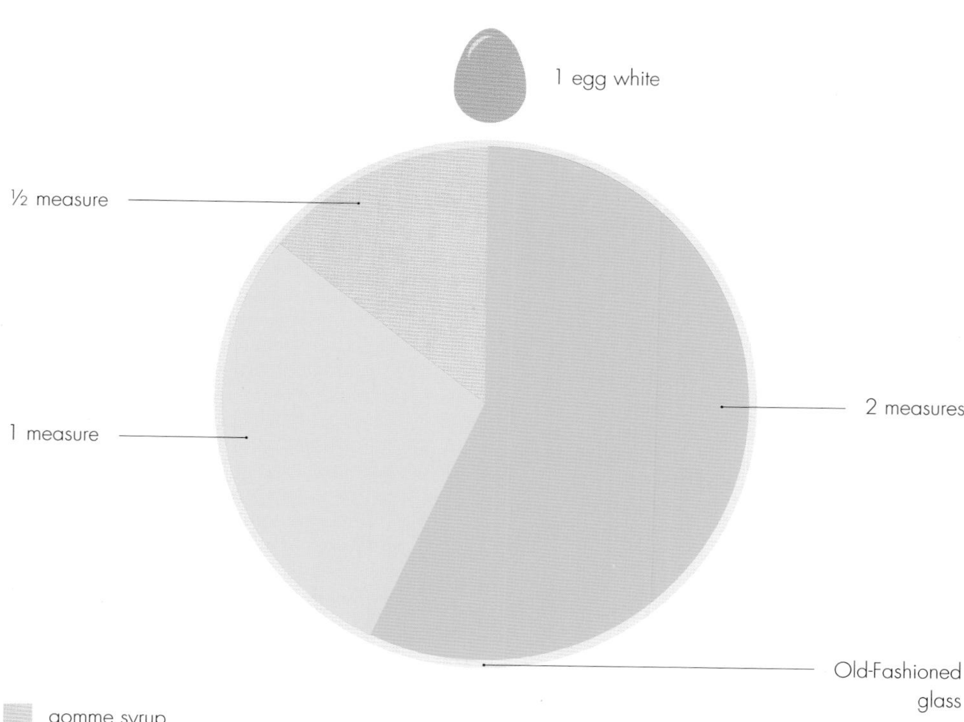
1 egg white
½ measure
1 measure
2 measures
Old-Fashioned glass
gomme syrup
fresh lemon juice
whisky

Instructions

1 Mix the whisky, lemon juice, and gomme in a shaker, then pour into an Old-Fashioned glass and serve.

VODKA

Aviation 2

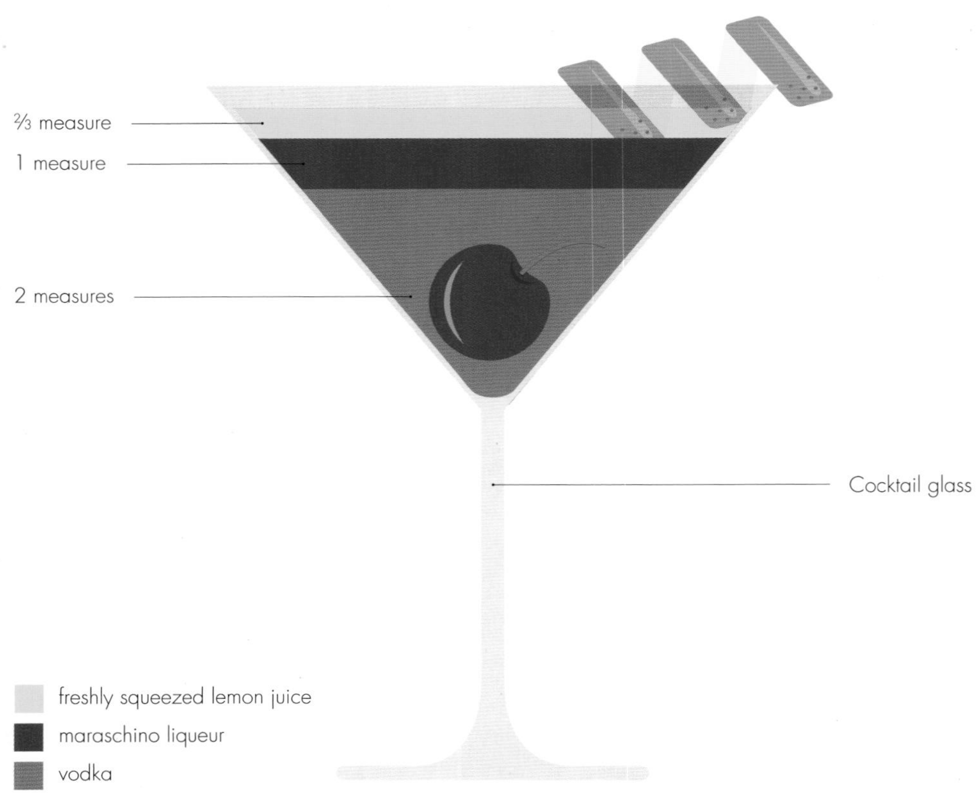

⅔ measure
1 measure
2 measures
Cocktail glass
freshly squeezed lemon juice
maraschino liqueur
vodka

Instructions

1 Shake all the ingredients. Strain into a cocktail glass. **2** Drop a maraschino cherry in the drink and a twist of lemon.

Bikini

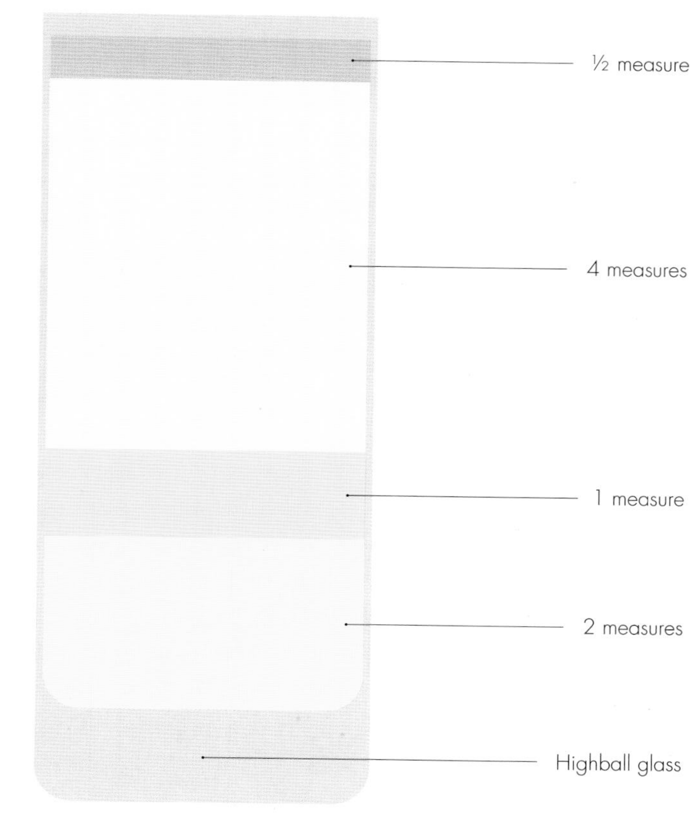

½ measure
4 measures
1 measure
2 measures
Highball glass

gomme

milk or single cream

white rum

vodka

Instructions

1. Shake the ingredients together, then strain into a highball glass and serve.

Black Magic

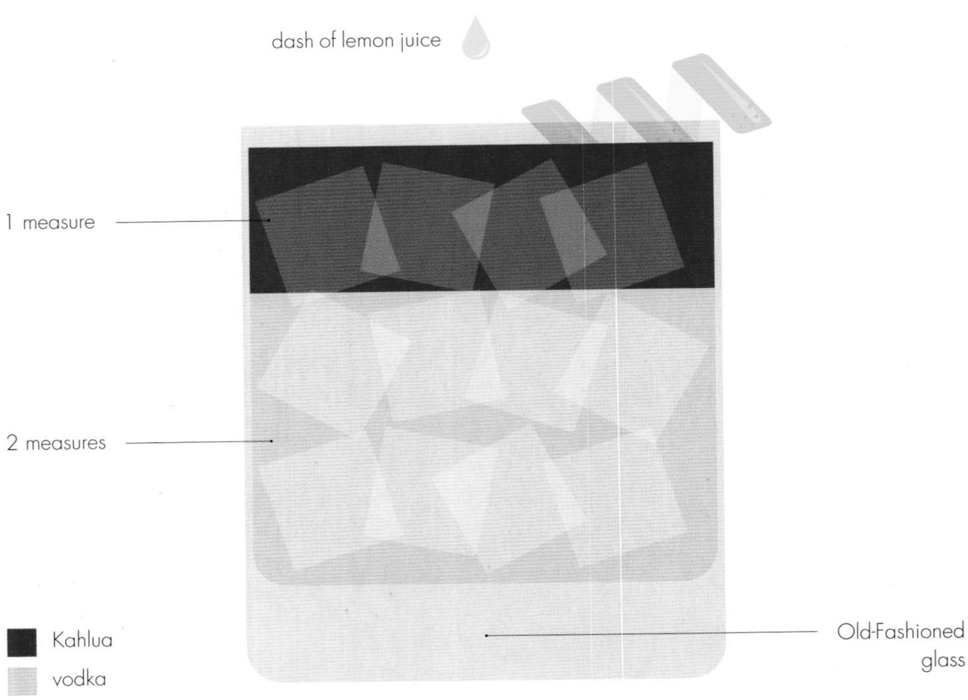

dash of lemon juice
1 measure
2 measures
Old-Fashioned glass
Kahlua
vodka

Instructions

1 Stir all the ingredients together, then pour into an ice-filled Old-Fashioned glass. **2** Serve with the lemon twist.

Black Russian

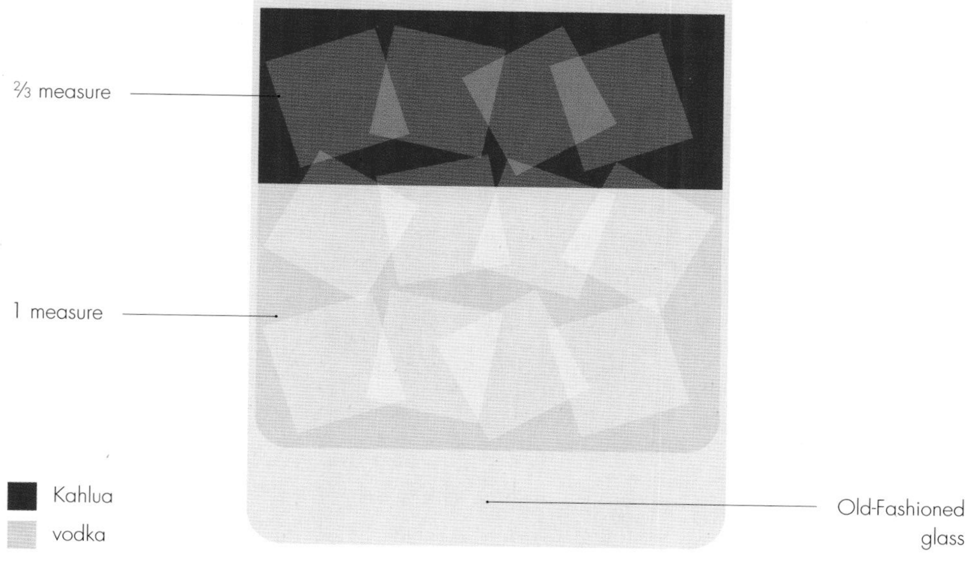

⅔ measure
1 measure
Kahlua
vodka
Old-Fashioned glass

Instructions

1 Pour the vodka, then the Kahlua into an Old-Fashioned glass straight up or over crushed ice, then serve.

Bullshot

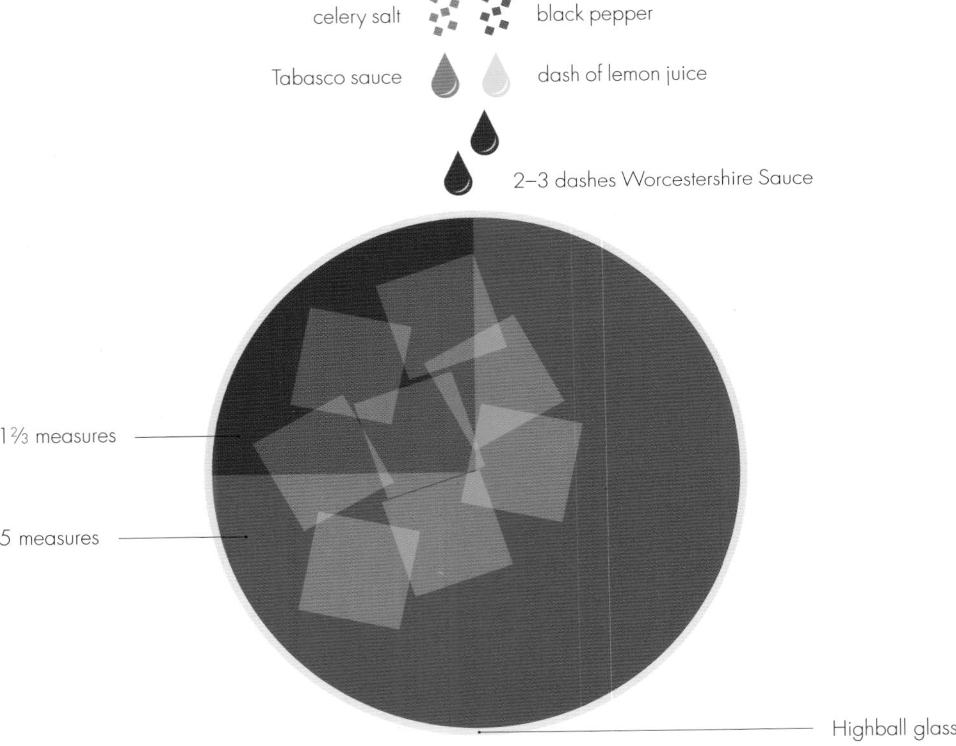

celery salt
black pepper
Tabasco sauce
dash of lemon juice
2–3 dashes Worcestershire Sauce
1⅔ measures
5 measures
Highball glass

vodka

beef bouillon

Instructions

1 Shake bouillon, lemon juice, Tabasco and Worcestershire sauces with vodka. **2** Strain into a highball glass full of ice cubes. **3** Add black pepper. **4** Serve with a stirrer.

Cape Codder

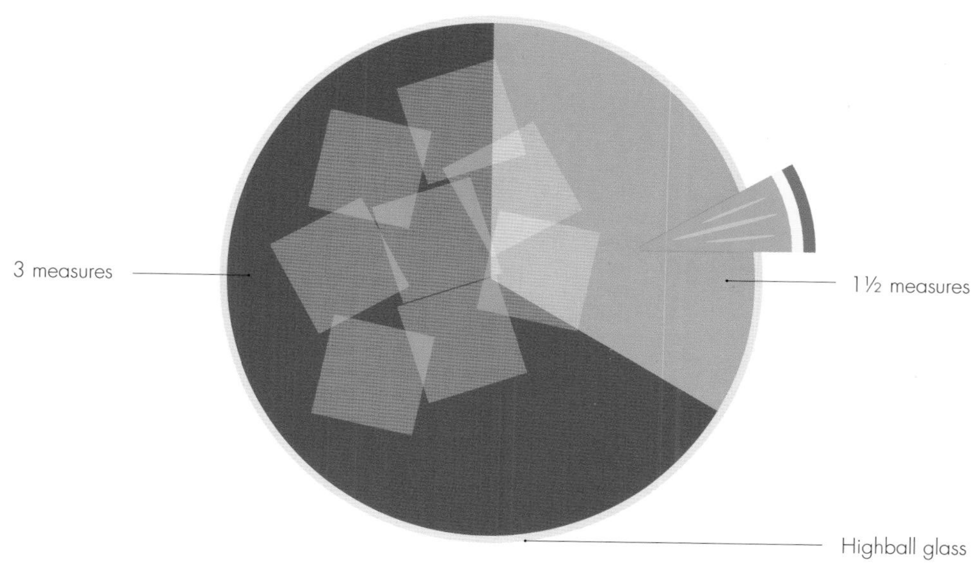

3 measures
1½ measures
Highball glass

cranberry juice

vodka

Instructions

1 Pour vodka and cranberry juice into a highball glass over ice. **2** Stir well, add the lime and serve.

French Kiss

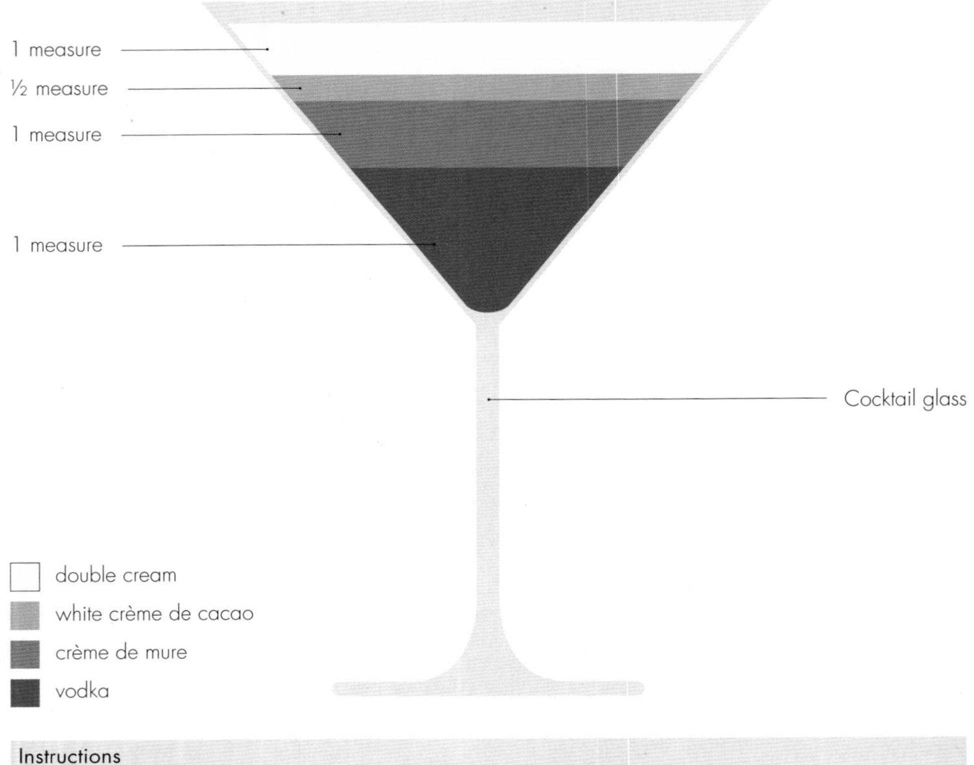
1 measure
½ measure
1 measure
1 measure
Cocktail glass
double cream
white crème de cacao
crème de mure
vodka

Instructions

1. Mix the ingredients together in a shaker, then strain into a cocktail glass.

French Martini

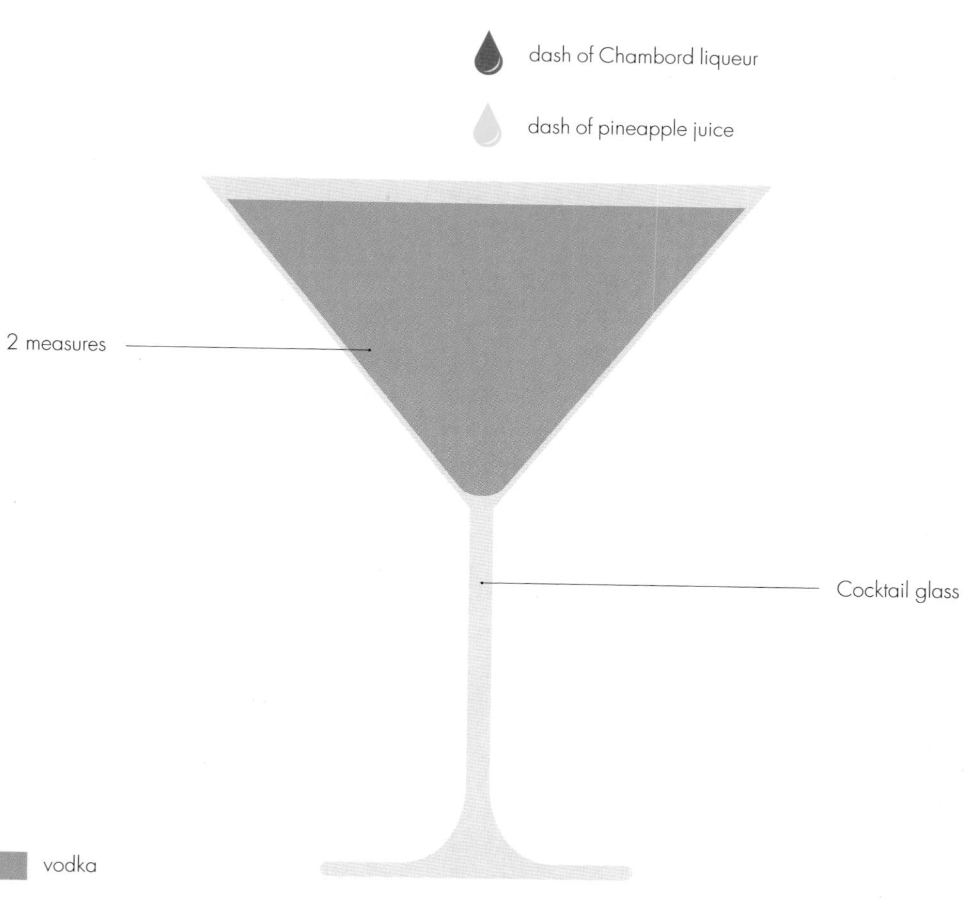
dash of Chambord liqueur
dash of pineapple juice
2 measures
Cocktail glass
vodka

Instructions

1 Shake all the ingredients together and strain into a cocktail glass.

Harvey Wallbanger

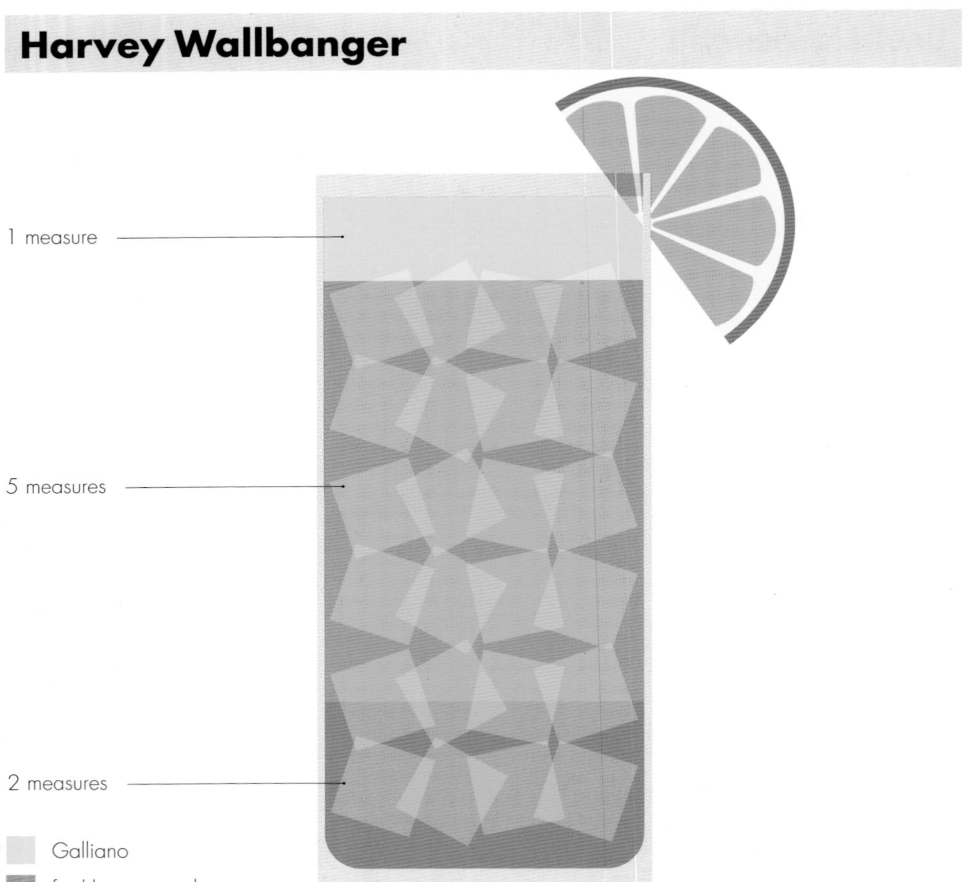

1 measure
5 measures
2 measures
Galliano
freshly squeezed orange juice
vodka
Highball glass

Instructions

1 Pour vodka and orange juice into a highball glass full of ice and stir. **2** Float Galliano on top. **3** Garnish with a slice of orange and serve with a stirrer.

Joe Collins

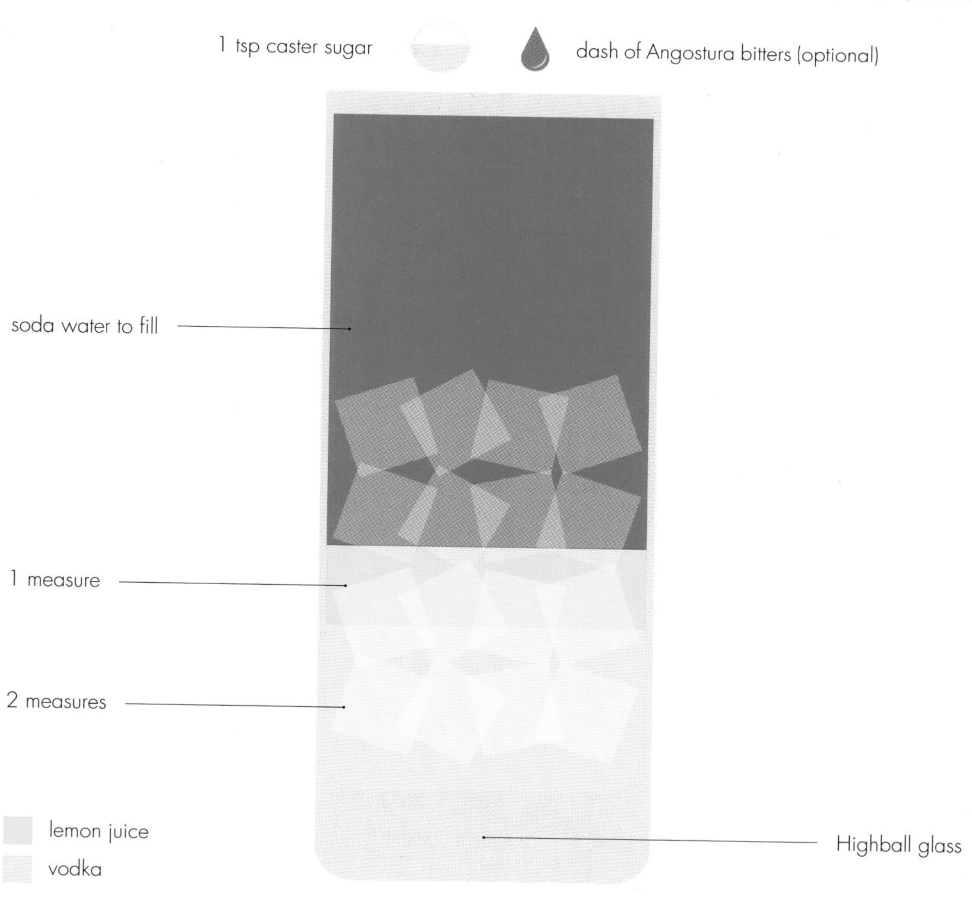
1 tsp caster sugar
dash of Angostura bitters (optional)
soda water to fill
1 measure
2 measures
lemon juice
vodka
Highball glass

Instructions

1 Place the vodka, juice, sugar and bitters in a tall glass half-filled with ice, and stir to mix. **2** Top up with soda. **3** Stir gently.

Love for Sale

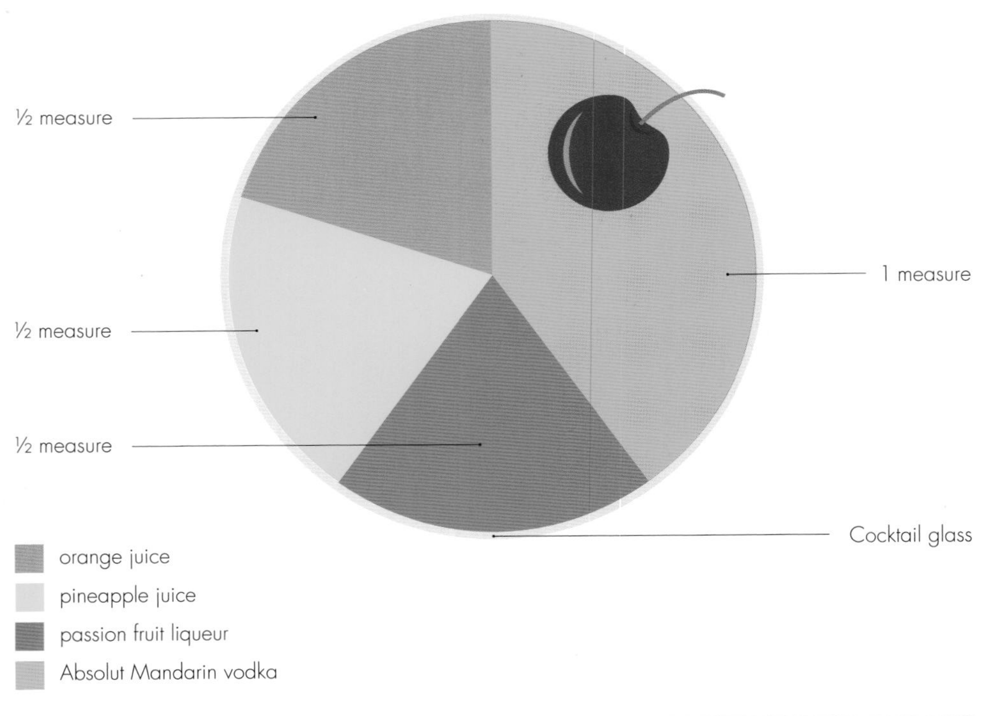
½ measure
½ measure
½ measure
1 measure
Cocktail glass
orange juice
pineapple juice
passion fruit liqueur
Absolut Mandarin vodka

Instructions

1 Shake all the ingredients with ice and strain into a chilled cocktail glass. 2 Garnish with a maraschino cherry.

Lychee Martini

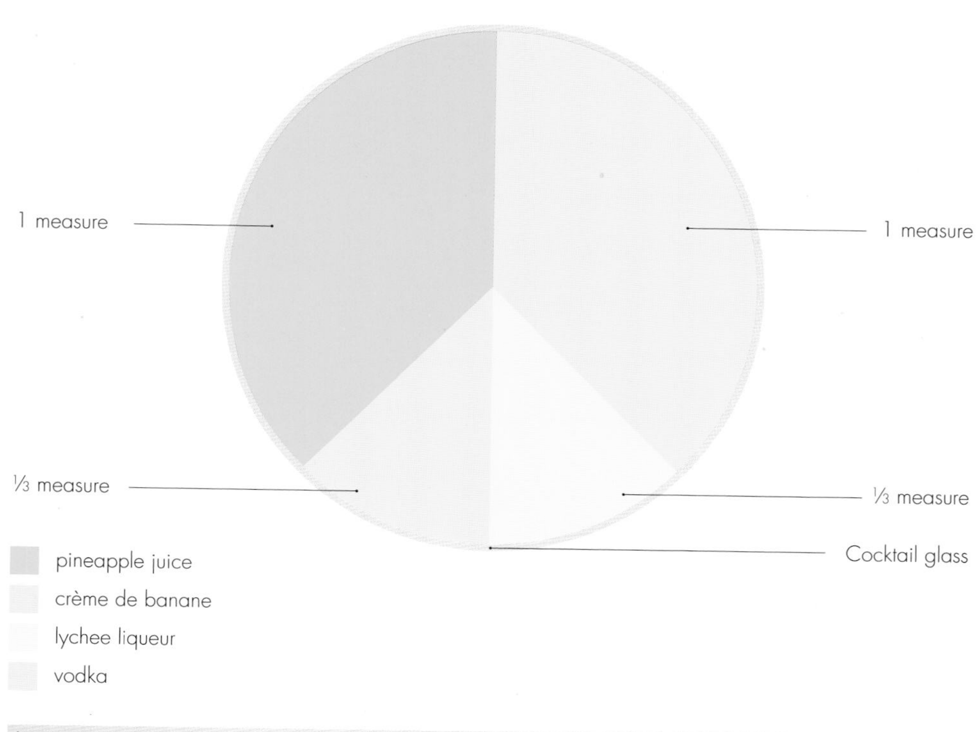
1 measure
1 measure
⅓ measure
⅓ measure
Cocktail glass
pineapple juice
crème de banane
lychee liqueur
vodka

Instructions

1 Shake all the ingredients. **2** Strain into a cocktail glass.

Metropolis

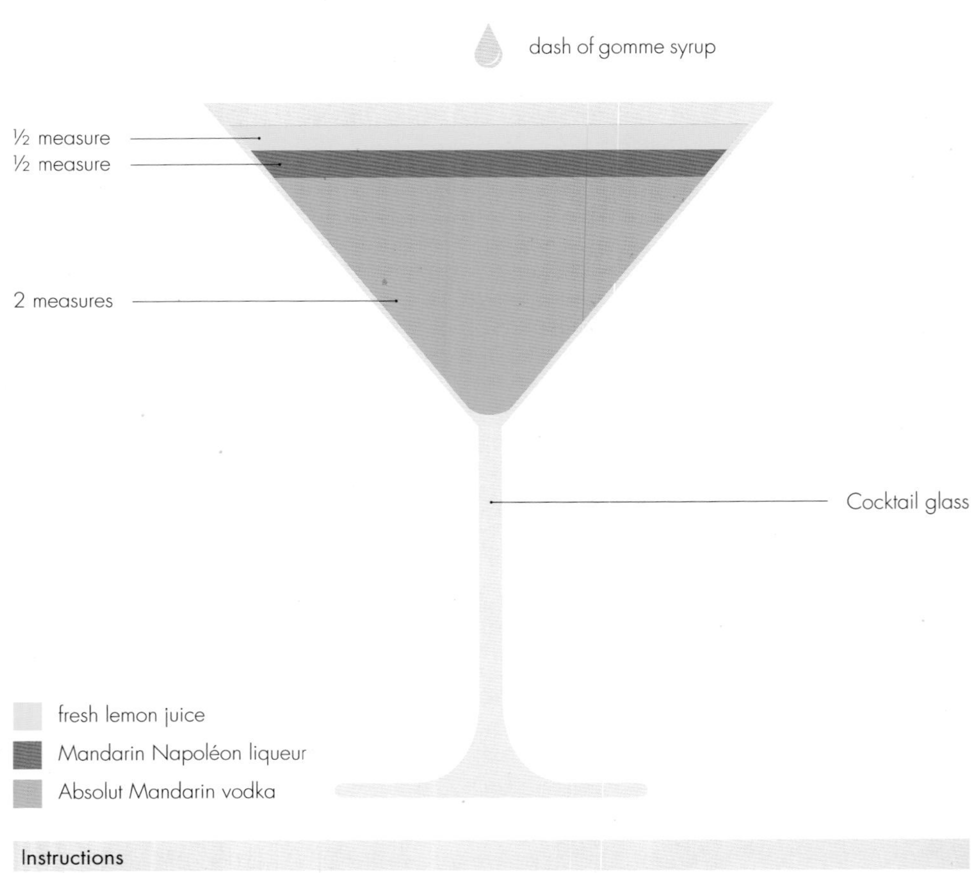
dash of gomme syrup
½ measure
½ measure
2 measures
Cocktail glass
fresh lemon juice
Mandarin Napoléon liqueur
Absolut Mandarin vodka

Instructions

1 Shake all ingredients with ice and strain into a cocktail glass.

Mudslide

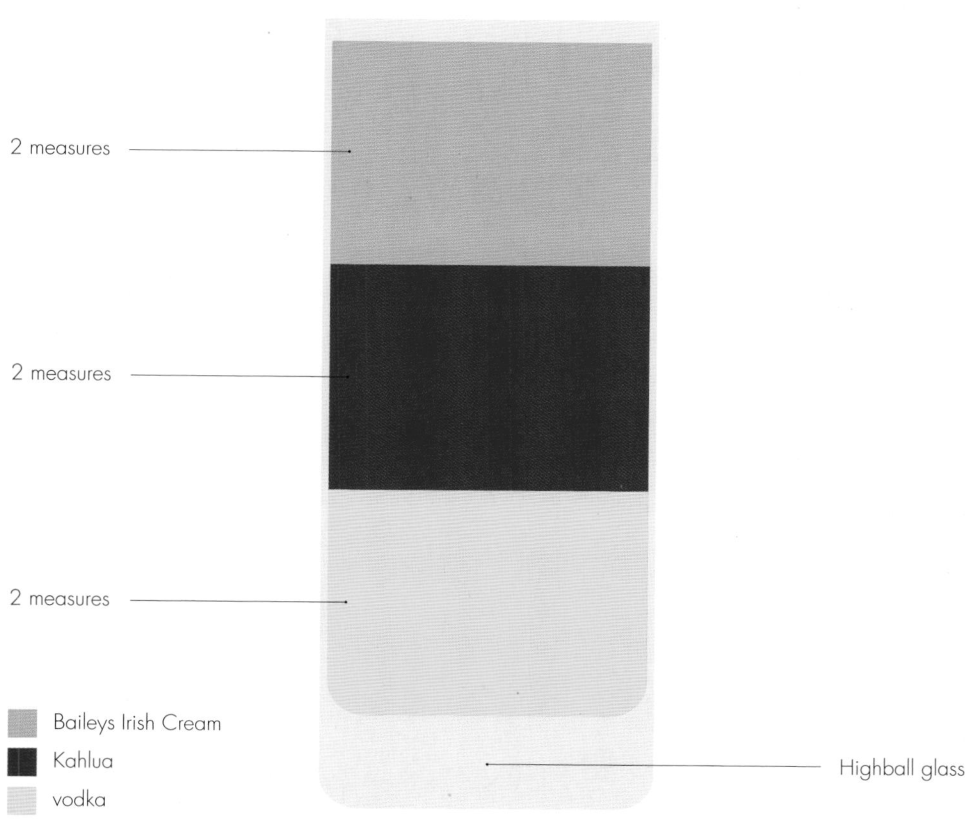

2 measures
2 measures
2 measures
Baileys Irish Cream
Kahlua
vodka
Highball glass

Instructions

1 Mix with cracked ice in a shaker. **2** Strain and serve in a chilled highball glass.

Poison Arrow

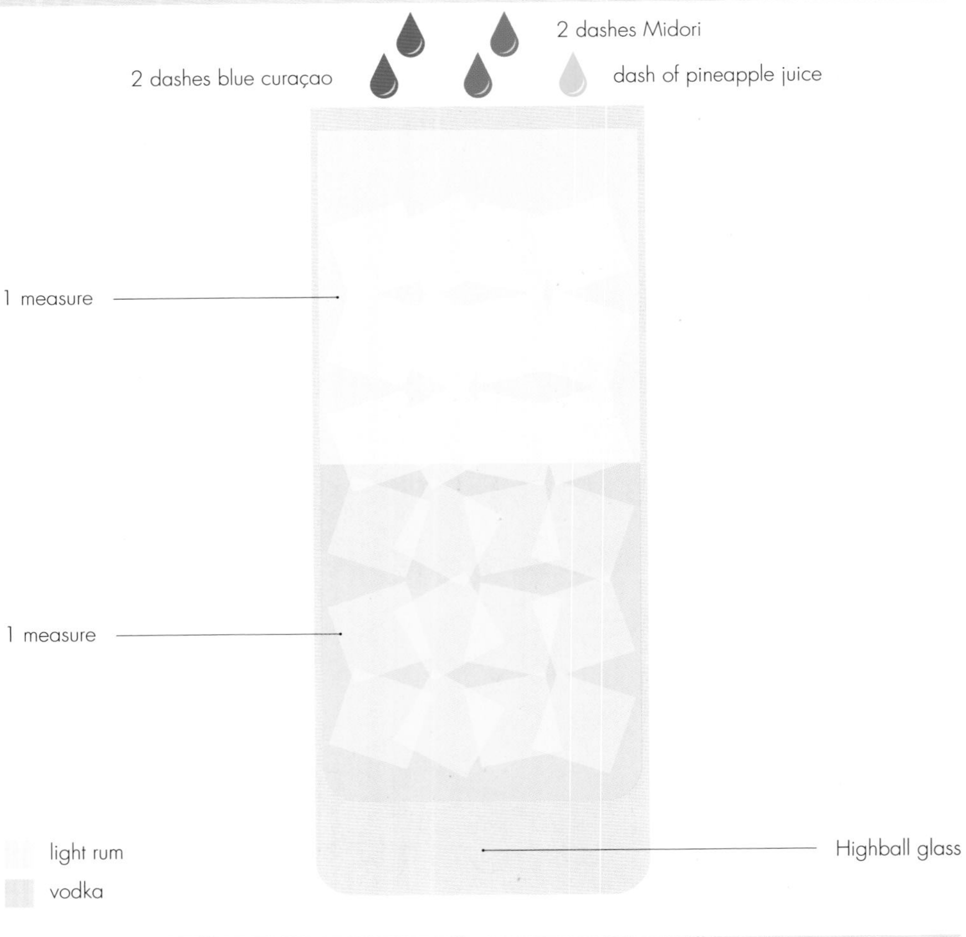

2 dashes Midori
2 dashes blue curaçao
dash of pineapple juice
1 measure
1 measure
light rum
vodka
Highball glass

Instructions

■ Shake all the ingredients with ice. ■ Strain into a chilled highball glass filled with crushed ice.

Salty Dog

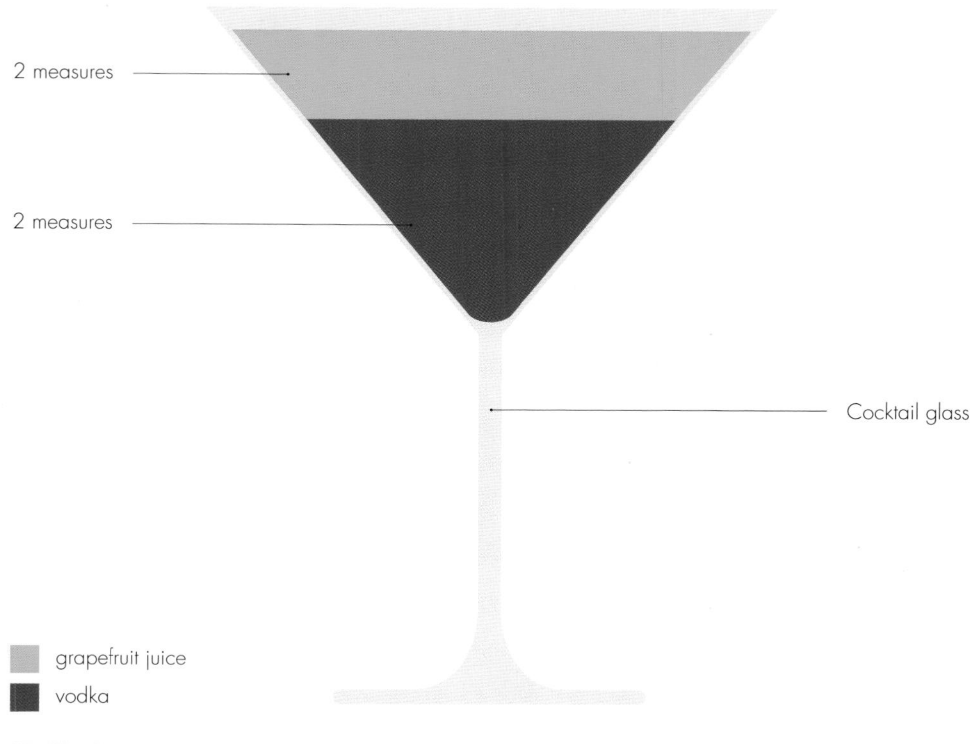
2 measures
2 measures
Cocktail glass
grapefruit juice
vodka

Instructions

1 Mix the vodka with the grapefruit juice in a shaker, then strain into a cocktail glass and serve.

Screwdriver

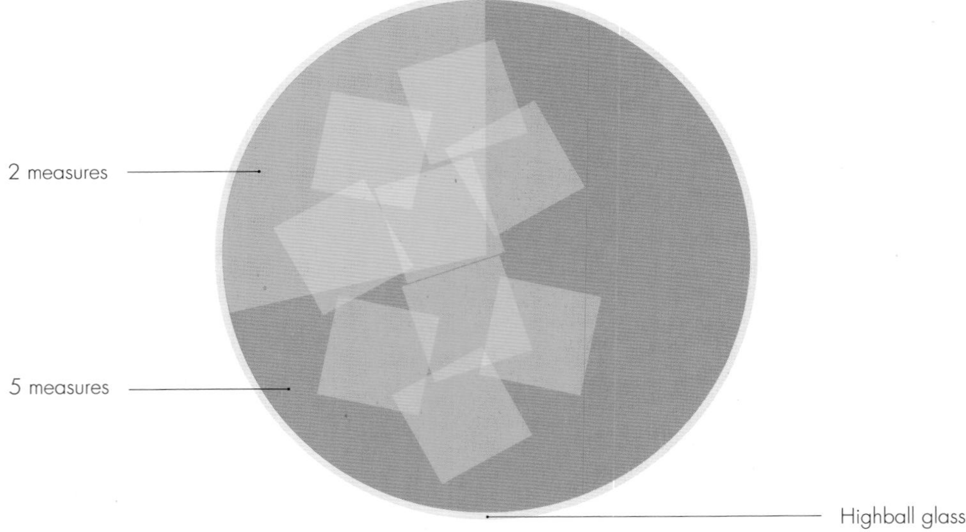
2 measures
5 measures
Highball glass

freshly squeezed orange juice

vodka

Instructions

1 Pour the vodka into a highball glass with ice. 2 Add orange juice, stir, and serve with a stirrer.

Sea Breeze

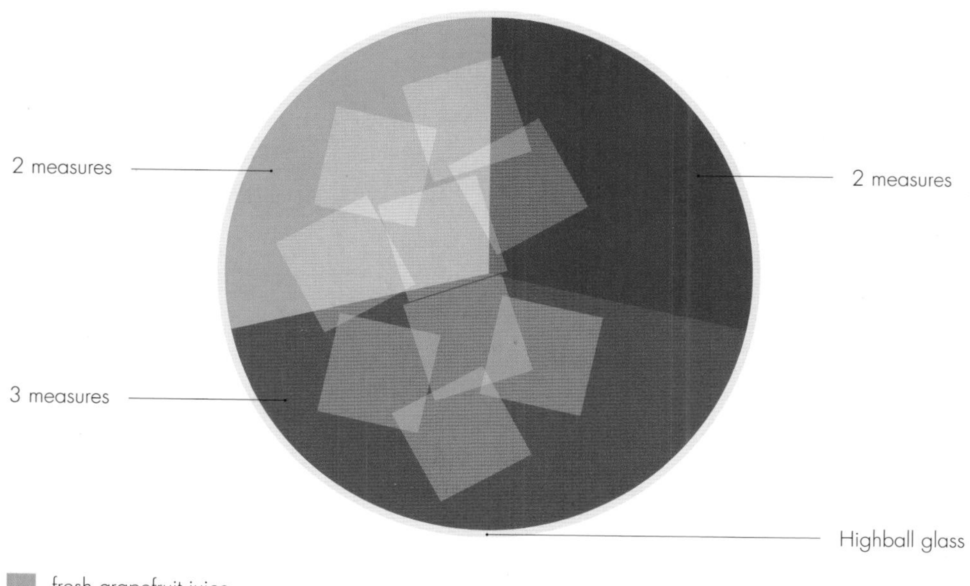
2 measures
2 measures
3 measures
Highball glass

- fresh grapefruit juice
- cranberry juice
- vodka

Instructions

1 Pour ingredients over ice into a highball glass. **2** Stir and serve with a stirrer.

Sea Horse

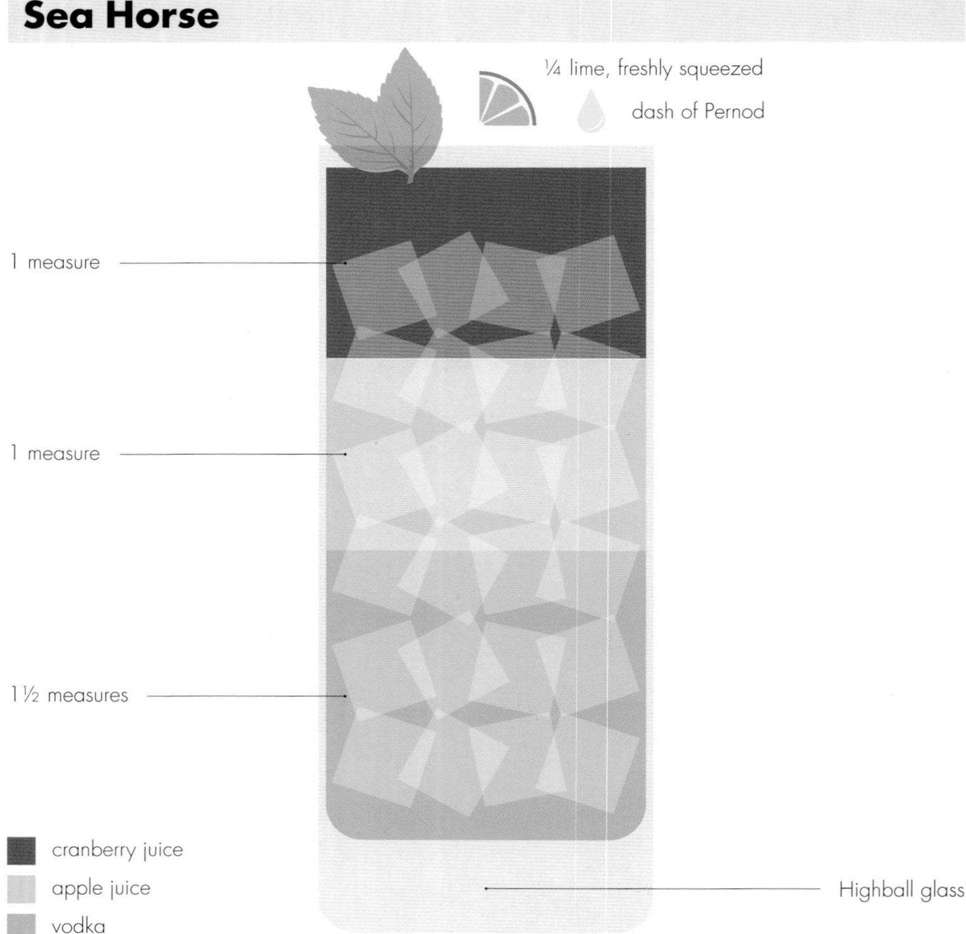

¼ lime, freshly squeezed
dash of Pernod
1 measure
1 measure
1½ measures
cranberry juice
apple juice
vodka
Highball glass

Instructions

1 Pour ingredients into a highball glass filled with ice. 2 Garnish with a sprig of mint.

Vesper

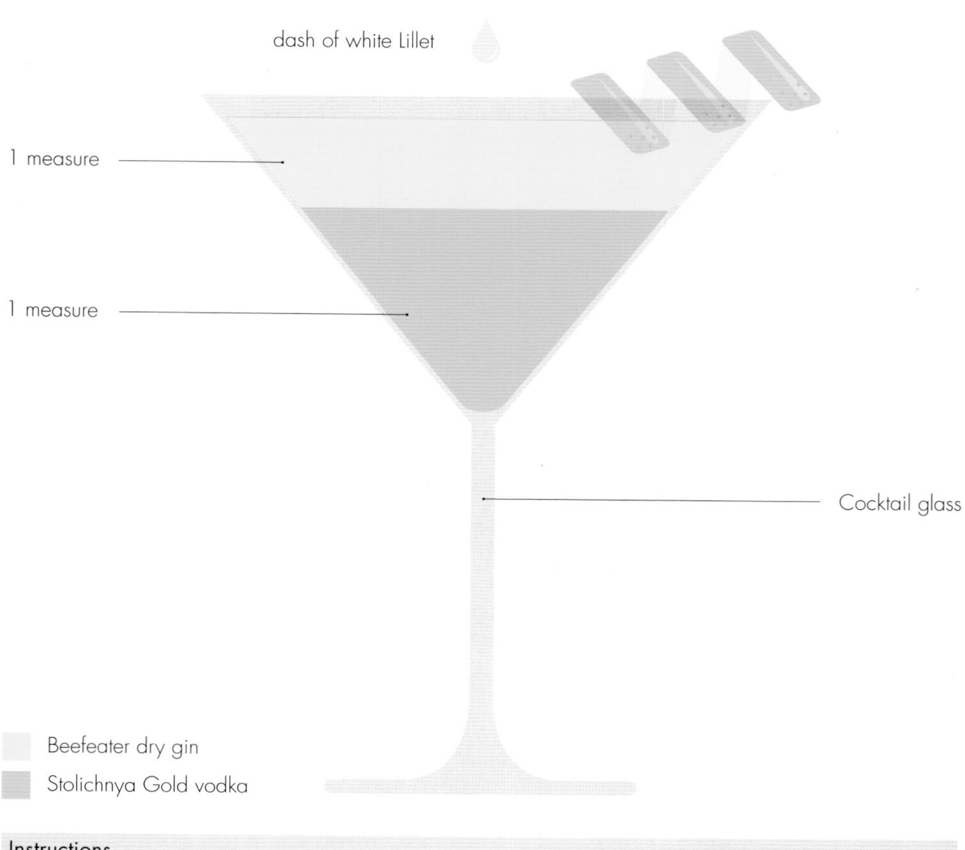

dash of white Lillet
1 measure
1 measure
Cocktail glass
Beefeater dry gin
Stolichnya Gold vodka

Instructions

1 Vigorously shake ingredients with ice and strain into a chilled cocktail glass. **2** Garnish with a lemon twist.

White Russian

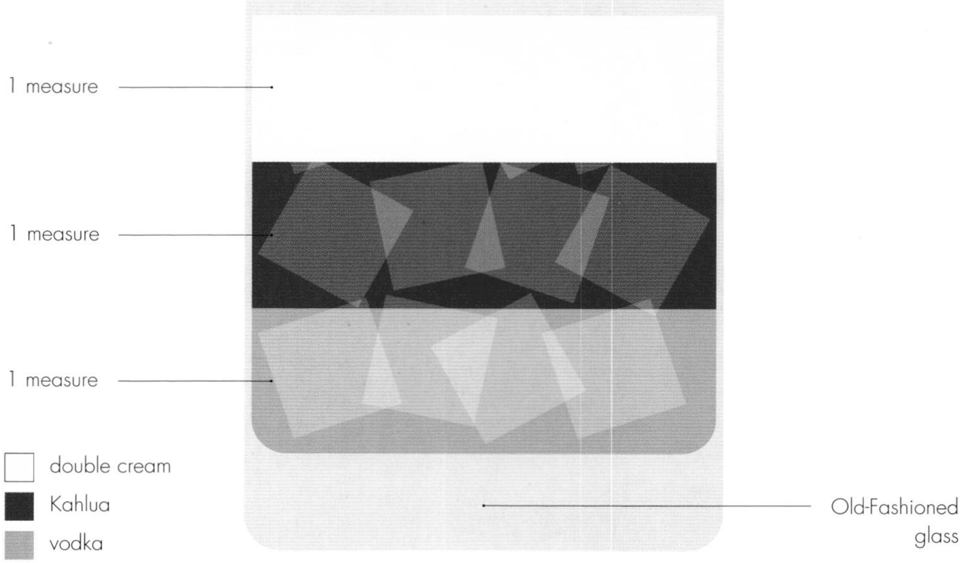
1 measure
1 measure
1 measure
double cream
Kahlua
vodka
Old-Fashioned glass

Instructions

■ Mix the ingredients together in a shaker, then strain into a cocktail glass and serve. ■ Alternatively, layer the ingredients in an ice-filled Old-Fashioned glass.

Woo Woo

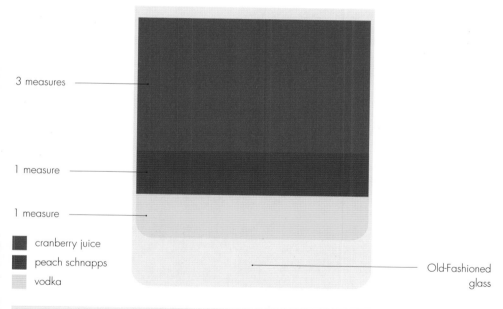

3 measures
1 measure
1 measure
cranberry juice
peach schnapps
vodka
Old-Fashioned glass

Instructions

■ Shake all the ingredients together, then strain into an Old-Fashioned glass and serve.

GIN

Alaska

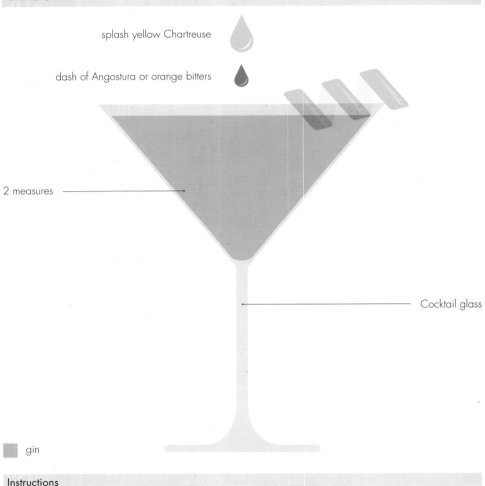

splash yellow Chartreuse

dash of Angostura or orange bitters

2 measures

Cocktail glass

gin

Instructions

1 Shake and strain into a cocktail glass. 2 Garnish with a lemon twist.

Astoria

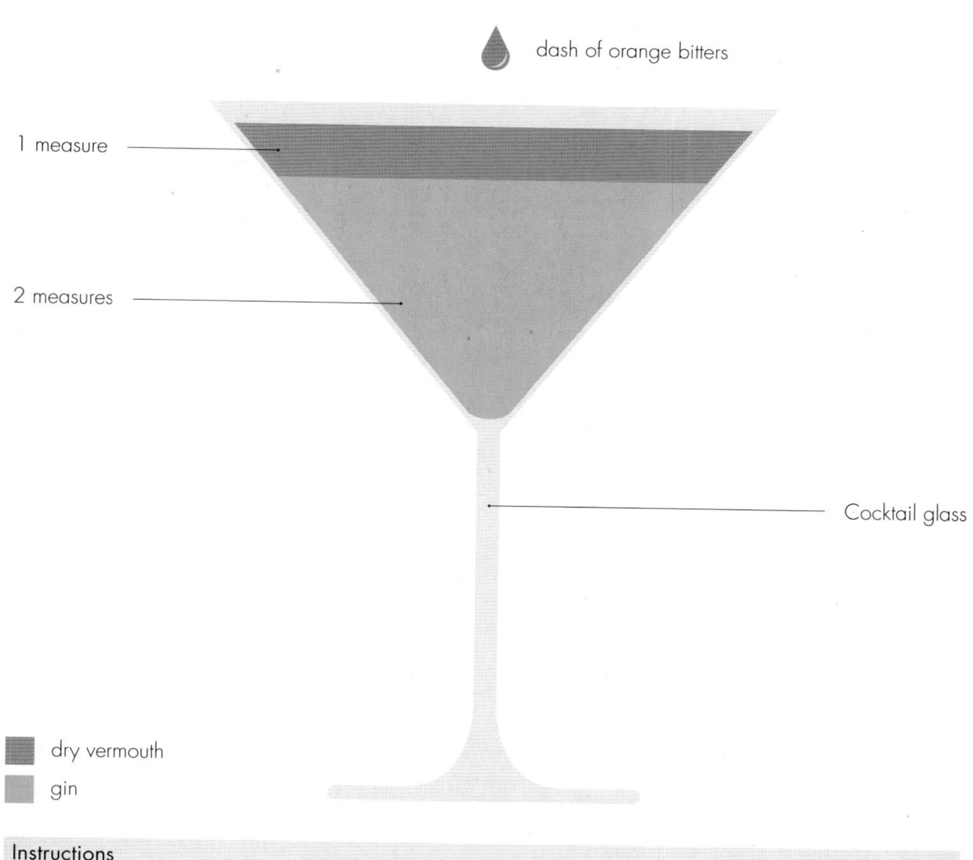
dash of orange bitters
1 measure
2 measures
Cocktail glass
dry vermouth
gin

Instructions

1. Shake all the ingredients together and strain into a cocktail glass.

Blue Monday

dash of blue curaçao

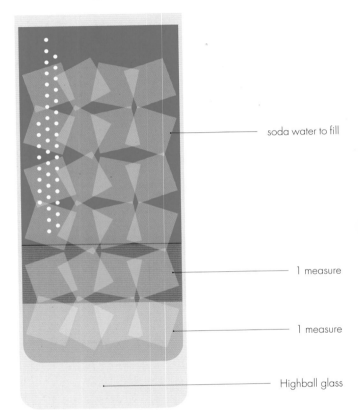

soda water to fill

1 measure

1 measure

Highball glass

soda water to fill

Cointreau

gin

Instructions

1 Pour the gin and Cointreau into a highball glass filled with ice, then fill with soda water, and stir. **2** Add a few drops of blue curaçao. **3** Stir again and serve with a stirrer in the glass.

Bombardier

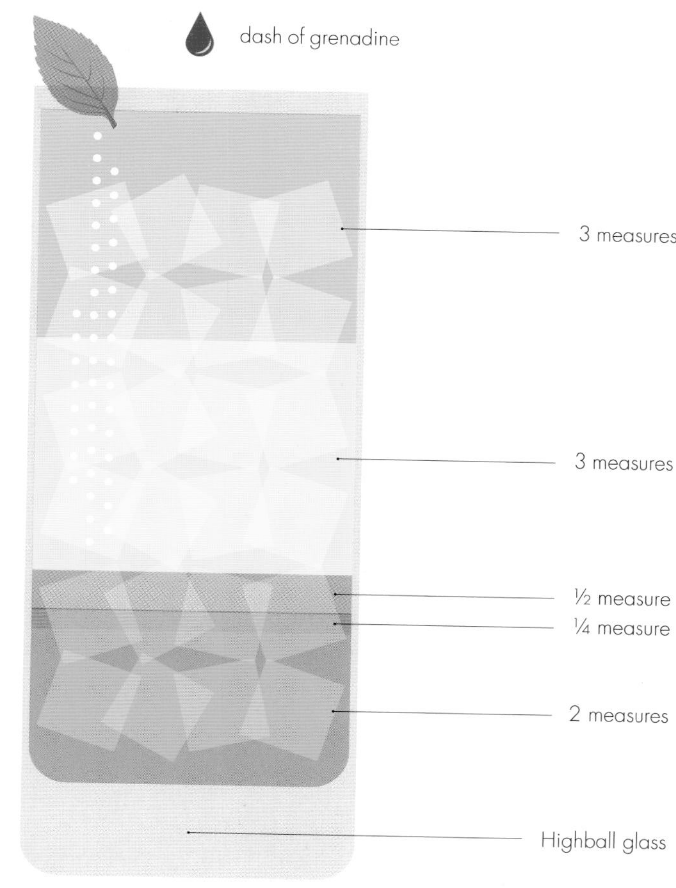

dash of grenadine
3 measures
3 measures
½ measure
¼ measure
2 measures
Highball glass

tonic water
soda water
fresh lime juice
orange juice
Bombay gin

Instructions

1 Shake all the liquid ingredients, except the tonic and soda, with ice and strain into an ice-filled highball glass. **2** Fill up with the tonic and soda waters. **3** Stir, then garnish with a mint leaf.

Broadway

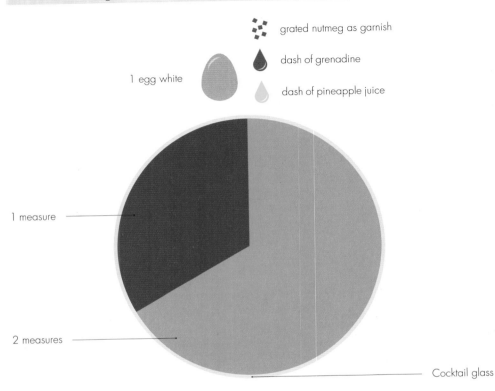

grated nutmeg as garnish

dash of grenadine

1 egg white

dash of pineapple juice

1 measure

2 measures

Cocktail glass

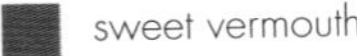

sweet vermouth

gin

Instructions

1 Shake all the liquid ingredients together, then strain into a cocktail glass. 2 Sprinkle with the nutmeg and serve.

Cadillac Lady

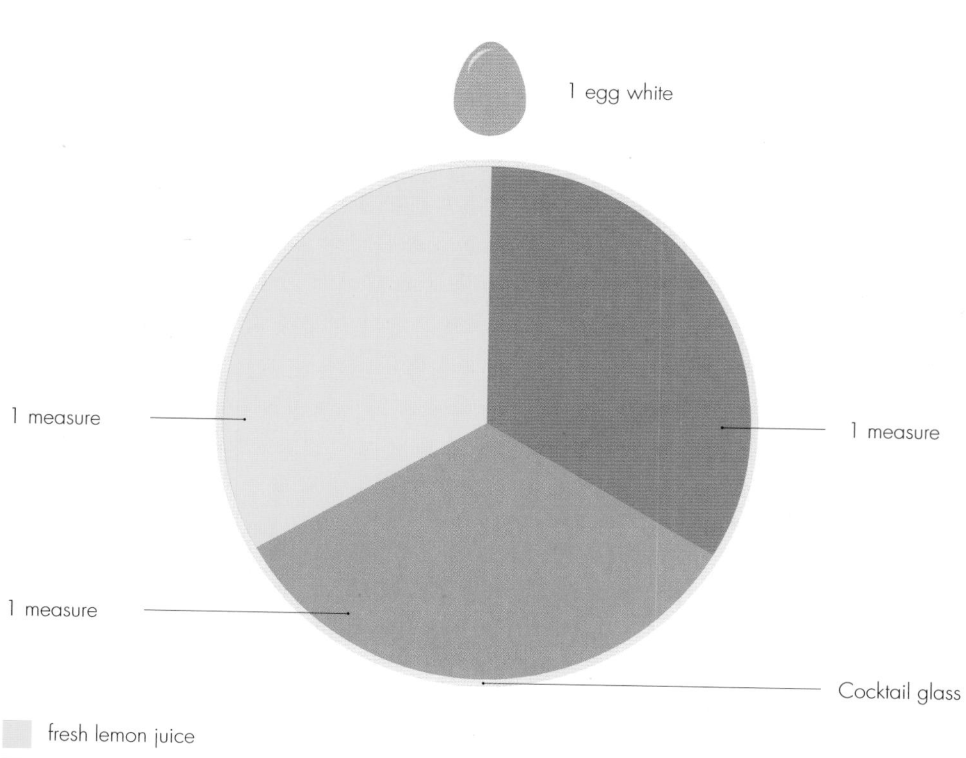
1 egg white
1 measure
1 measure
1 measure
Cocktail glass

- fresh lemon juice
- Grand Marnier
- gin

Instructions

1 Shake all the ingredients together, then strain into a cocktail glass and serve.

Dirty Martini

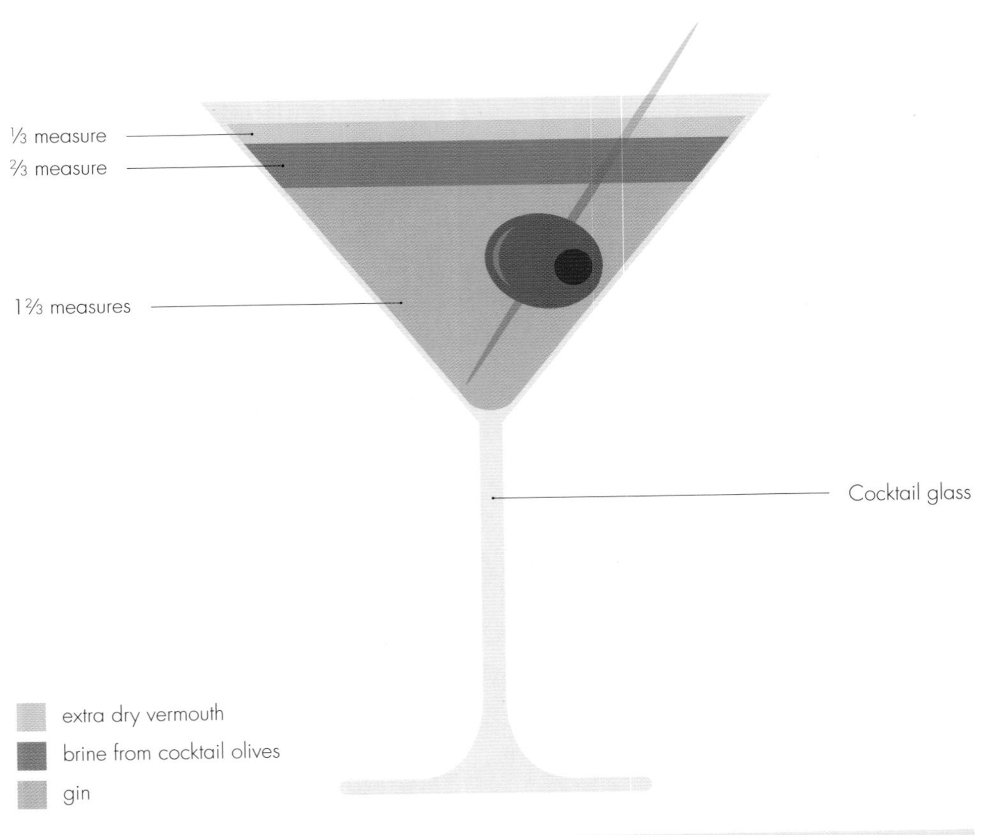

⅓ measure
⅔ measure
1⅔ measures
Cocktail glass
extra dry vermouth
brine from cocktail olives
gin

Instructions

1 Pour ingredients into a mixing glass with ice and stir. **2** Strain into a cocktail glass. **3** Add an olive on a cocktail stick.

Fluffy Duck (international)

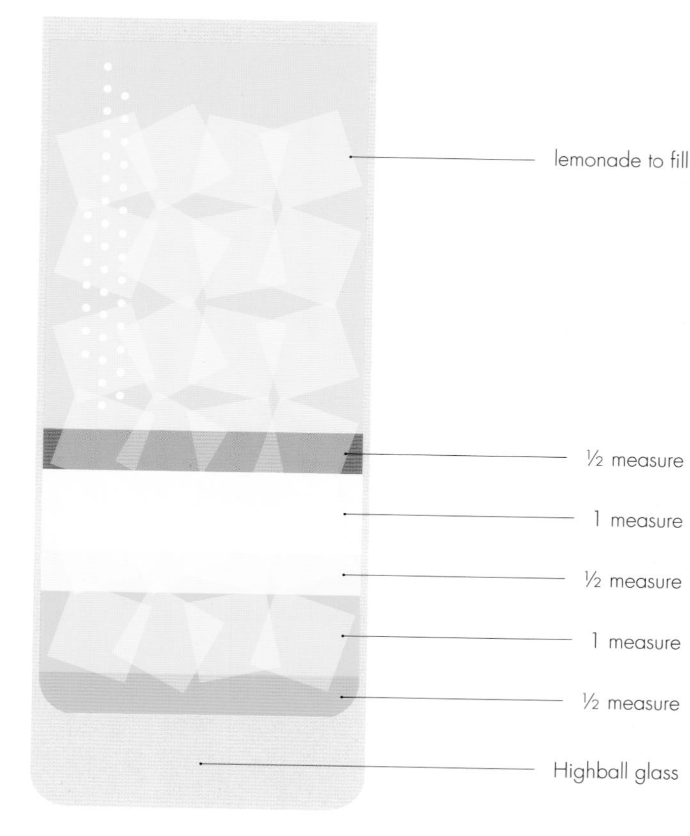
lemonade to fill
½ measure
1 measure
½ measure
1 measure
½ measure
Highball glass

lemonade
Cointreau
cream
vodka
advocaat
gin

Instructions

1 Pour all ingredients, except the lemonde, into a highball glass over ice. **2** Stir, then top up with lemonade.

French 75

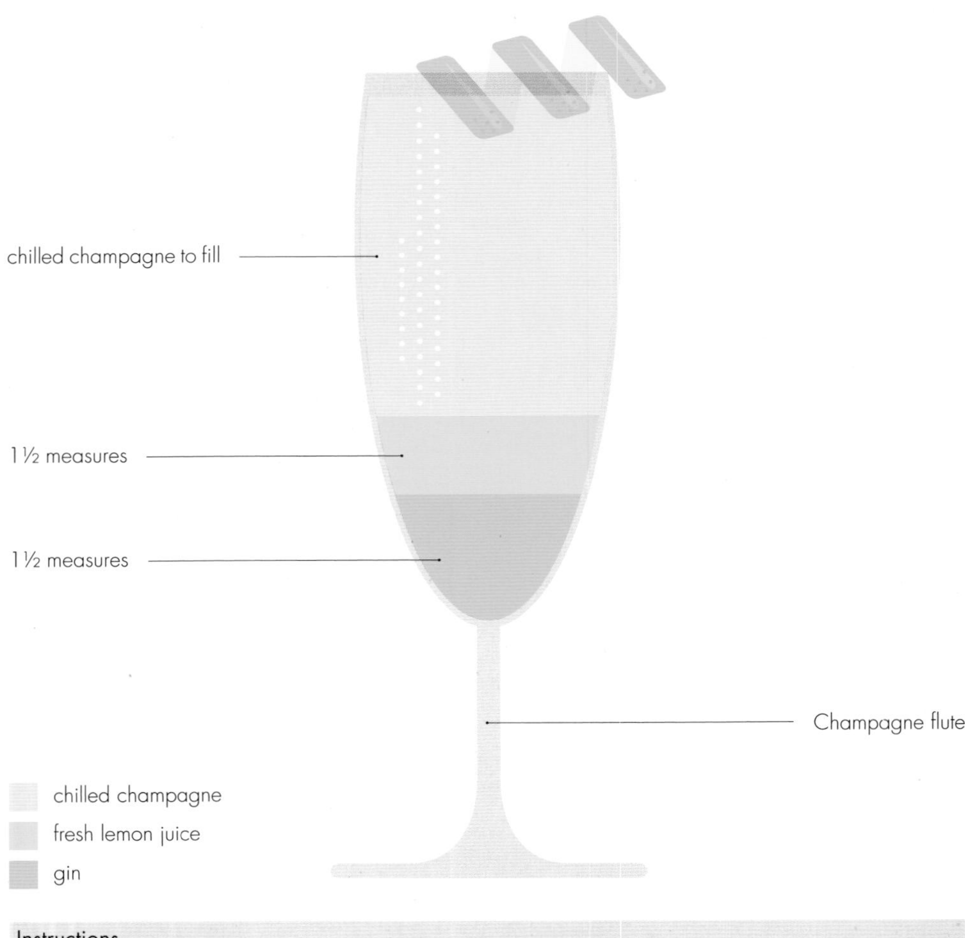
chilled champagne to fill
1 ½ measures
1 ½ measures
Champagne flute
chilled champagne
fresh lemon juice
gin

Instructions

1 Mix the gin and lemon juice together in a champagne flute. **2** Top up with champagne, garnish with a lemon twist and serve.

Harry's Cocktail

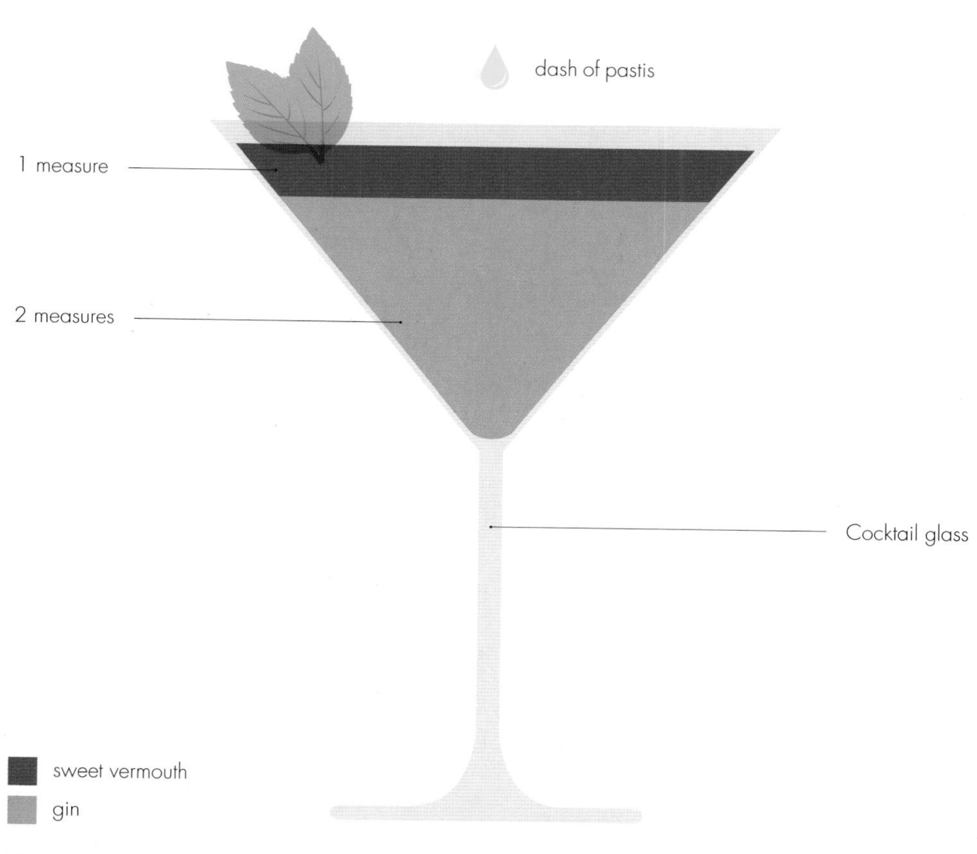
dash of pastis
1 measure
2 measures
Cocktail glass
sweet vermouth
gin

Instructions

1 Shake all the liquids together, then strain into a cocktail glass and serve. **2** Garnish with a sprig of mint.

Imperial

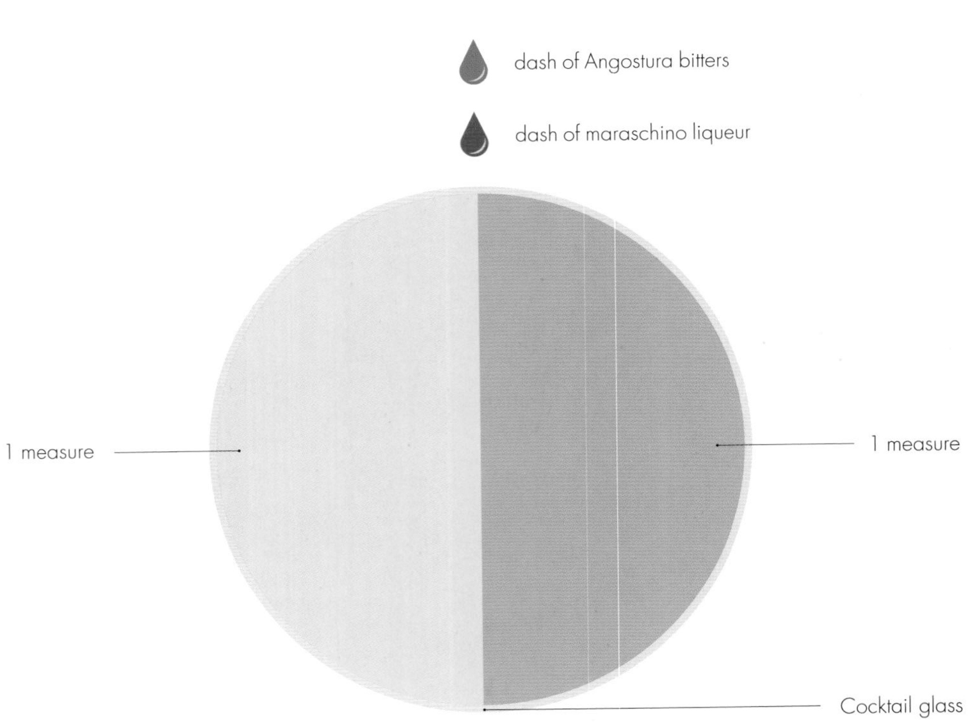
dash of Angostura bitters
dash of maraschino liqueur
1 measure
1 measure
Cocktail glass

dry vermouth

gin

Instructions

1 Shake all the ingredients together, then strain into a cocktail glass and serve.

Jacuzzi

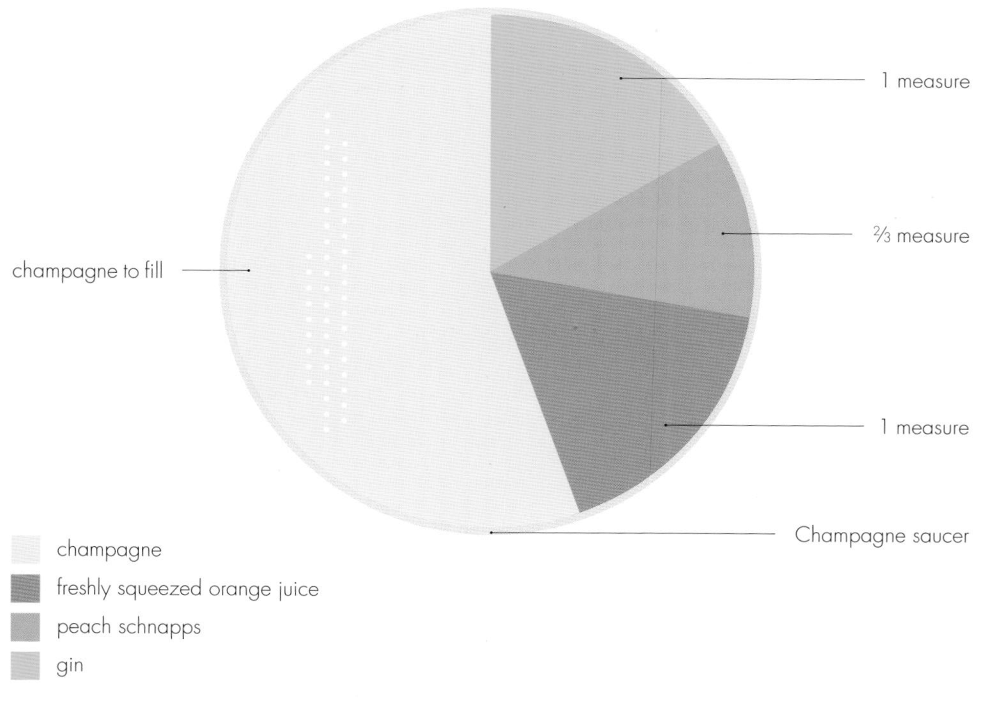

1 measure
2/3 measure
champagne to fill
1 measure
Champagne saucer
champagne
freshly squeezed orange juice
peach schnapps
gin

Instructions

1 Pour the gin, schnapps and juice into a shaker with ice. **2** Shake, then strain into a champagne saucer. **3** Stir gently and fill with champagne. Stir again.

Jasmine

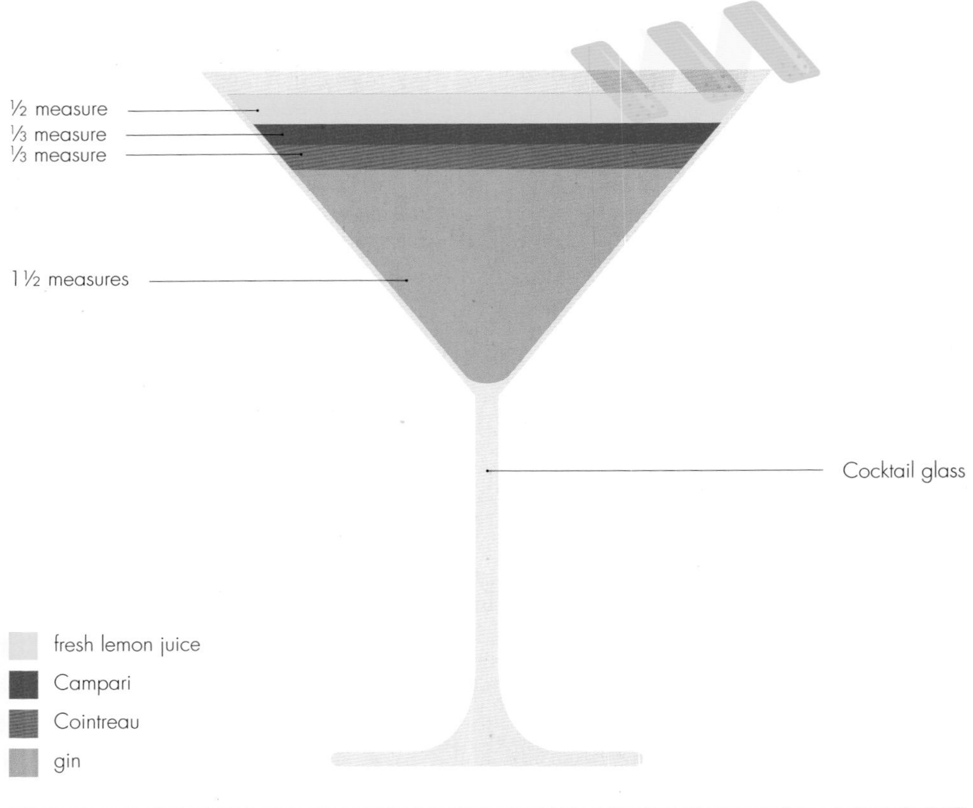

½ measure
⅓ measure
⅓ measure
1 ½ measures
Cocktail glass
fresh lemon juice
Campari
Cointreau
gin

Instructions

1 Shake with all the ingredients together with ice and strain into a cocktail glass. **2** Add a lemon twist.

Juniper Royale

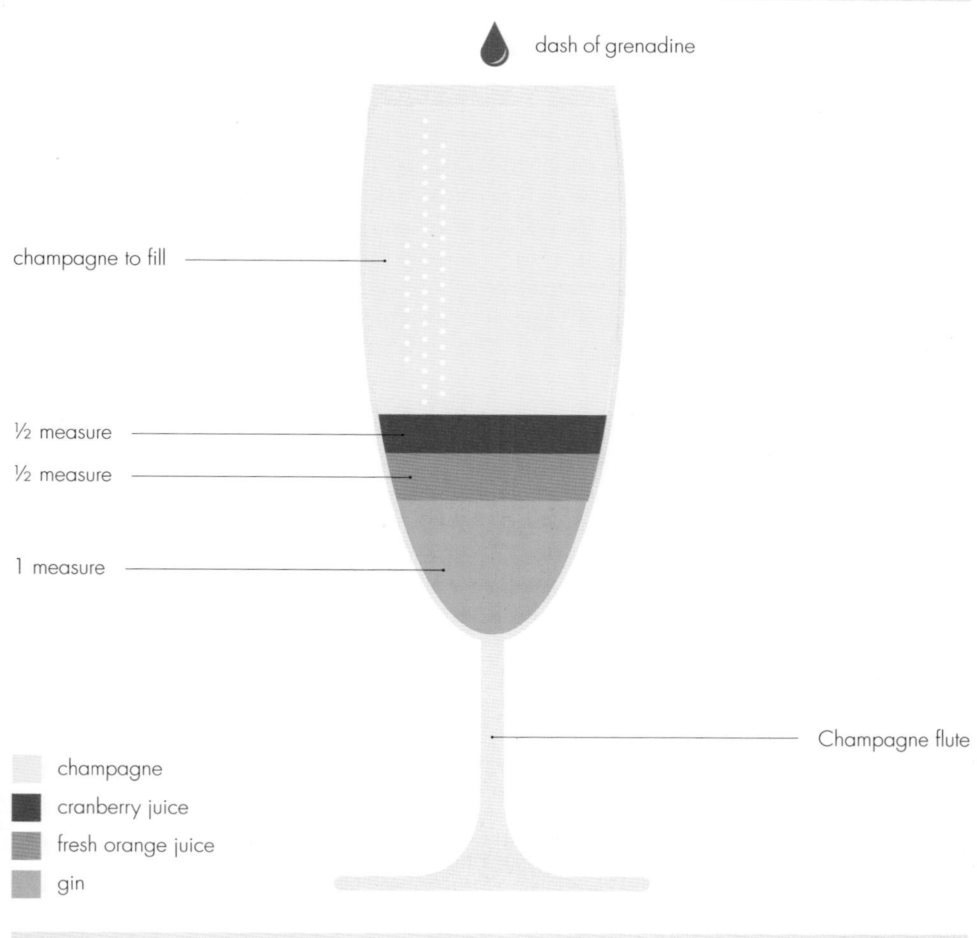

dash of grenadine
champagne to fill
½ measure
½ measure
1 measure
Champagne flute
champagne
cranberry juice
fresh orange juice
gin

Instructions

1 Pour the gin, juices, and grenadine into a shaker with ice and shake. **2** Strain into a champagne flute and stir gently. **3** Top up with champagne and stir again.

Kaiser

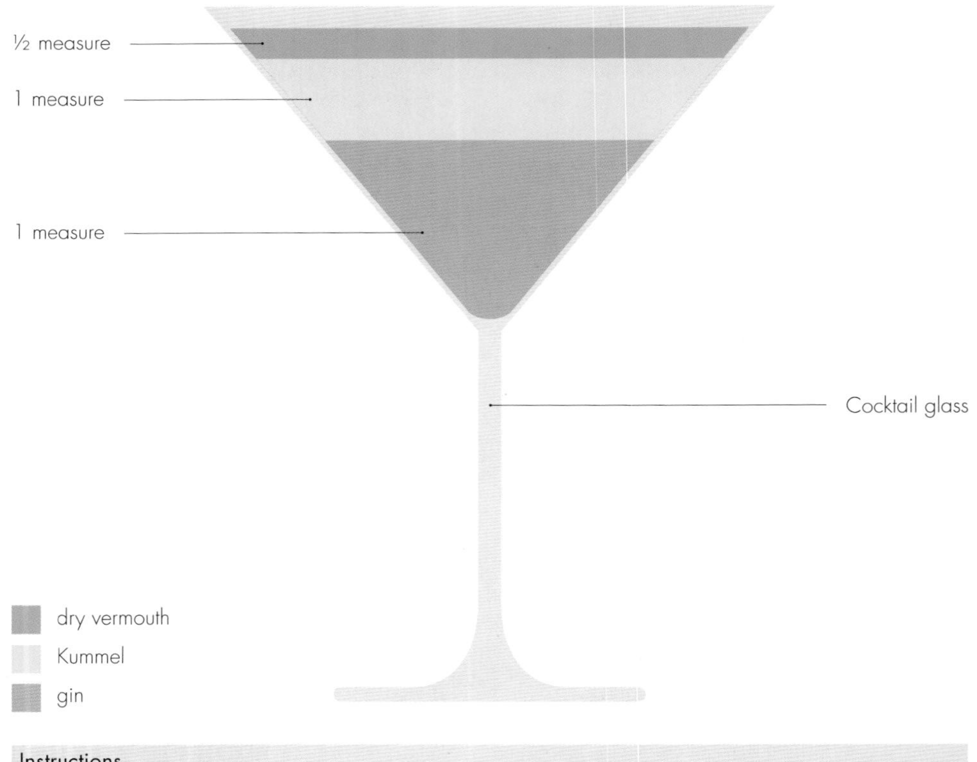

½ measure
1 measure
1 measure
Cocktail glass
dry vermouth
Kummel
gin

Instructions

1. Stir all the ingredients together, then strain into a cocktail glass and serve.

Leap Year

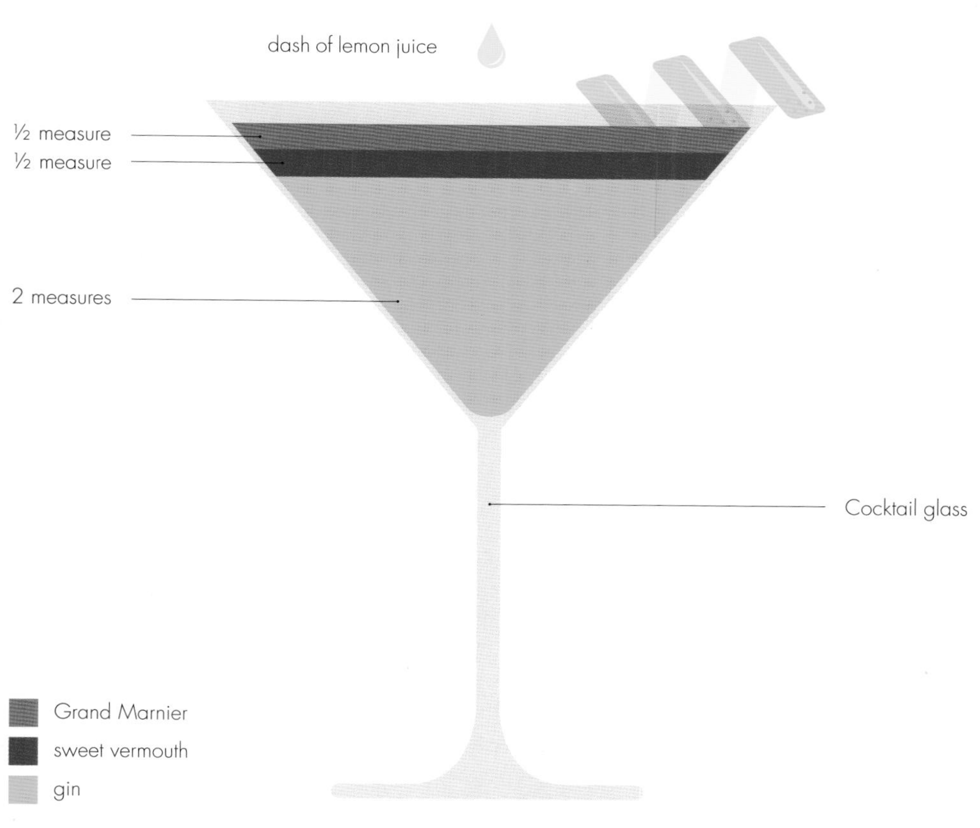

dash of lemon juice
½ measure
½ measure
2 measures
Cocktail glass
Grand Marnier
sweet vermouth
gin

Instructions

1 Shake all ingredients with ice and strain into a chilled cocktail glass. **2** Garnish with a twist of lemon or orange.

Moulin Rouge

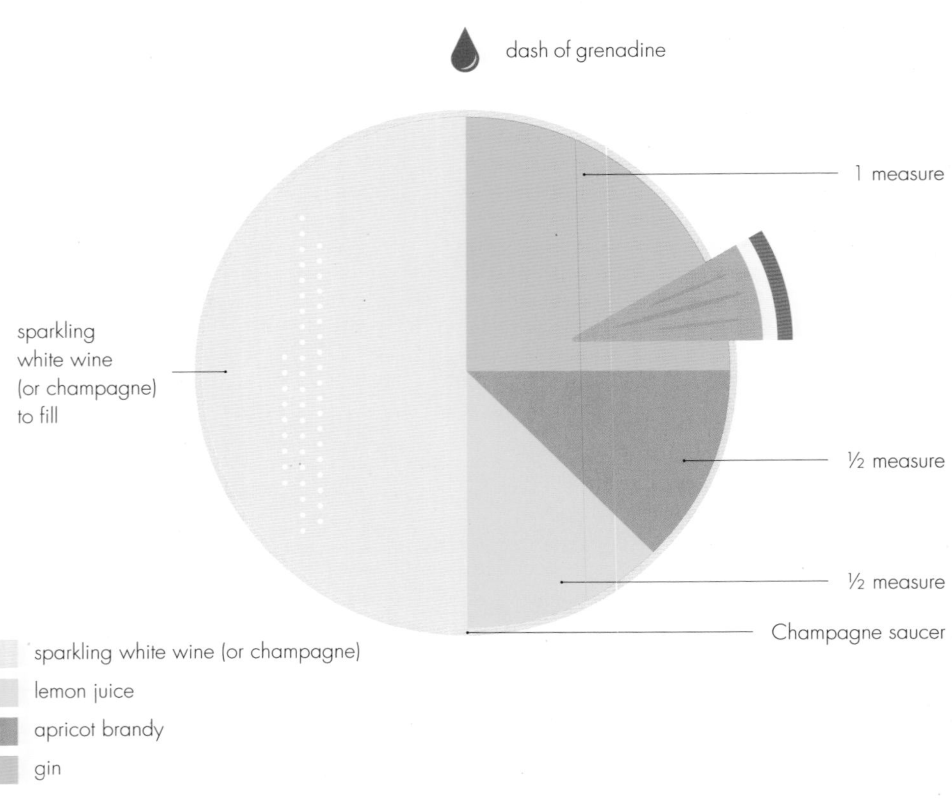

dash of grenadine
1 measure
sparkling
white wine
(or champagne)
to fill
½ measure
½ measure
Champagne saucer
sparkling white wine (or champagne)
lemon juice
apricot brandy
gin

Instructions

1 Shake all the ingredients, except the sparkling wine (or champagne), together, and strain into a champagne saucer. **2** Top with sparkling wine. **3** Garnish with an orange slice.

Old Vermouth

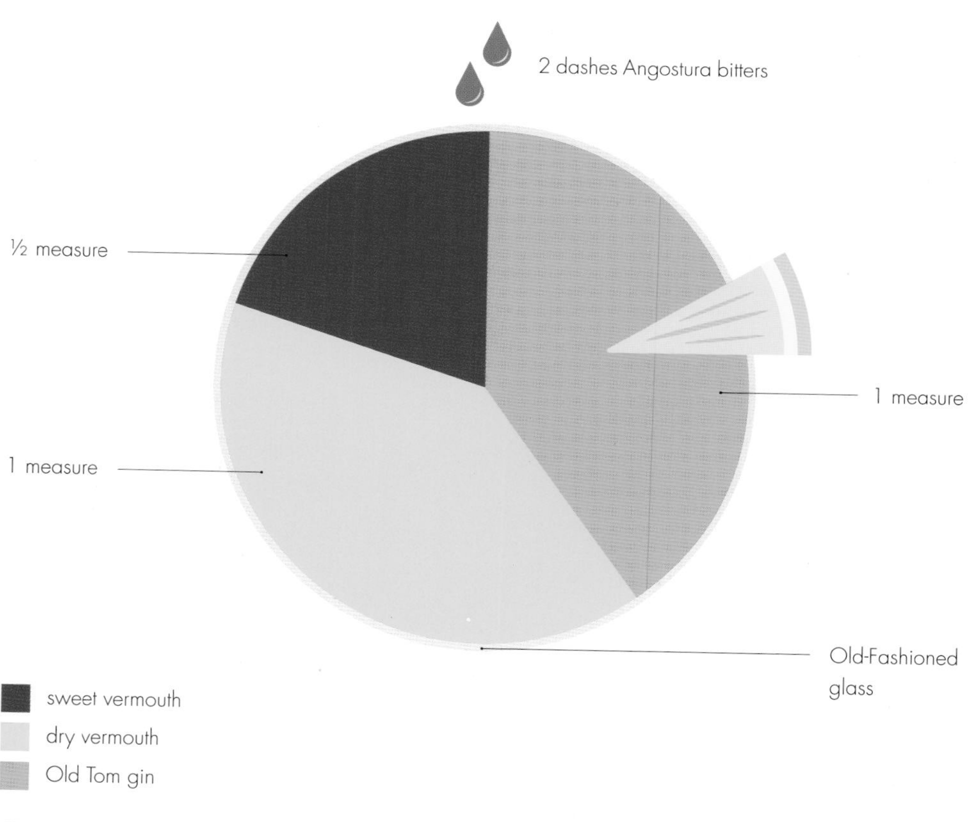
2 dashes Angostura bitters
½ measure
1 measure
1 measure
Old-Fashioned glass
sweet vermouth
dry vermouth
Old Tom gin

Instructions

1 Pour the gin, vermouths and bitters into an Old-Fashioned glass. **2** Garnish with the lemon slice and serve.

Red Snapper

1–2 pinches salt and pepper

2–3 dashes Worcestershire sauce

2–3 drops Tabasco sauce

stick of celery (optional garnish)

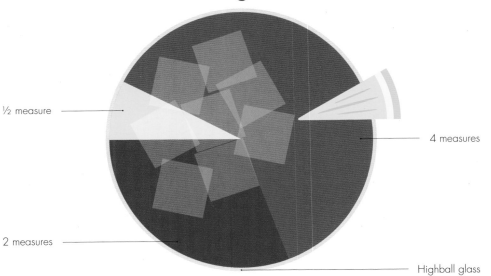

½ measure

4 measures

2 measures

Highball glass

- lemon juice
- tomato juice
- gin

Instructions

1 Shake the gin, tomato juice, and lemon juice with ice and strain into a chilled highball glass filled with ice. 2 Stir in the Worcestershire, Tabasco, and salt and pepper. 3 Add a stick of celery (if needed) and a lemon slice.

The Swinger

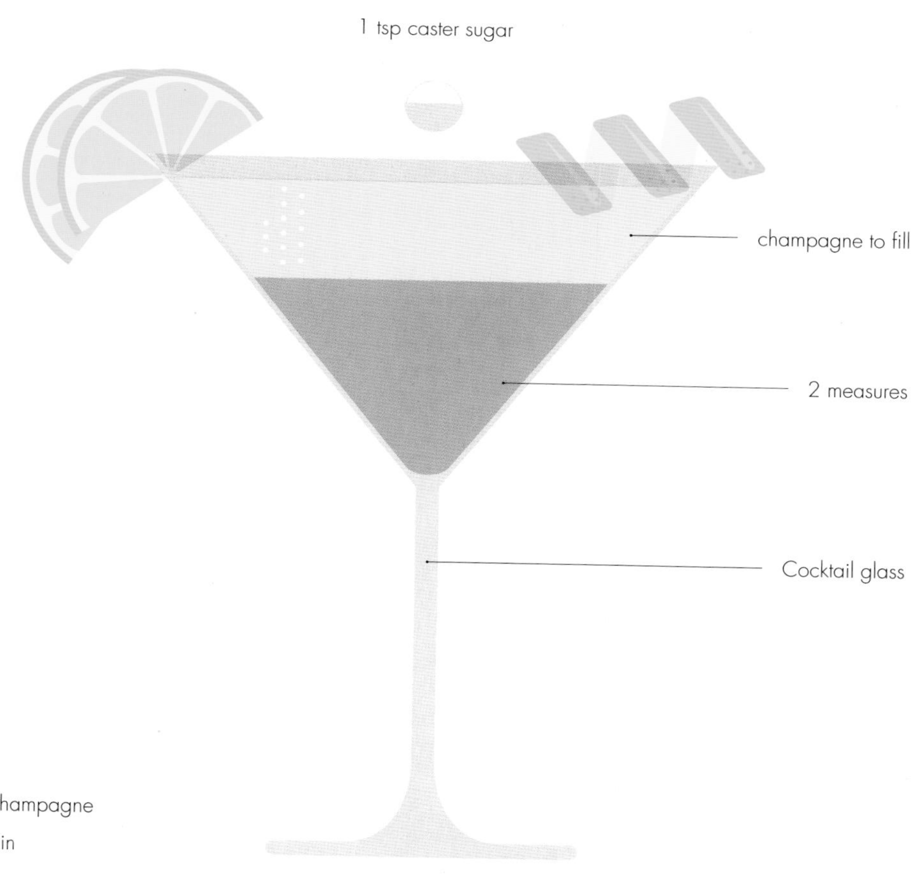
1 tsp caster sugar
champagne to fill
2 measures
Cocktail glass
champagne
gin

Instructions

■ Fill a shaker with ice, add sugar, squeezed lemon wedges, and gin. ■ Shake and strain into a cocktail glass. ■ Top up with champagne and garnish with a lemon twist.

Tom Fizz

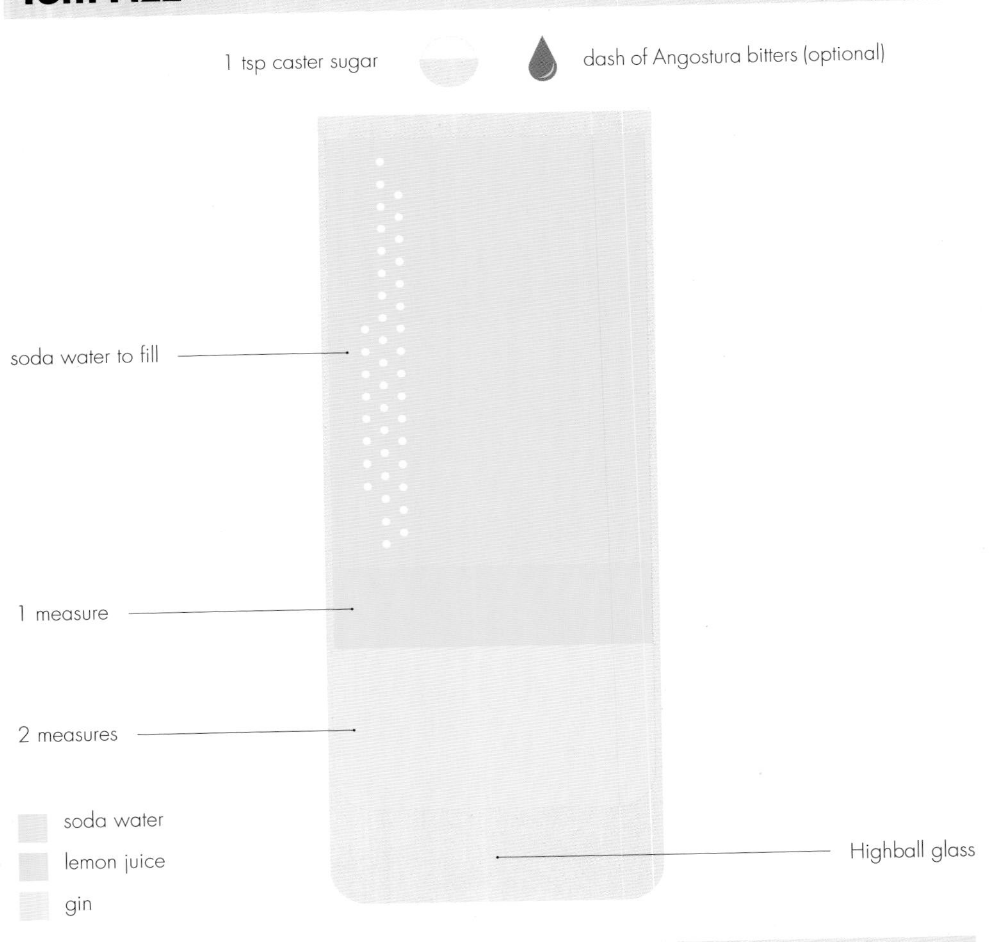

1 tsp caster sugar
dash of Angostura bitters (optional)
soda water to fill
1 measure
2 measures
soda water
lemon juice
gin
Highball glass

Instructions

1 Shake the gin, juice, sugar and bitters, strain into a tall glass, and top up with soda.

Union Jack

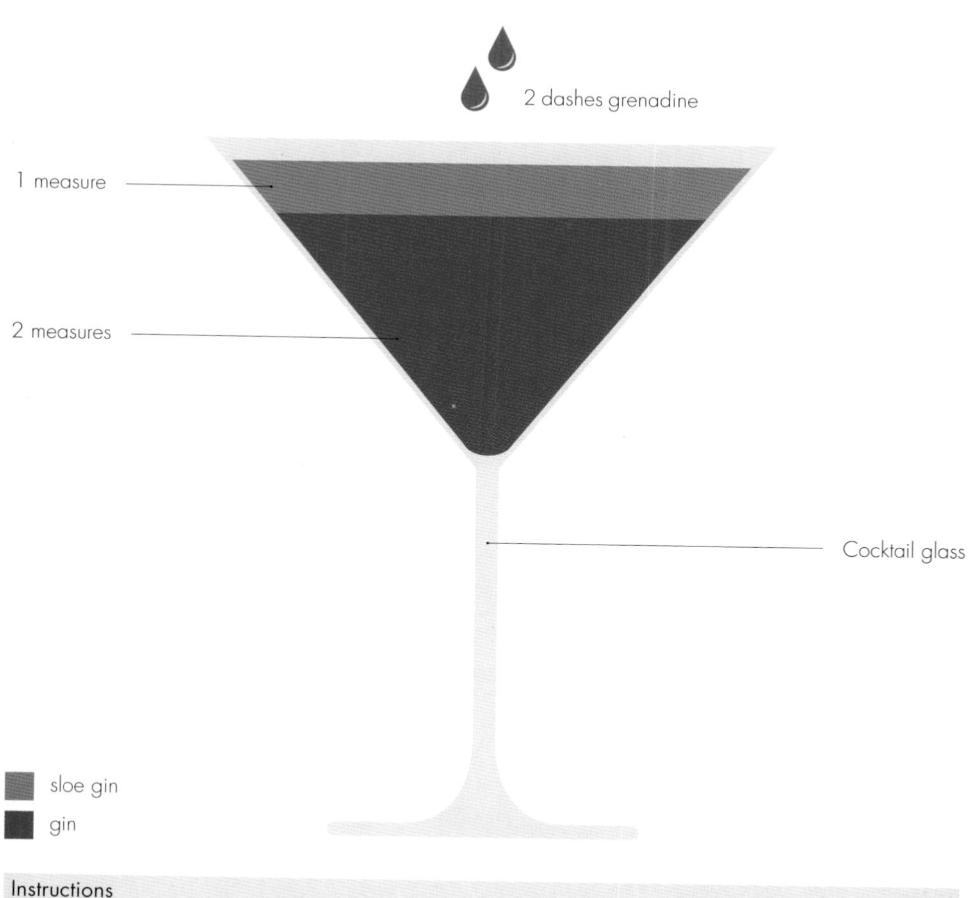
2 dashes grenadine
1 measure
2 measures
Cocktail glass
sloe gin
gin

Instructions

1 Mix the gins and grenadine together in a shaker, then strain into a cocktail glass and serve.

White Velvet

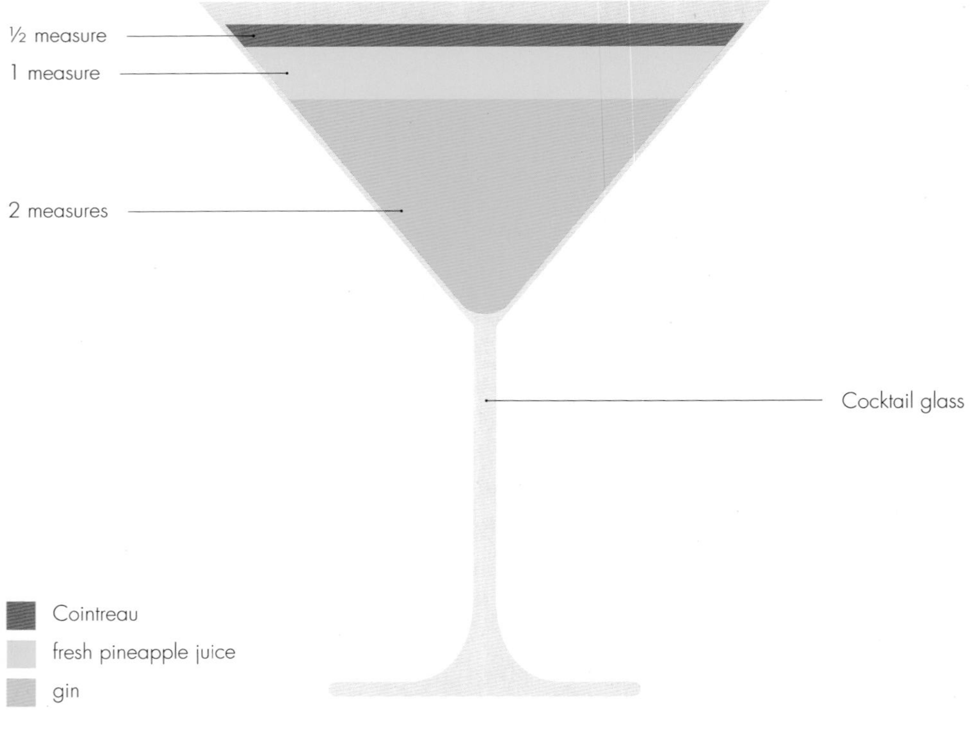

½ measure
1 measure
2 measures
Cocktail glass
Cointreau
fresh pineapple juice
gin

Instructions

1 Pour all the ingredients together, then strain into a cocktail glass and serve.

Woodstock

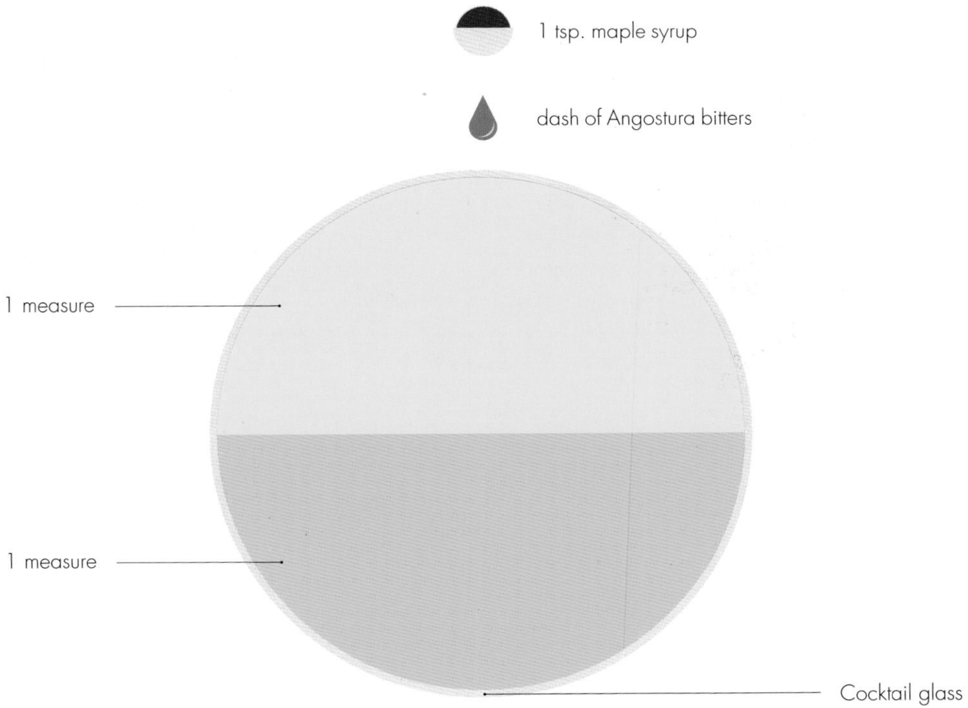

1 tsp. maple syrup

dash of Angostura bitters

1 measure

1 measure

Cocktail glass

lemon juice

gin

Instructions

1. Shake all the ingredients together, then strain into a cocktail glass and serve.

BRANDY

Adam and Eve

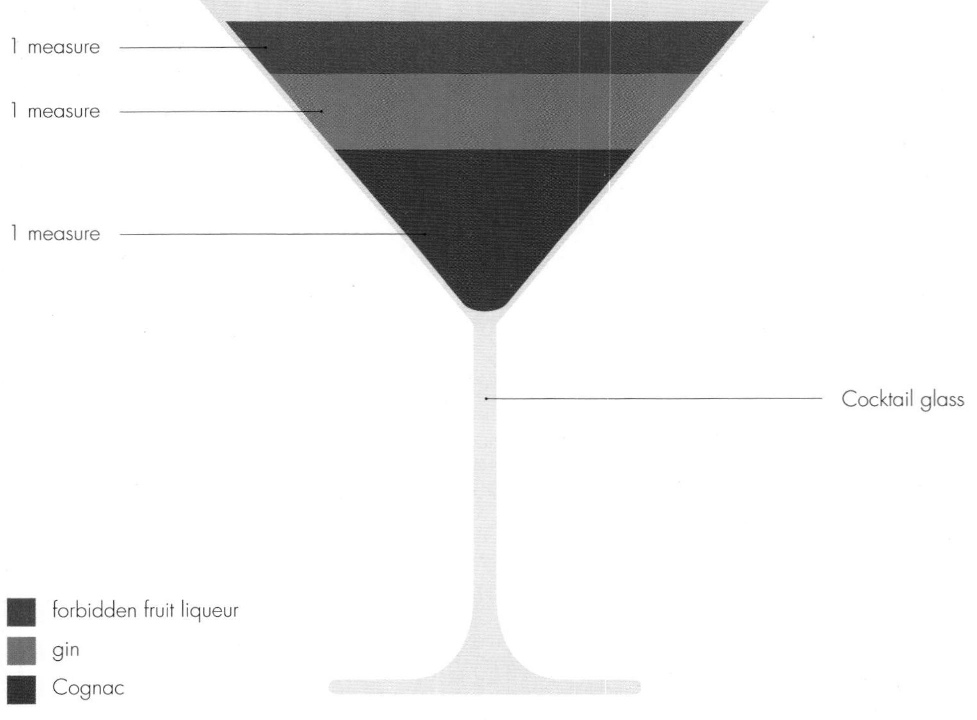
1 measure
1 measure
1 measure
Cocktail glass
forbidden fruit liqueur
gin
Cognac

Instructions

1. Shake all the liquids together, then strain into a cocktail glass and serve.

American Beauty

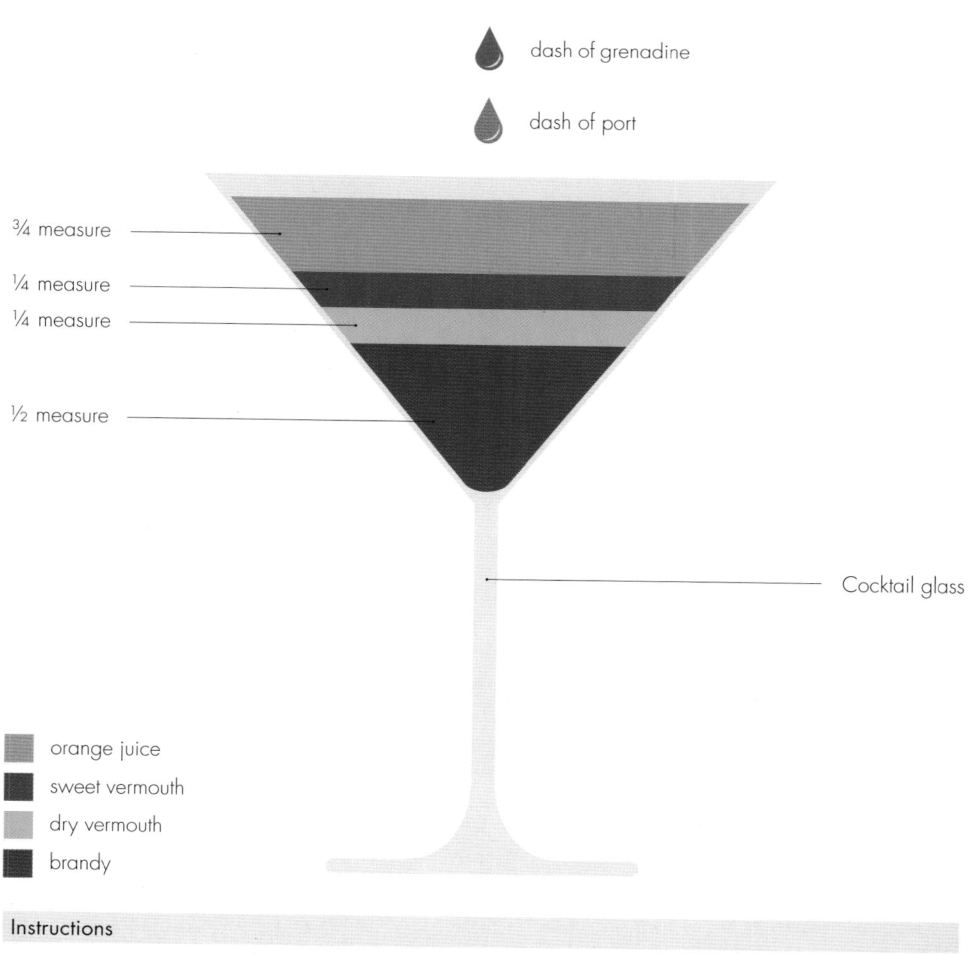

dash of grenadine
dash of port
¾ measure
¼ measure
¼ measure
½ measure
Cocktail glass
orange juice
sweet vermouth
dry vermouth
brandy

Instructions

1 Shake and strain all the ingredients, except the port, into a cocktail glass. **2** Float the port on top.

April Shower

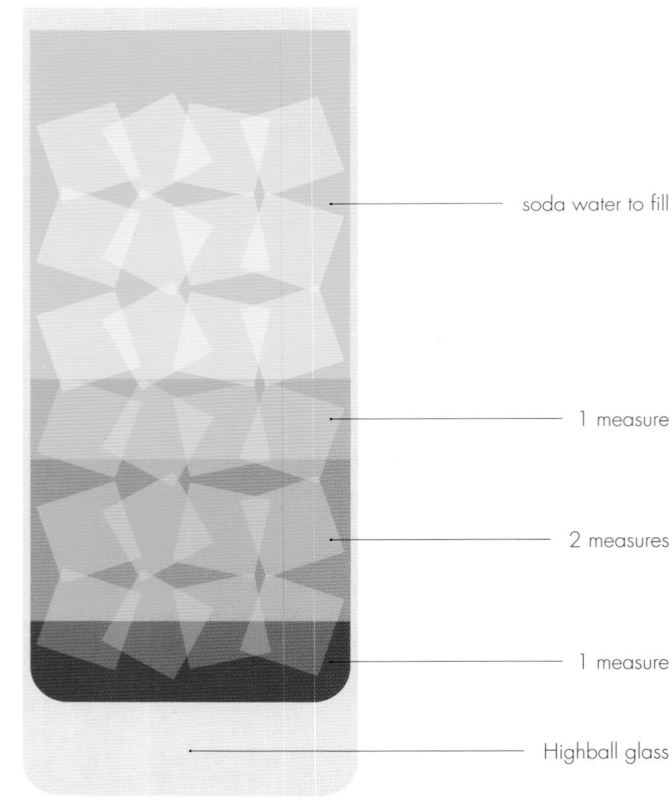
soda water to fill
1 measure
2 measures
1 measure
Highball glass

soda water
Benedictine
orange juice
brandy

Instructions

1 Pour the brandy, orange juice, and Benedictine into a highball glass with ice. **2** Stir and top up with soda.

B & B

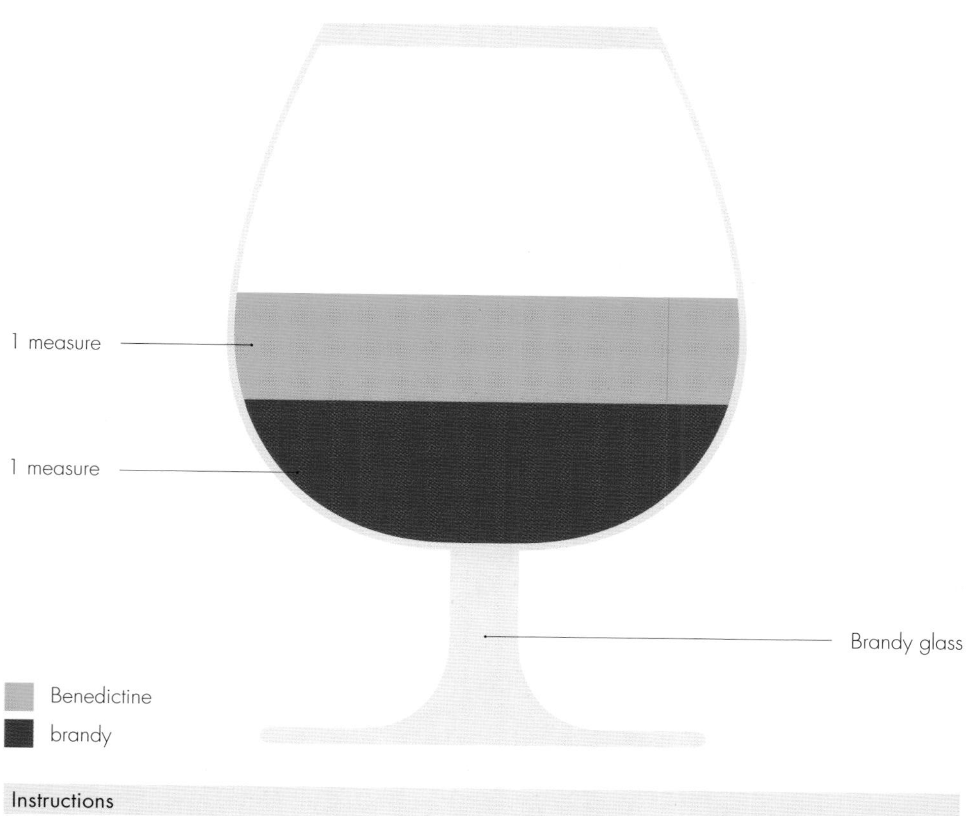

1 measure
1 measure
Brandy glass
Benedictine
brandy

Instructions

1. Pour the brandy and Benedictine into a brandy glass and serve.

Between the Sheets

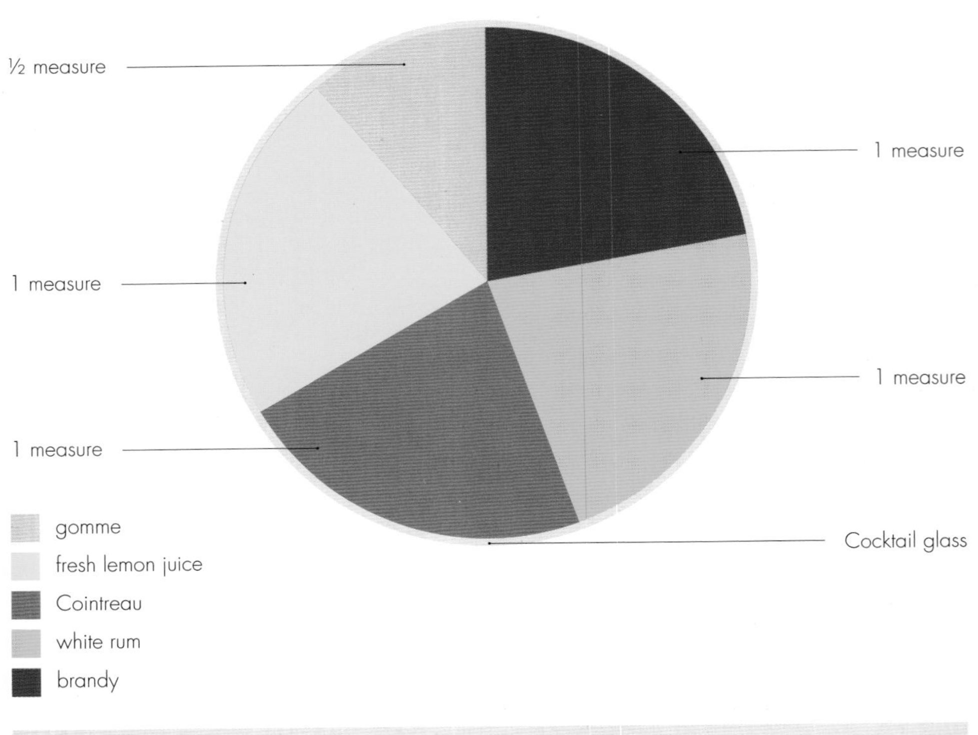

½ measure
1 measure
1 measure
1 measure
1 measure
Cocktail glass
gomme
fresh lemon juice
Cointreau
white rum
brandy

Instructions

1 Shake all the ingredients together, then strain into a cocktail glass, and serve.

Brandy Cocktail

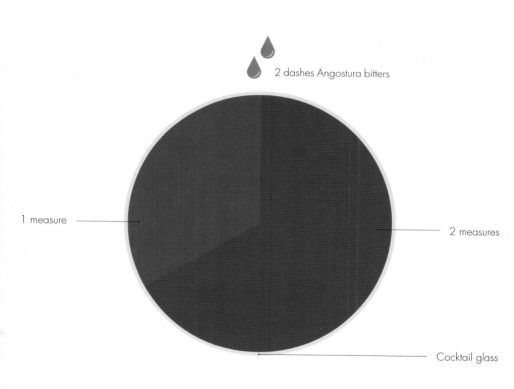

2 dashes Angostura bitters

1 measure

2 measures

Cocktail glass

sweet vermouth

Cognac

Instructions

1. Stir the Cognac, vermouth, and bitters together, then strain into a cocktail glass and serve.

Brandy Daisy

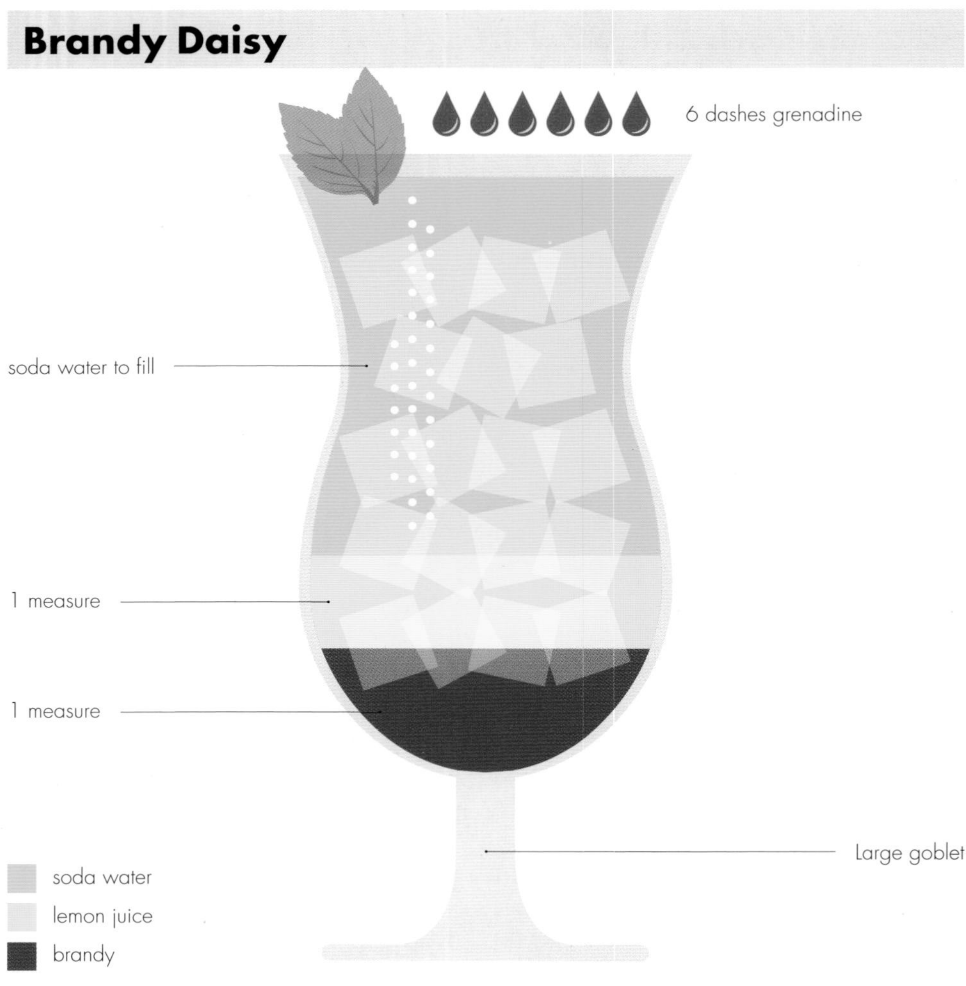
6 dashes grenadine
soda water to fill
1 measure
1 measure
Large goblet
soda water
lemon juice
brandy

Instructions

1 Shake the brandy, lemon juice, and grenadine and strain into a goblet over ice. **2** Top up with soda and garnish with a sprig of mint.

Brandy Kiss

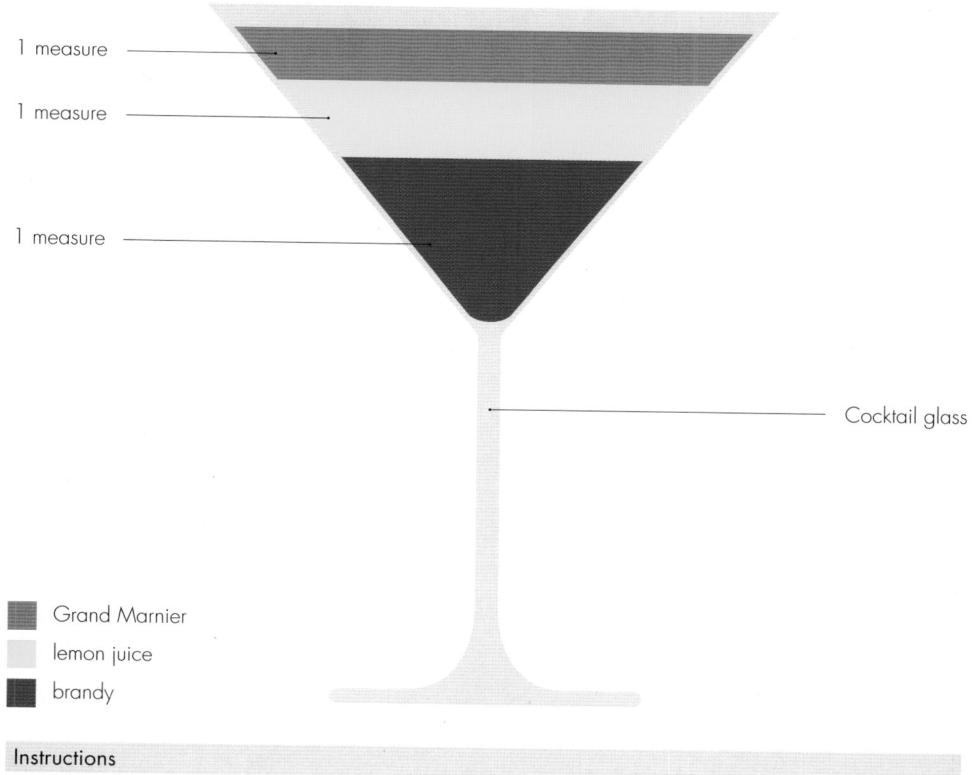

1 measure
1 measure
1 measure
Cocktail glass
Grand Marnier
lemon juice
brandy

Instructions

1. Shake all the ingredients together with ice and strain into a cocktail glass.

Cherry Picker

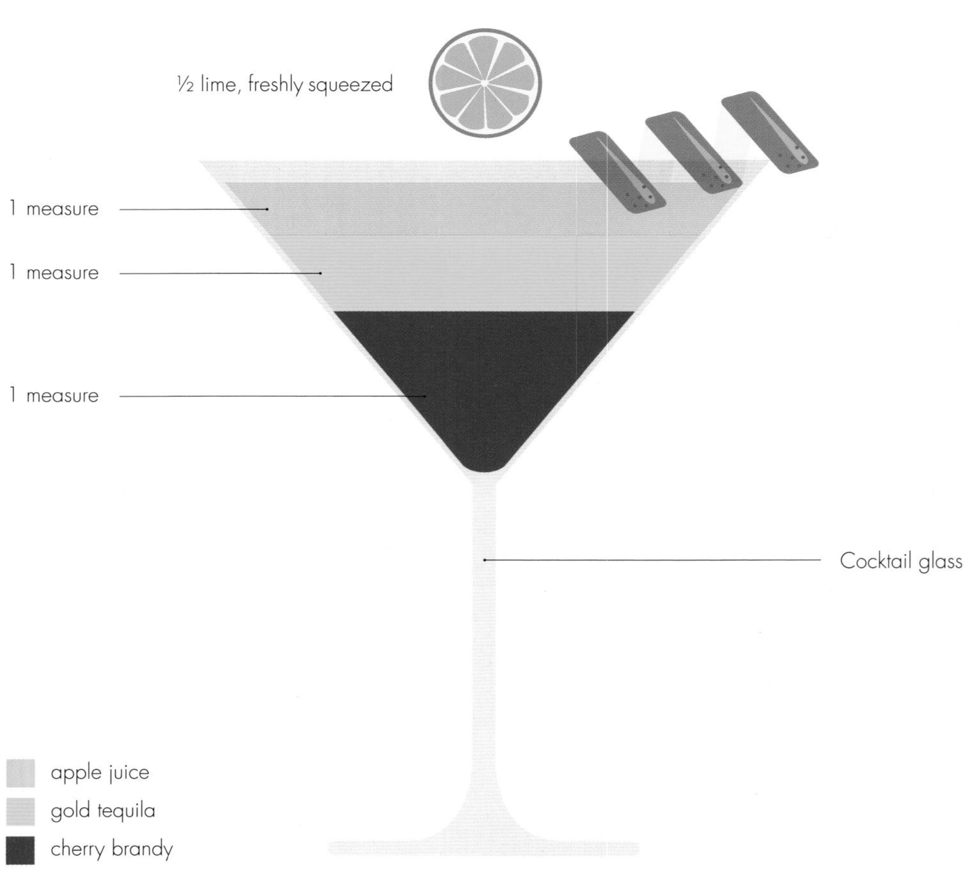
½ lime, freshly squeezed
1 measure
1 measure
1 measure
Cocktail glass
apple juice
gold tequila
cherry brandy

Instructions

1 Put all the ingredients in a shaker. **2** Shake, then strain into a cocktail glass and add a twist of lime to serve.

Chicago

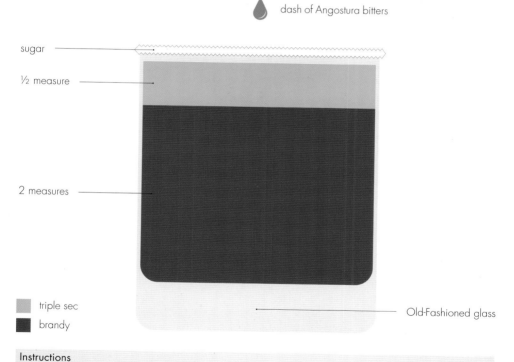
dash of Angostura bitters
sugar
½ measure
2 measures
triple sec
brandy
Old-Fashioned glass

Instructions

1 Shake all the ingredients together, then pour into a sugar-rimmed Old-Fashioned glass and serve.

Corpse Reviver

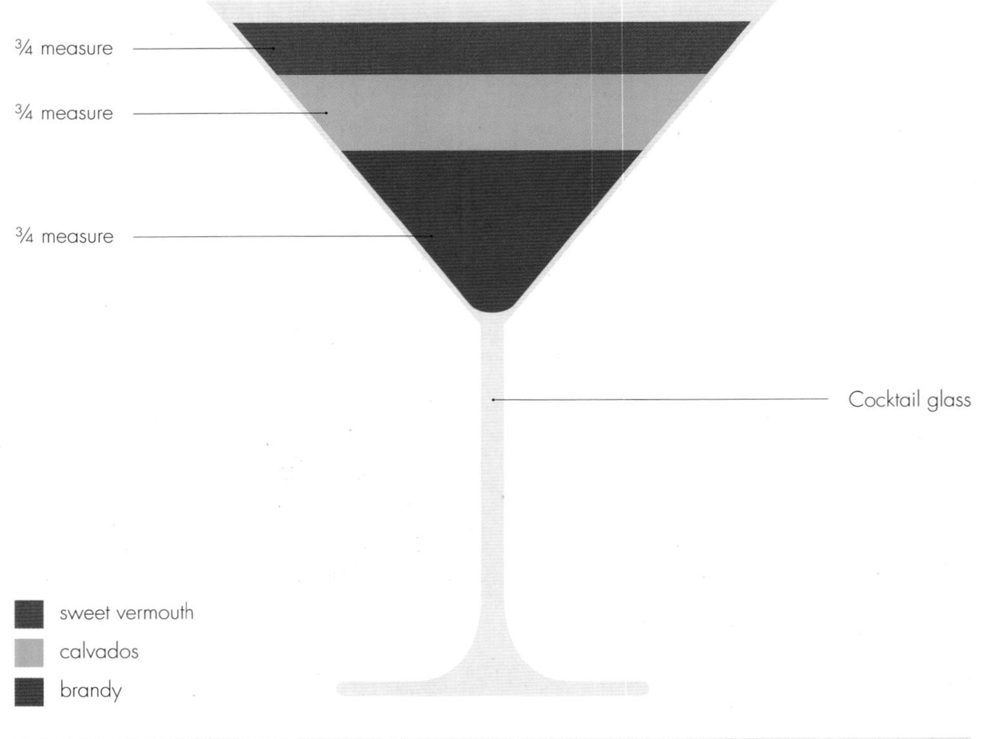

¾ measure
¾ measure
¾ measure
Cocktail glass
sweet vermouth
calvados
brandy

Instructions

1. Shake all the ingredients together and strain into a cocktail glass.

Dizzy Dame

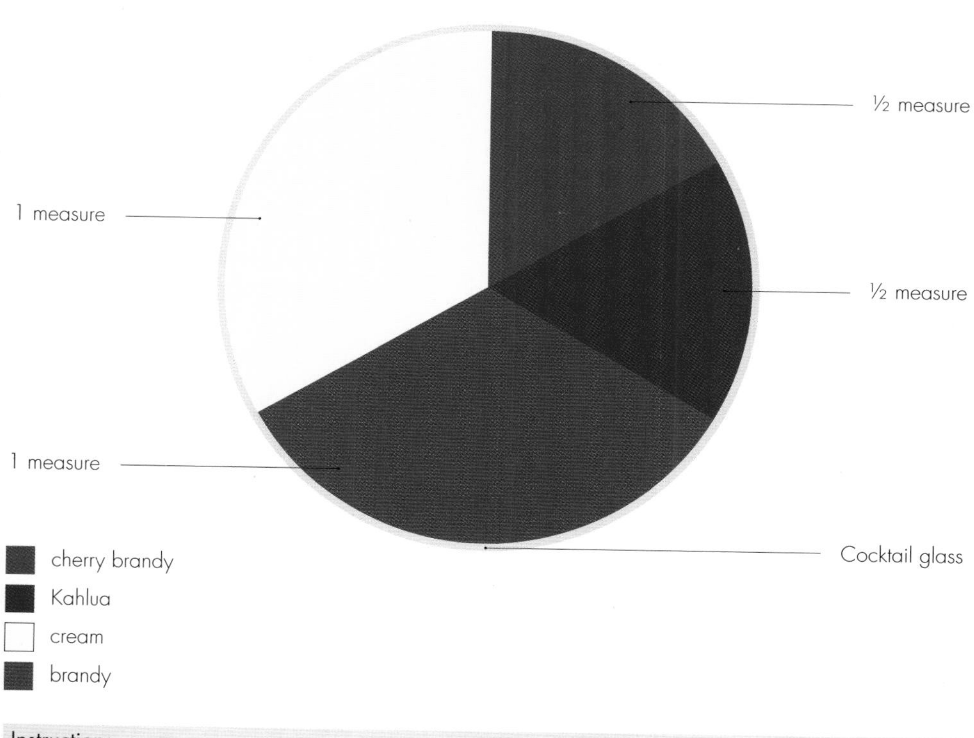
½ measure
1 measure
½ measure
1 measure
Cocktail glass
cherry brandy
Kahlua
cream
brandy

Instructions

1. Shake all the ingredients together with ice and strain into a cocktail glass.

Eggnog

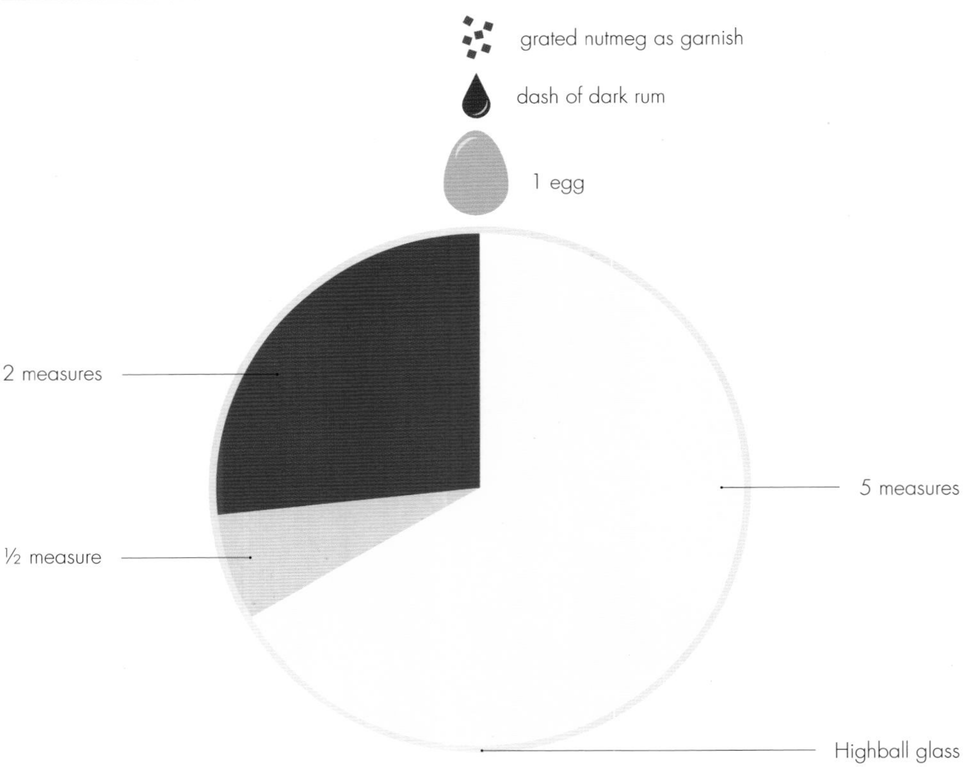

grated nutmeg as garnish
dash of dark rum
1 egg
2 measures
5 measures
½ measure
Highball glass

milk or single cream

gomme

Cognac

Instructions

1 Mix the ingredients together in a shaker, then pour into a highball glass. **2** Sprinkle on the grated nutmeg and serve.

Frenchie

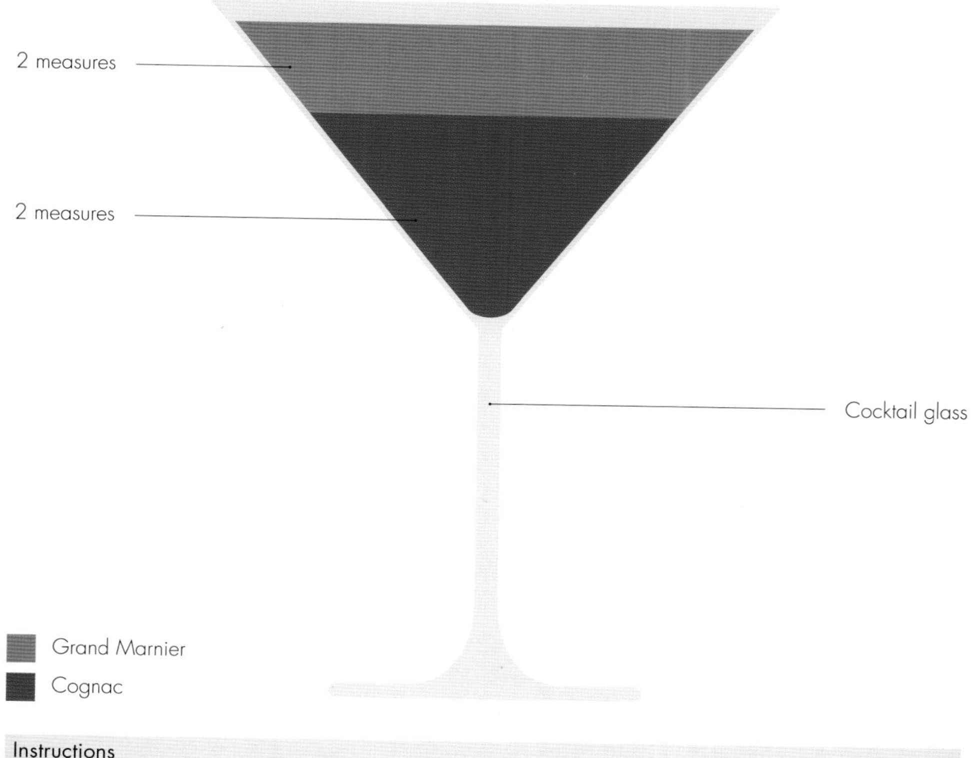

2 measures
2 measures
Cocktail glass
Grand Marnier
Cognac

Instructions

1. Pour the ingredients into a cocktail glass and stir.

Jack Rose

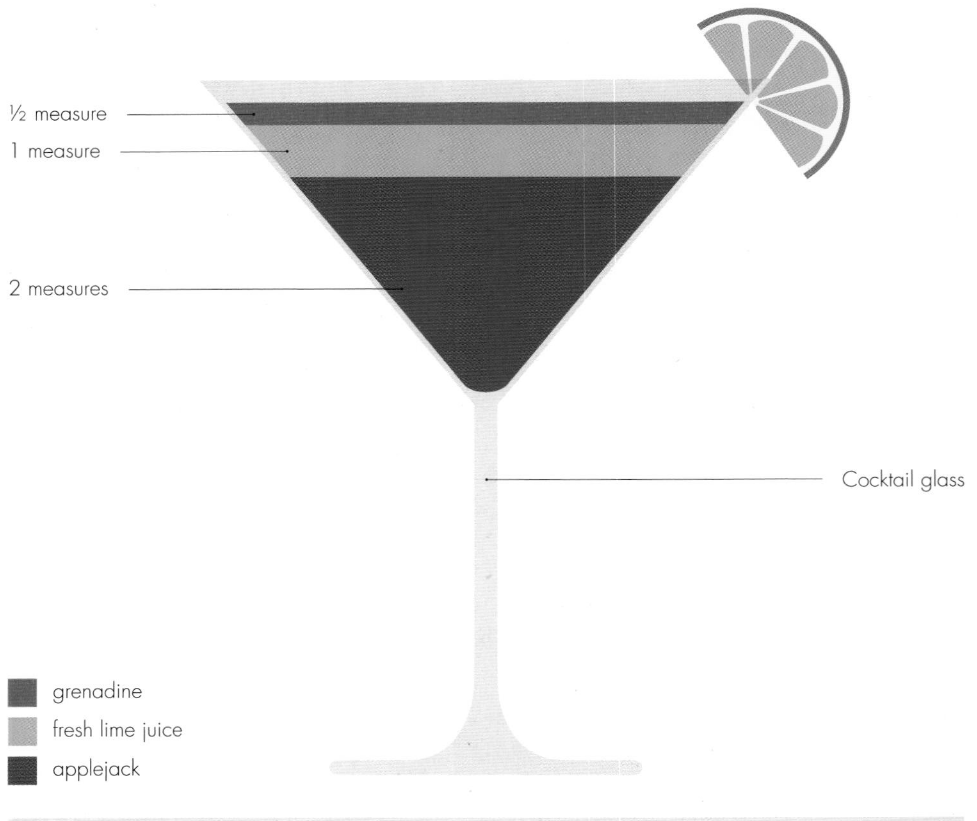
½ measure
1 measure
2 measures
Cocktail glass
grenadine
fresh lime juice
applejack

Instructions

1 Shake ingredients with ice and strain into a cocktail glass. **2** Garnish with a slice of lime.

Lieutenant

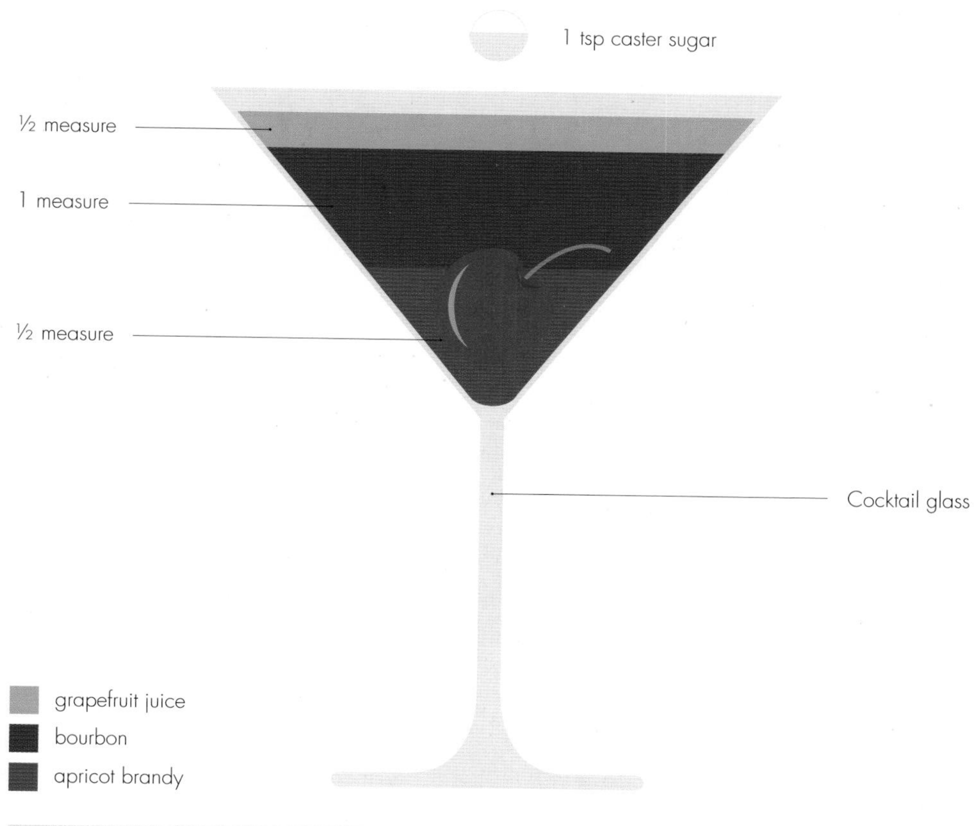
1 tsp caster sugar
½ measure
1 measure
½ measure
Cocktail glass
grapefruit juice
bourbon
apricot brandy

Instructions

1 Shake all the ingredients together with ice and strain into a cocktail glass. **2** Garnish with a cherry and serve.

Mikado

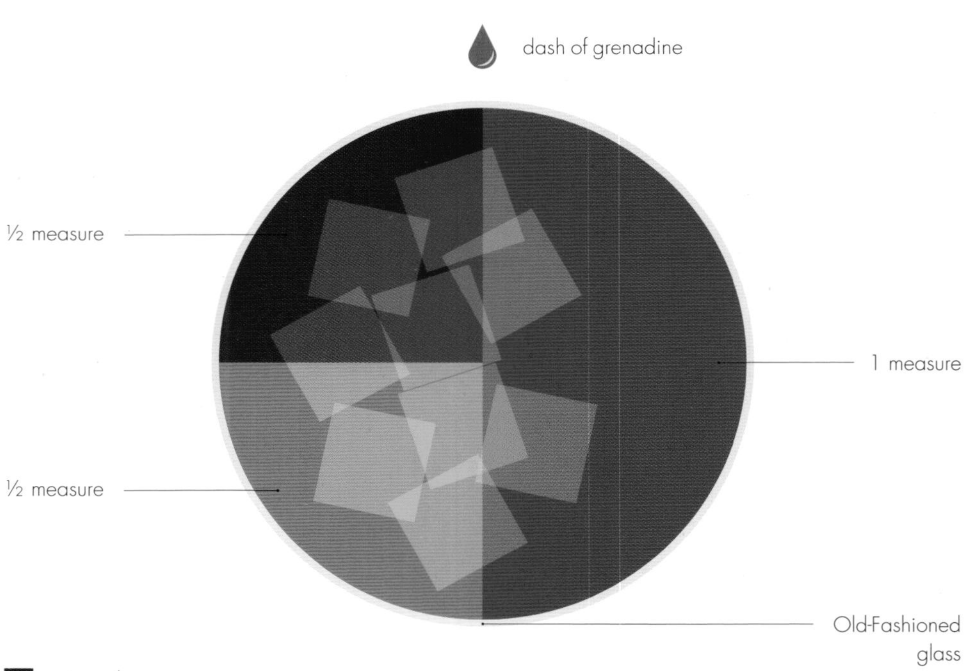

dash of grenadine
½ measure
1 measure
½ measure
Old-Fashioned glass

crème de noyaux

Cointreau

cognac

Instructions

1. Stir all the ingredients together, then strain into an ice-filled Old-Fashioned glass and serve.

Nicky Finn

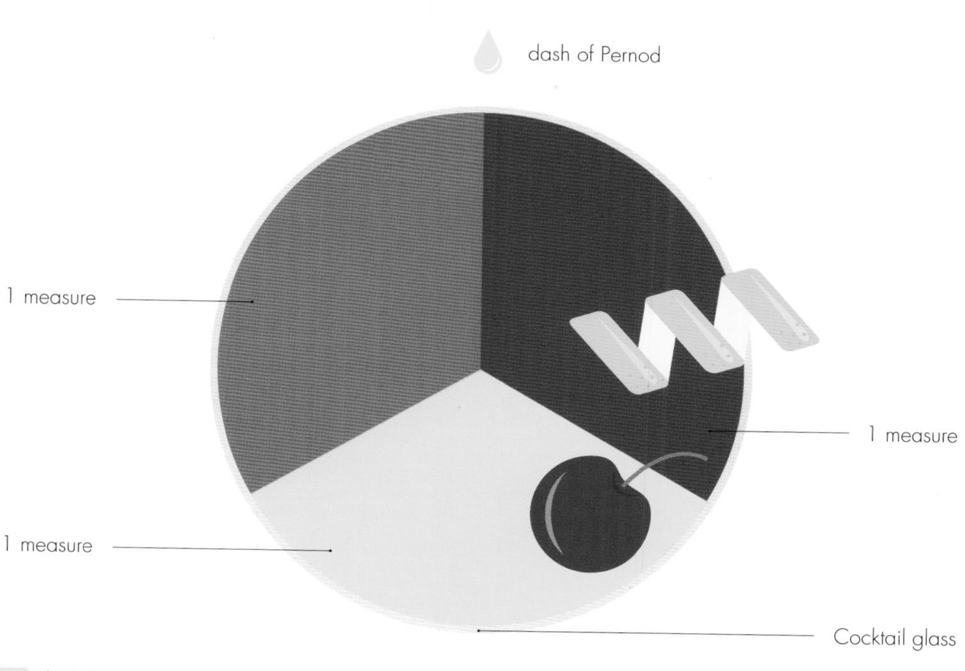
dash of Pernod
1 measure
1 measure
1 measure
Cocktail glass

fresh lemon juice

Cointreau

brandy

Instructions

1 Shake with ice and strain into a chilled cocktail glass. **2** Garnish with a lemon twist or a maraschino cherry.

Raja

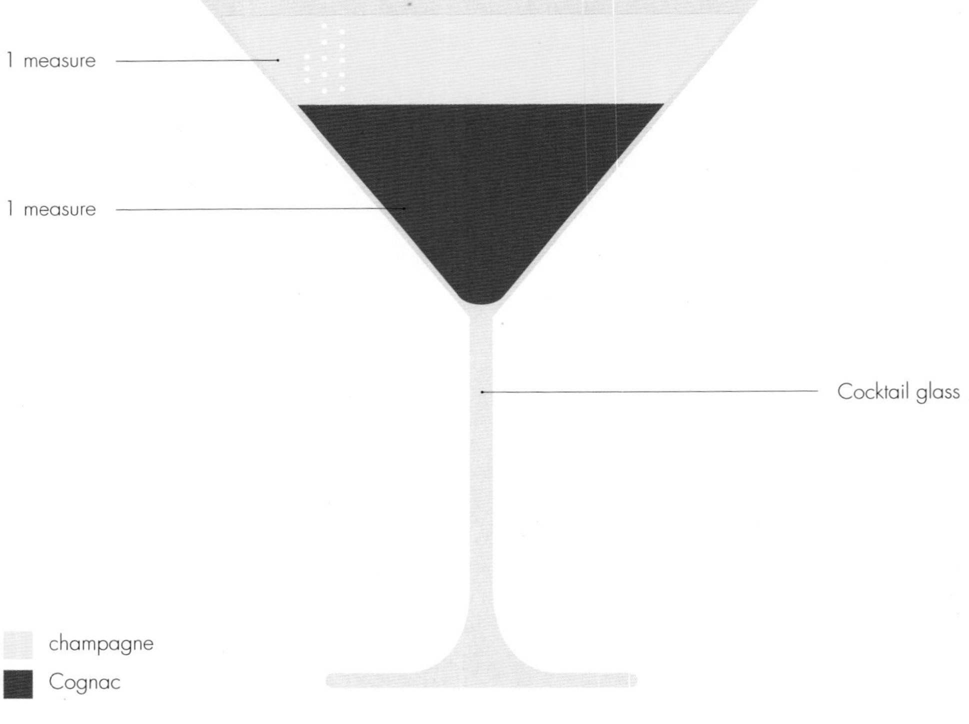
1 measure
1 measure
Cocktail glass
champagne
Cognac

Instructions

1 Stir the Cognac and champagne together, then strain into a cocktail glass and serve.

Tulip

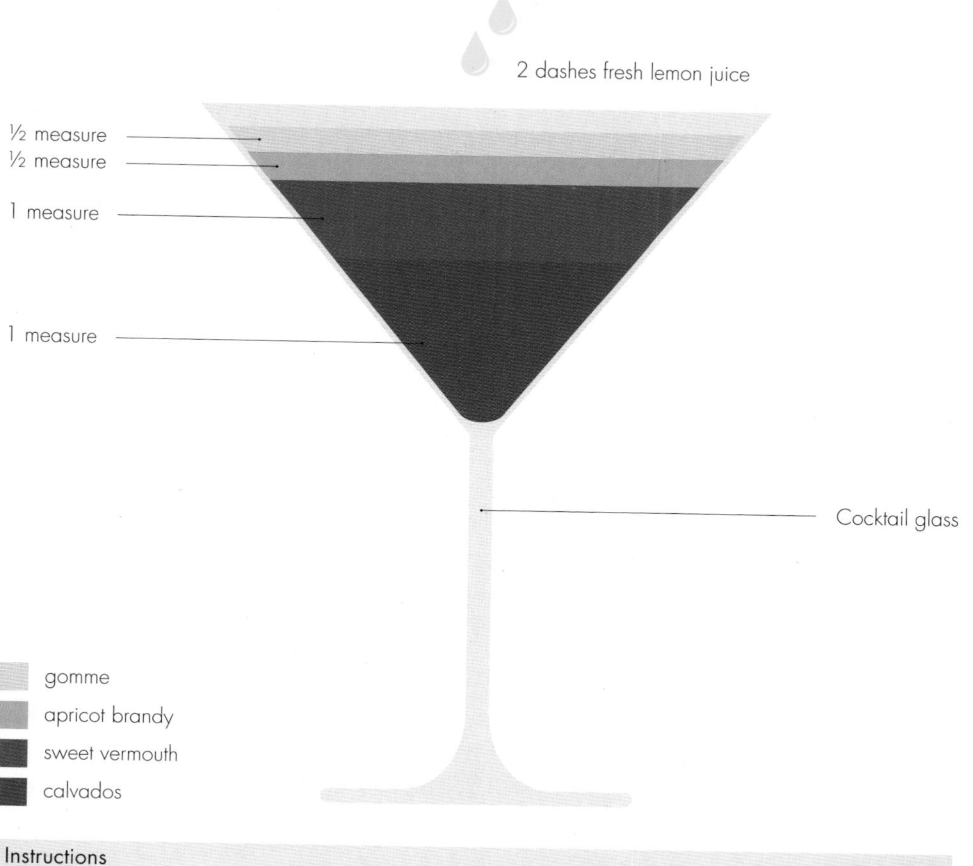

2 dashes fresh lemon juice
½ measure
½ measure
1 measure
1 measure
Cocktail glass
gomme
apricot brandy
sweet vermouth
calvados

Instructions

1 Shake all the ingredients together, then strain into a cocktail glass and serve.

RUM

Afternoon Delight

6 strawberries

½ measure

½ measure

1 measure

1 measure

1 measure

Small goblet

- double cream
- crème de fraise
- coconut cream
- freshly squeezed orange juice
- dark rum

Instructions

1 Place all the ingredients, except one strawberry, into a blender. **2** Add crushed ice and blend. Pour into a goblet. **3** Garnish with a strawberry and serve with a straw.

Apollo 13

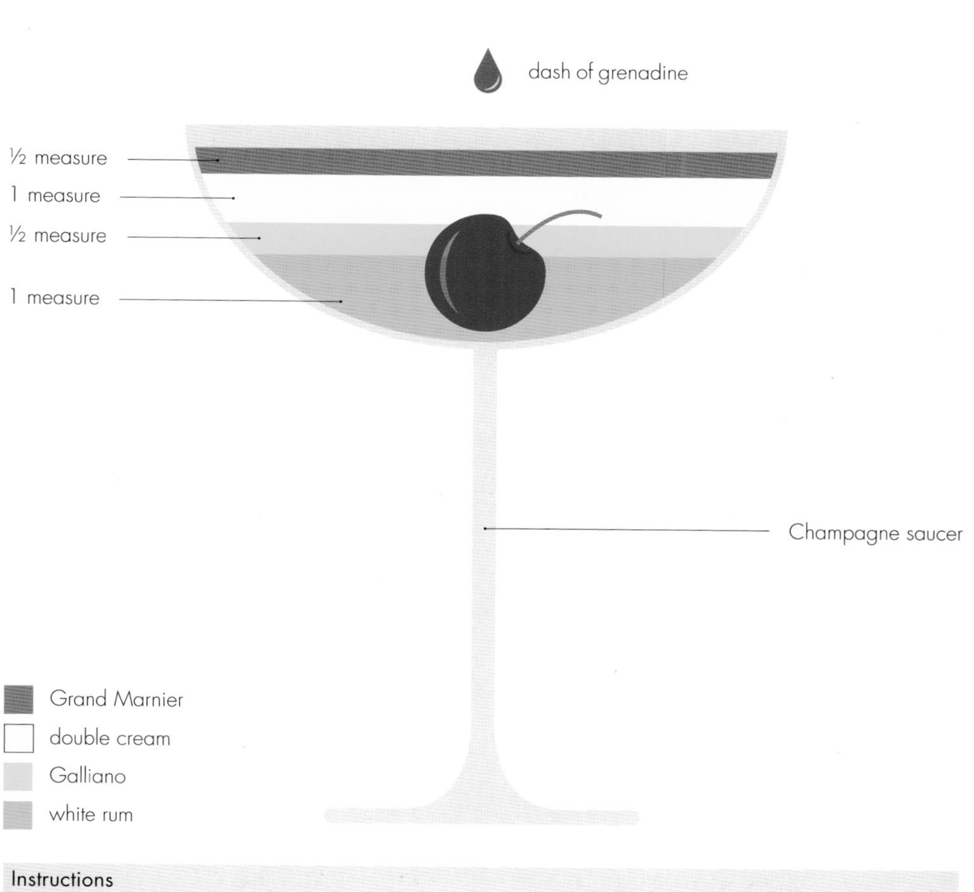

dash of grenadine
½ measure
1 measure
½ measure
1 measure
Champagne saucer
Grand Marnier
double cream
Galliano
white rum

Instructions

1 Shake all the ingredients together with ice and strain into a champagne saucer. 2 Garnish with a maraschino cherry.

Bahia

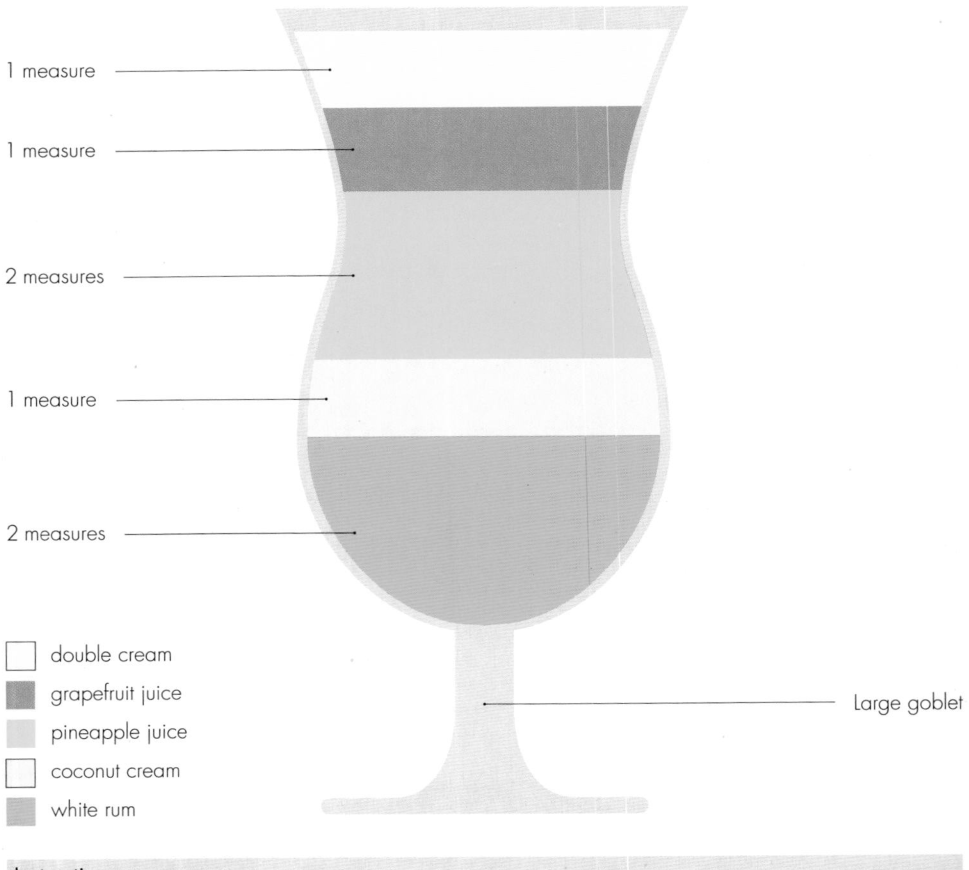

1 measure
1 measure
2 measures
1 measure
2 measures
double cream
grapefruit juice
pineapple juice
coconut cream
white rum
Large goblet

Instructions

1. Blend all the ingredients together and pour into a large goblet.

Barracuda

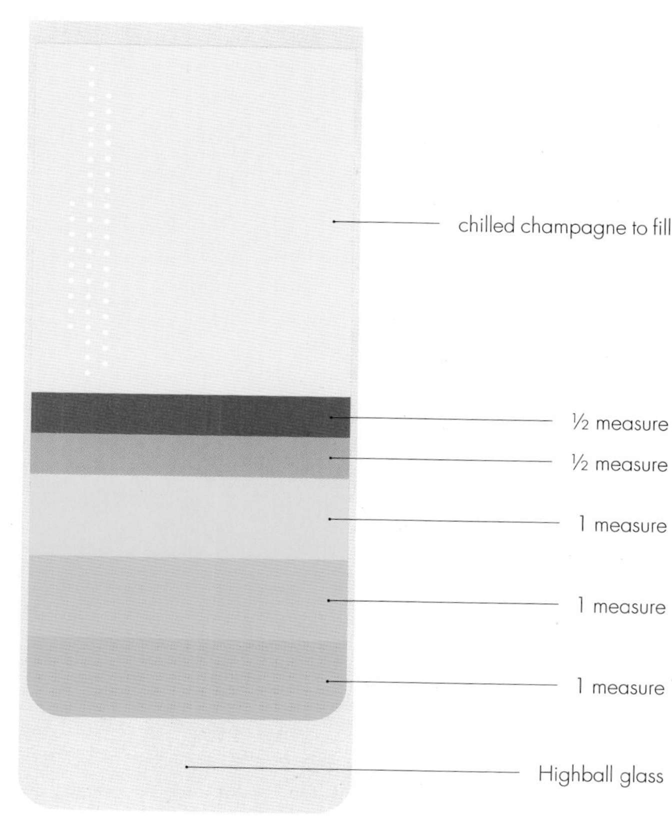

chilled champagne to fill
½ measure
½ measure
1 measure
1 measure
1 measure
Highball glass

- chilled champagne
- grenadine
- fresh lime juice
- pineapple juice
- Galliano
- white rum

Instructions

1. Pour each of the ingredients into a highball glass, top up with champagne and serve.

Bee's Kiss

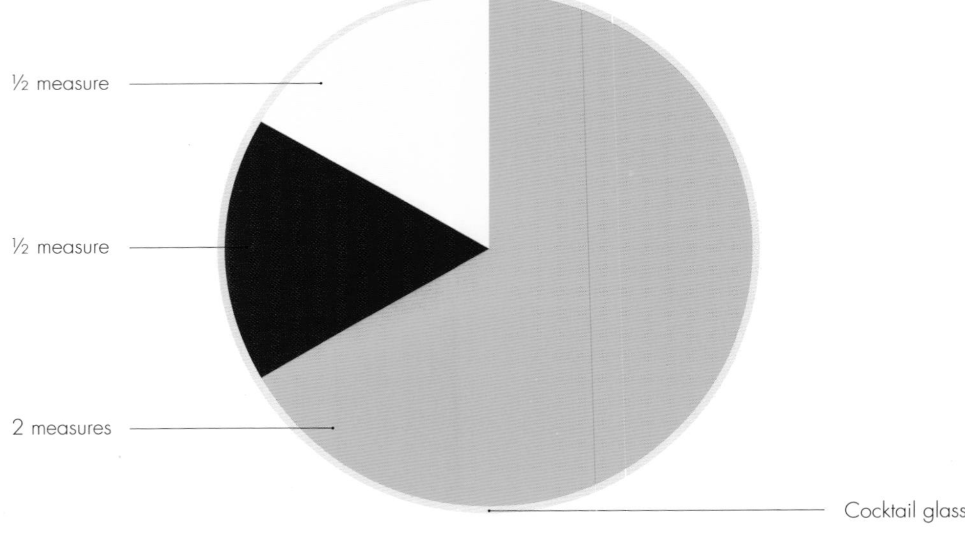

½ measure
½ measure
2 measures
Cocktail glass

- double cream
- cold black coffee
- white rum

Instructions

1. Shake all the ingredients well and strain into a cocktail glass.

Bella Donna

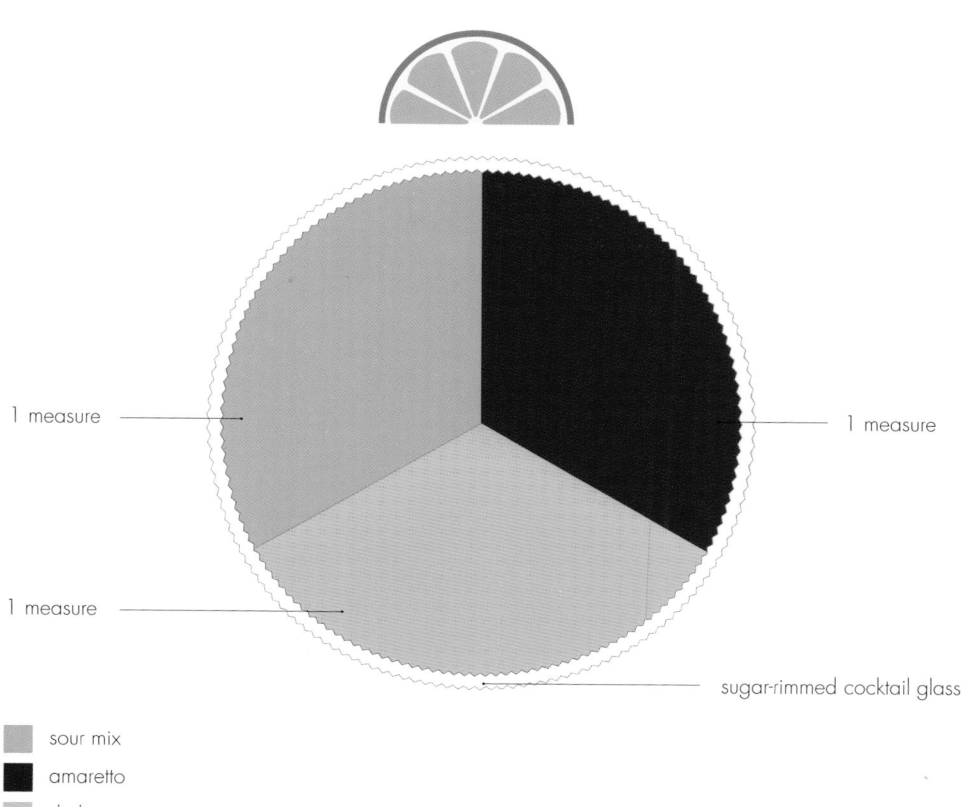

1 measure
1 measure
1 measure
sugar-rimmed cocktail glass

sour mix
amaretto
dark rum

Instructions

1. Rub the rim of a cocktail glass with a wedge of lime and then dip it into a saucer of sugar to coat the rim.
2. Shake all ingredients with ice and strain into the glass.

Blue Hawaiian

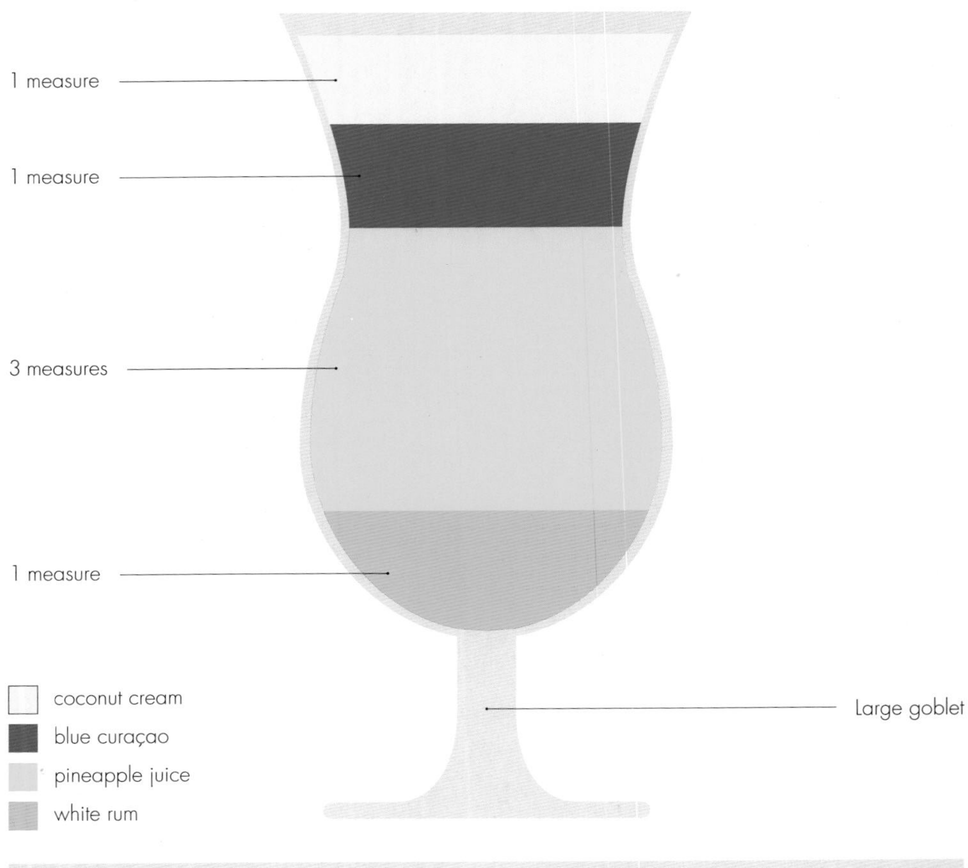
1 measure
1 measure
3 measures
1 measure
coconut cream
blue curaçao
pineapple juice
white rum
Large goblet

Instructions

1. Blend all the ingredients together and pour into a large goblet.

Casablanca

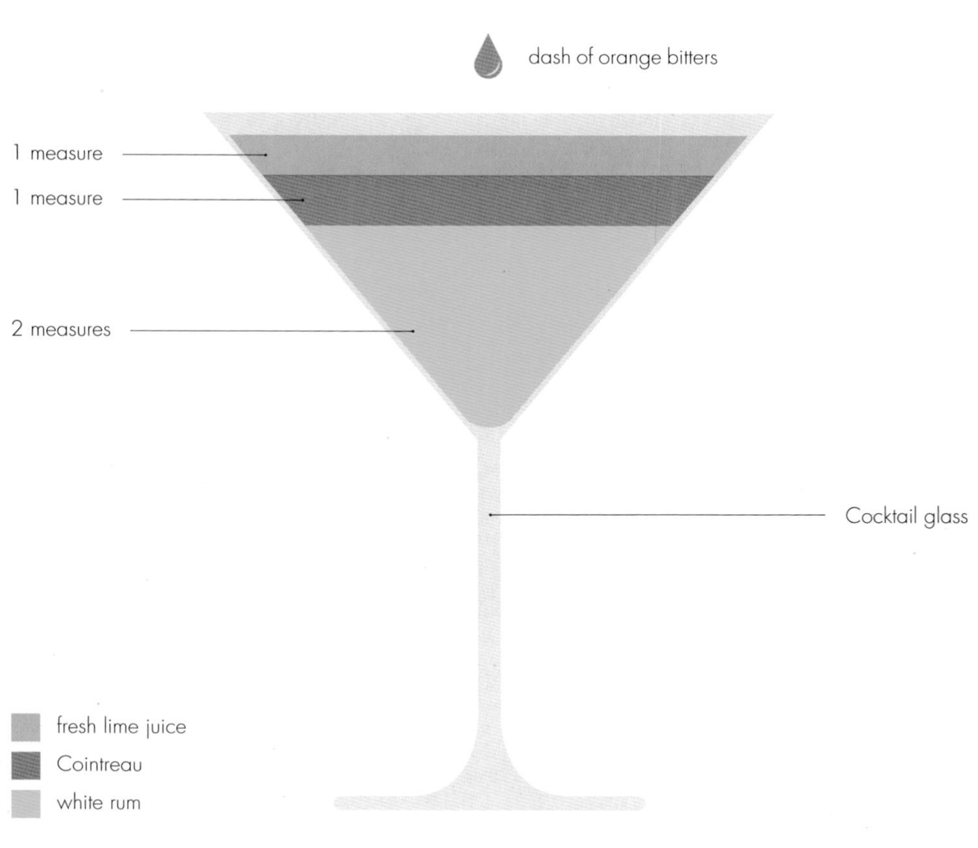
dash of orange bitters
1 measure
1 measure
2 measures
Cocktail glass
fresh lime juice
Cointreau
white rum

Instructions

1 Shake all the ingredients together, then strain into a cocktail glass, and serve.

Cocoloco

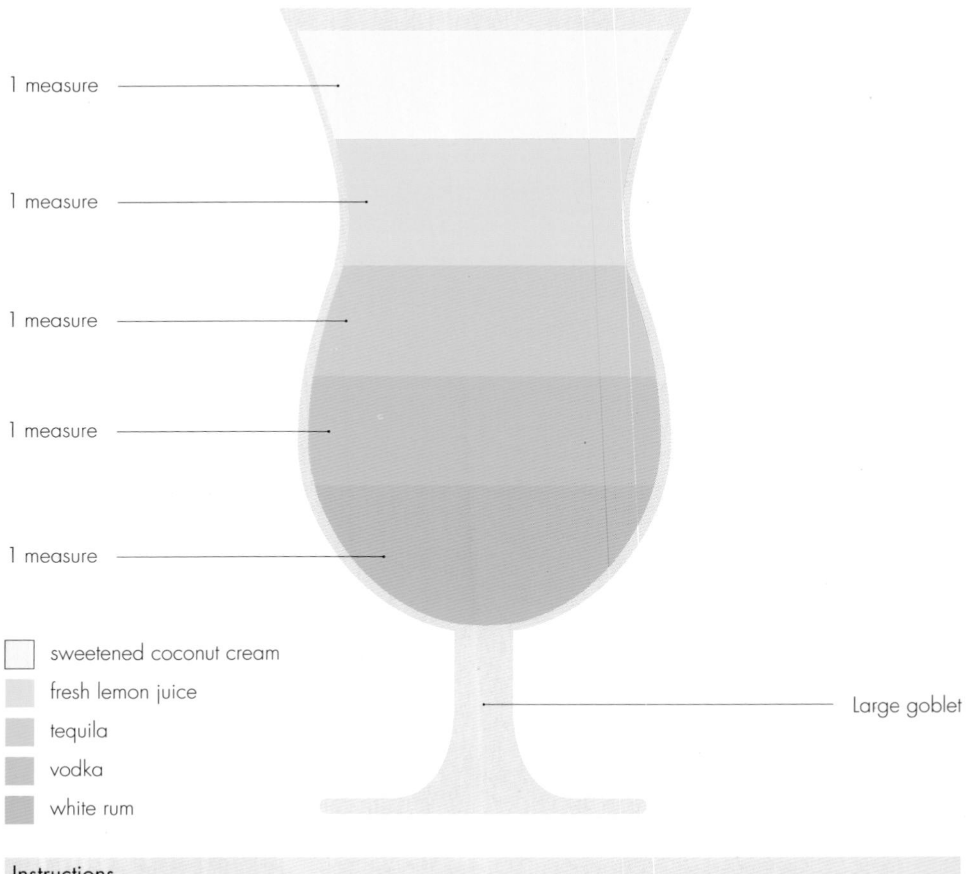

1 measure
1 measure
1 measure
1 measure
1 measure
sweetened coconut cream
fresh lemon juice
tequila
vodka
white rum
Large goblet

Instructions

1 Blend all the ingredients together until smooth, then pour into a large goblet.

Cuba Libre

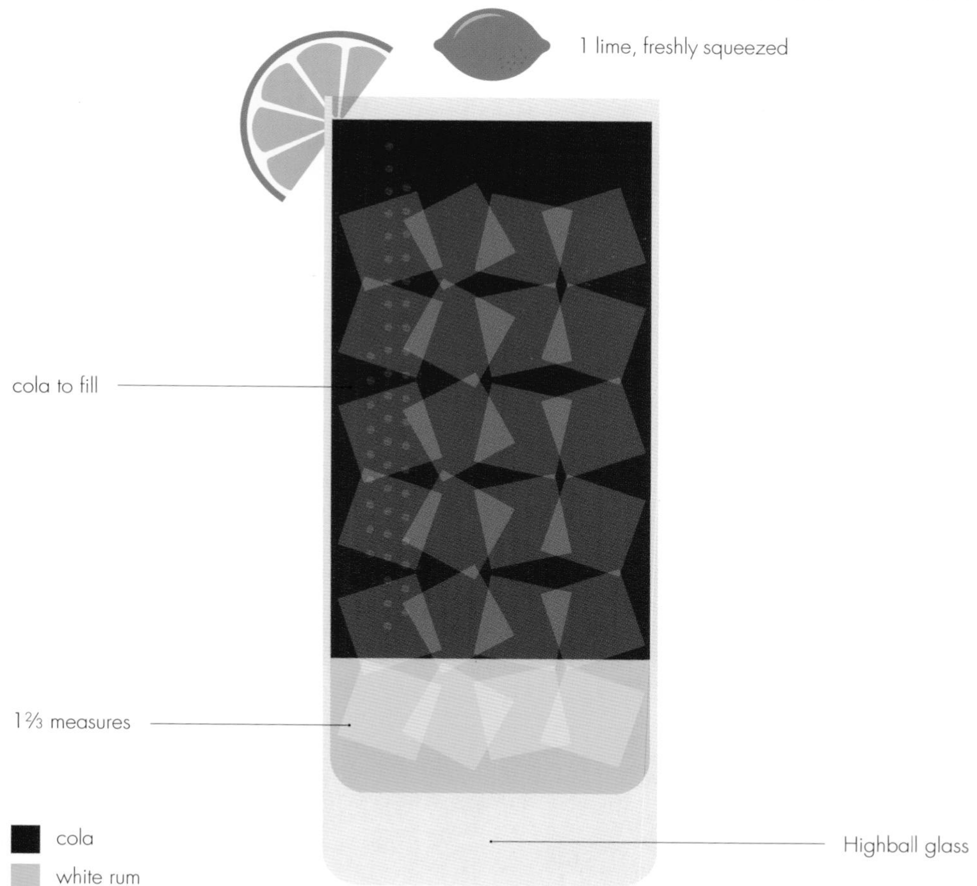

1 lime, freshly squeezed
cola to fill
1⅔ measures
cola
white rum
Highball glass

Instructions

1 Pour the juice, then the rum into a highball glass filled with ice. **2** Top up with cola, add a wedge of lime, then serve with a stirrer.

Dizzy Gillespie

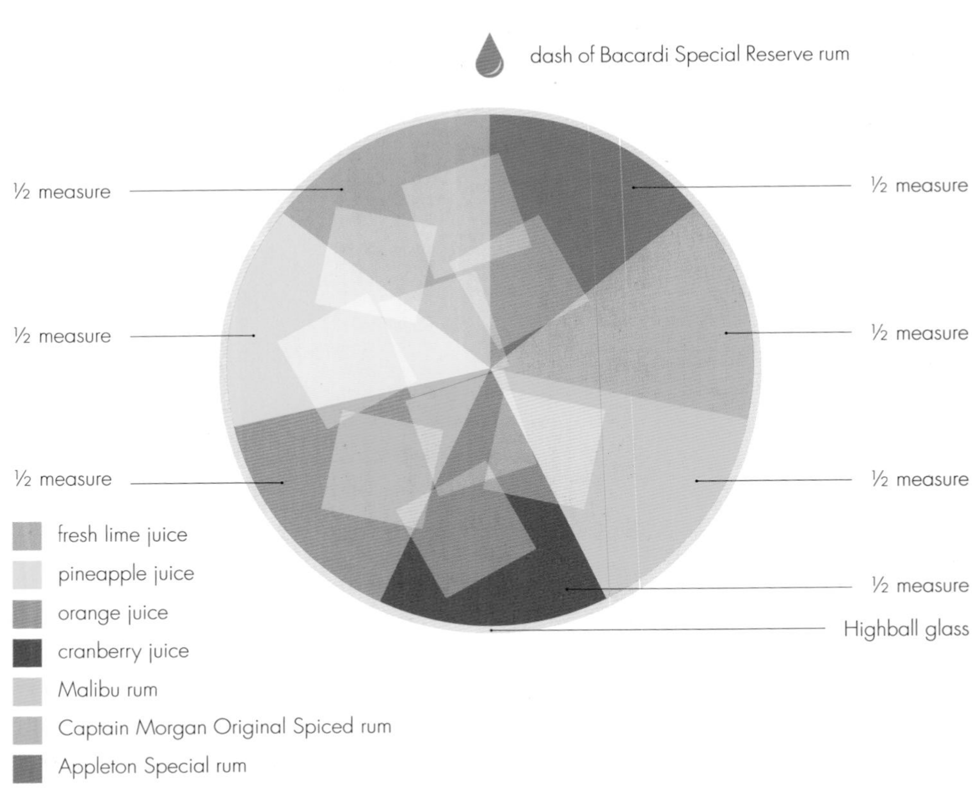

dash of Bacardi Special Reserve rum
½ measure
½ measure
½ measure
½ measure
½ measure
½ measure
½ measure
Highball glass
fresh lime juice
pineapple juice
orange juice
cranberry juice
Malibu rum
Captain Morgan Original Spiced rum
Appleton Special rum

Instructions

1. Shake all the ingredients, except the Bacardi, with ice and strain into a highball glass with ice.
2. Float the Bacardi Special Reserve.

El Presidente

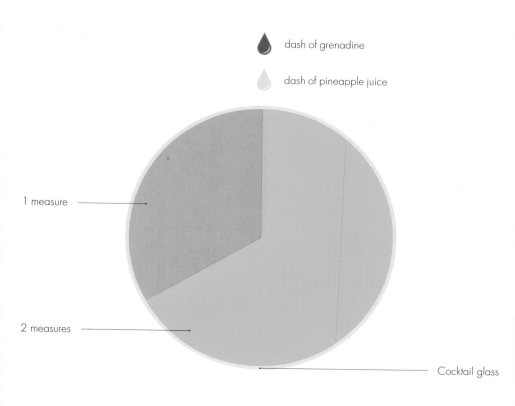

dash of grenadine

dash of pineapple juice

1 measure

2 measures

Cocktail glass

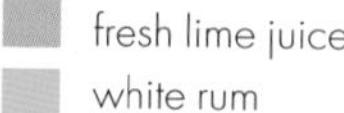

fresh lime juice
white rum

Instructions

1 Pour the grenadine into a cocktail glass. In an ice-filled shaker, mix the rum and the lime and pineapple juices, then strain into the glass and serve.

Floridita

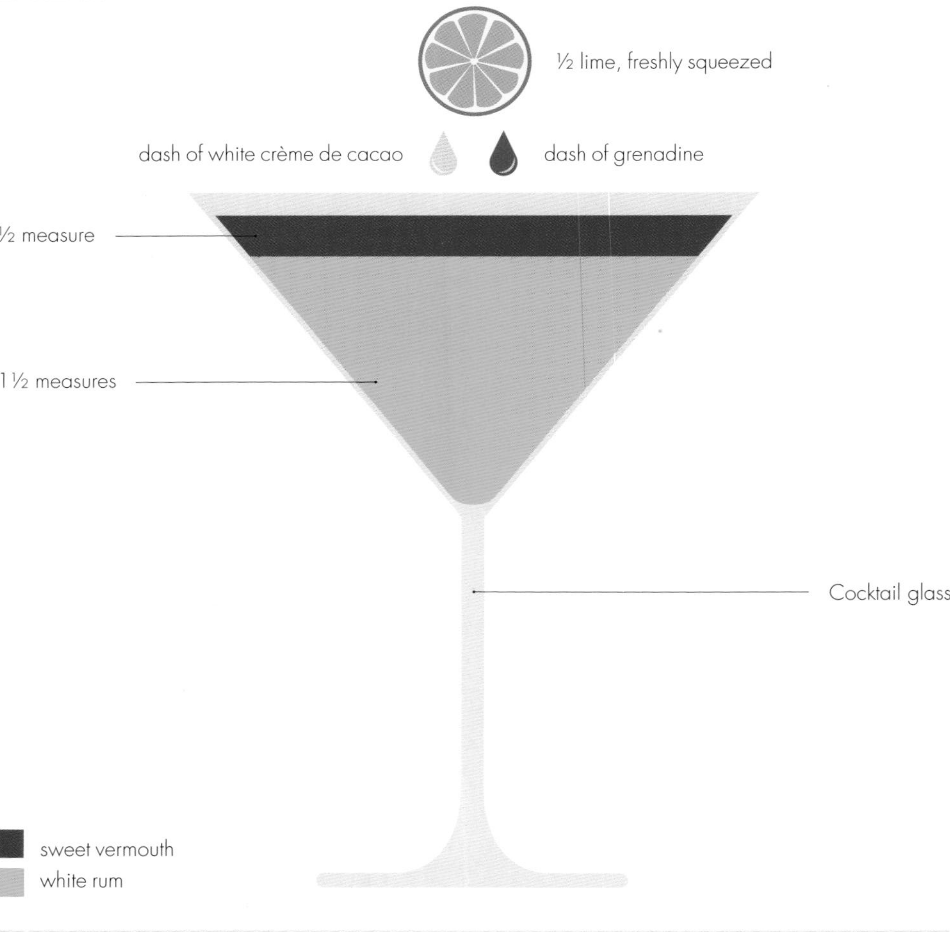

½ lime, freshly squeezed
dash of white crème de cacao
dash of grenadine
½ measure
1 ½ measures
Cocktail glass
sweet vermouth
white rum

Instructions

1. Shake all the ingredients over ice cubes and strain into a cocktail glass.

Hurricane

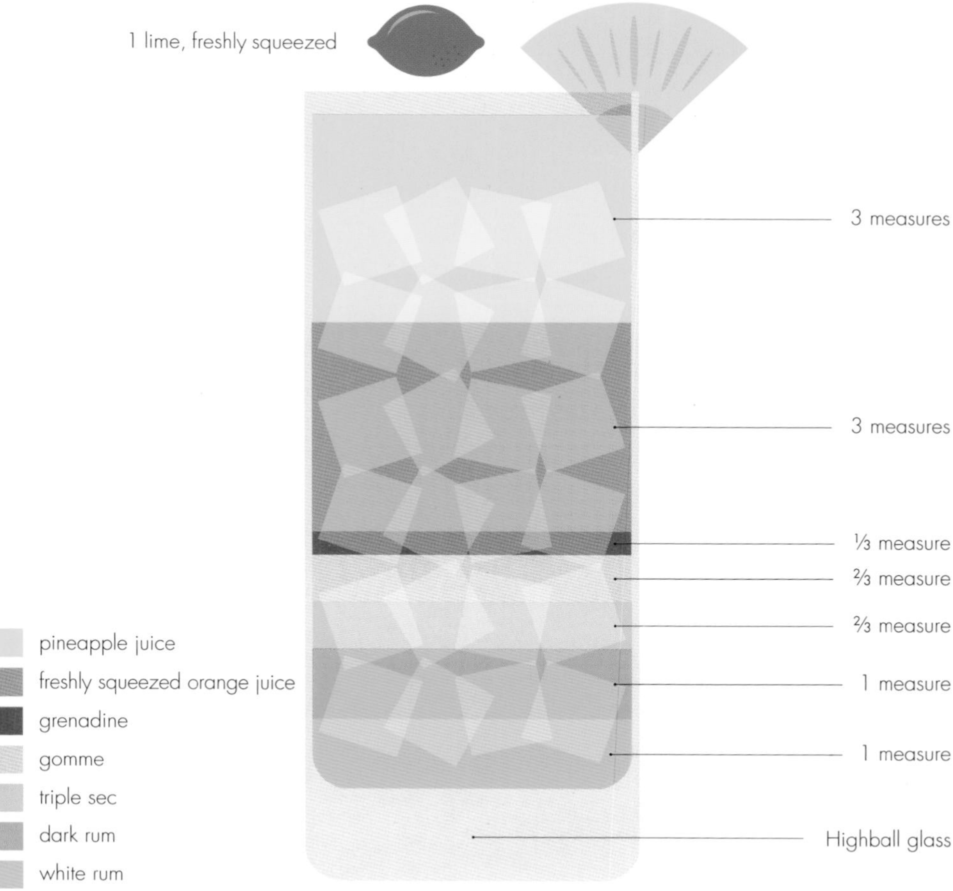

1 lime, freshly squeezed
3 measures
3 measures
⅓ measure
⅔ measure
⅔ measure
1 measure
1 measure
Highball glass
pineapple juice
freshly squeezed orange juice
grenadine
gomme
triple sec
dark rum
white rum

Instructions

1 Shake all the ingredients together and strain into a highball glass filled with ice. **2** Add a pineapple wedge to decorate.

Jungle Juice

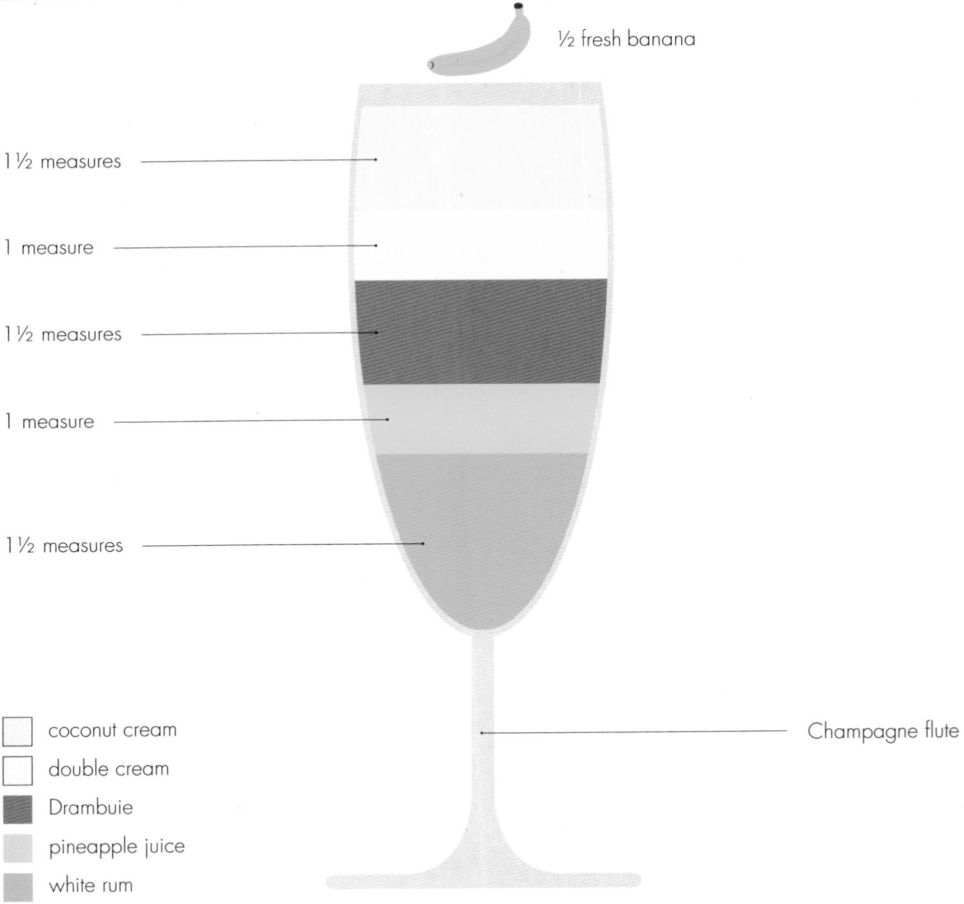

½ fresh banana

1½ measures

1 measure

1½ measures

1 measure

1½ measures

Champagne flute

- coconut cream
- double cream
- Drambuie
- pineapple juice
- white rum

Instructions

1. Blend all the ingredients together until smooth, then pour into a champagne flute.

Madonna

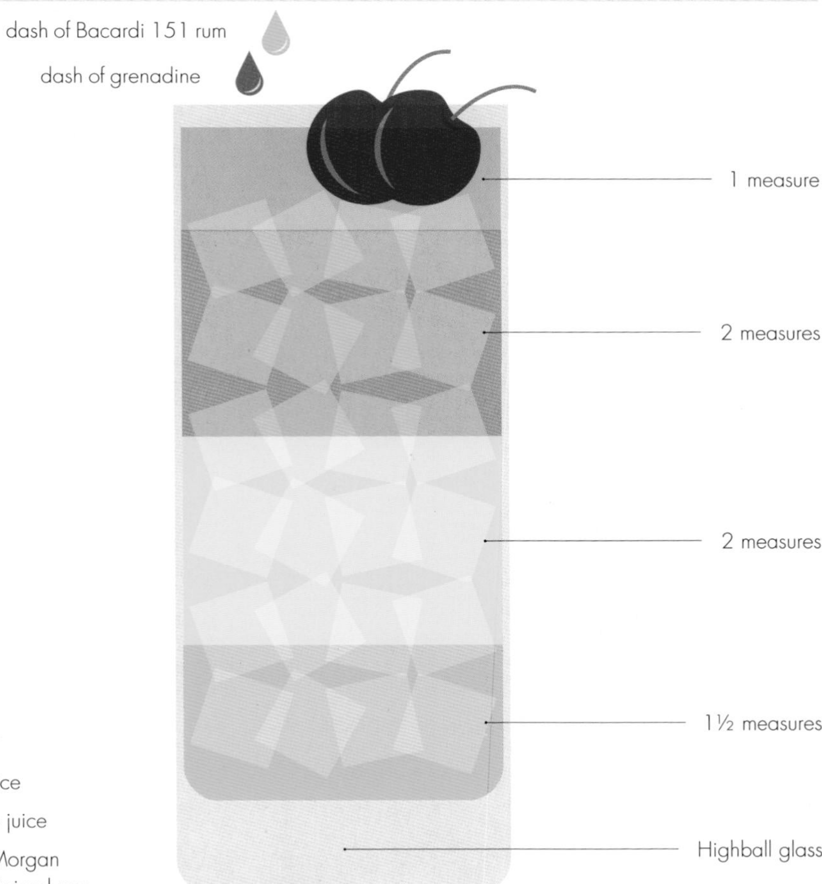

dash of Bacardi 151 rum
dash of grenadine
1 measure
2 measures
2 measures
1½ measures
Highball glass
sour mix
orange juice
pineapple juice
Captain Morgan Original Spiced rum

Instructions

1 Shake the Captain Morgan, pineapple juice, orange juice and sour mix with ice and strain into an ice-filled highball glass. **2** Float the Bacardi over the top, then the grenadine and garnish with two maraschino cherries.

Mojito

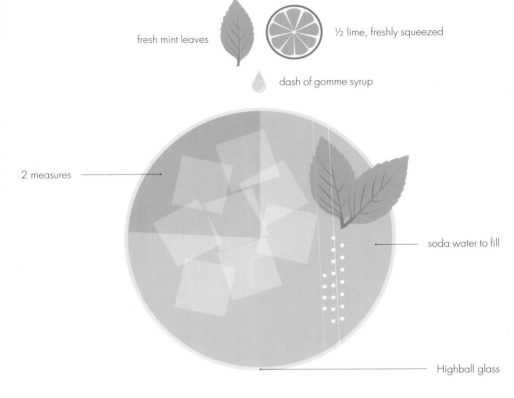

fresh mint leaves

½ lime, freshly squeezed

dash of gomme syrup

2 measures

soda water to fill

Highball glass

soda water

white rum

Instructions

1 In a large highball glass, muddle the mint leaves and gomme. **2** Squeeze lime juice into the glass and add lime half. **3** Then add the rum and some ice. **4** Stir, then add the soda, stir again briefly, and garnish with a sprig of mint.

Naked Lady

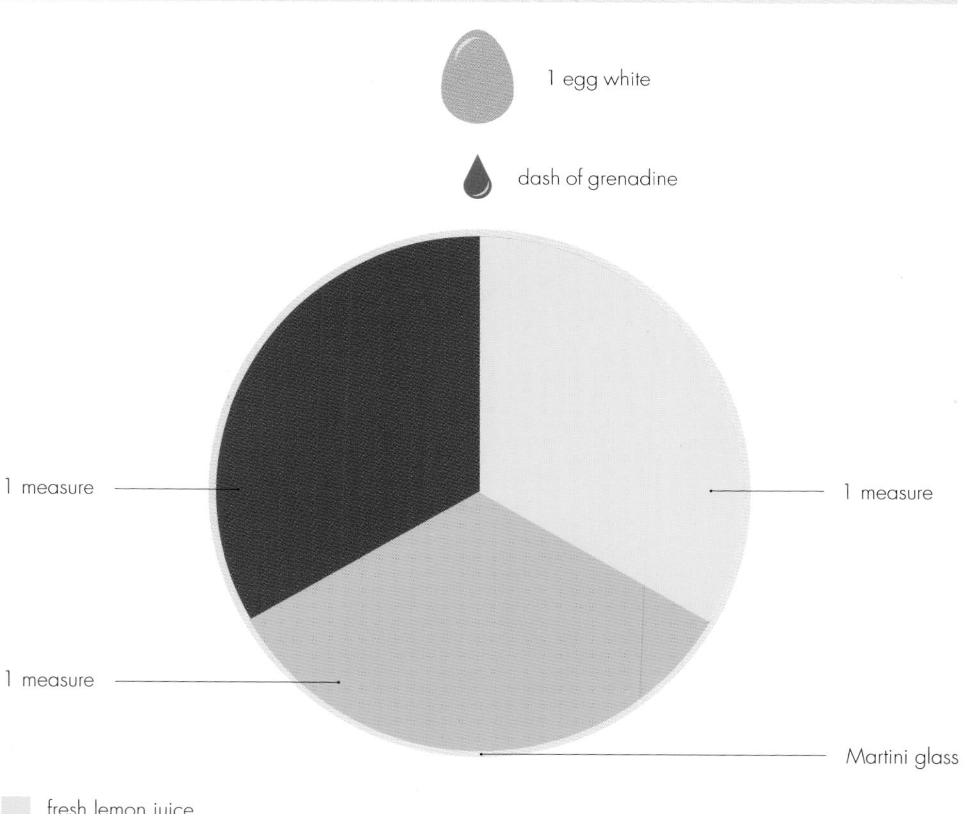

1 egg white
dash of grenadine
1 measure
1 measure
1 measure
Martini glass

fresh lemon juice
apricot brandy
white rum

Instructions

1. Shake all the ingredients together, then strain into a cocktail glass and serve.

Painkiller

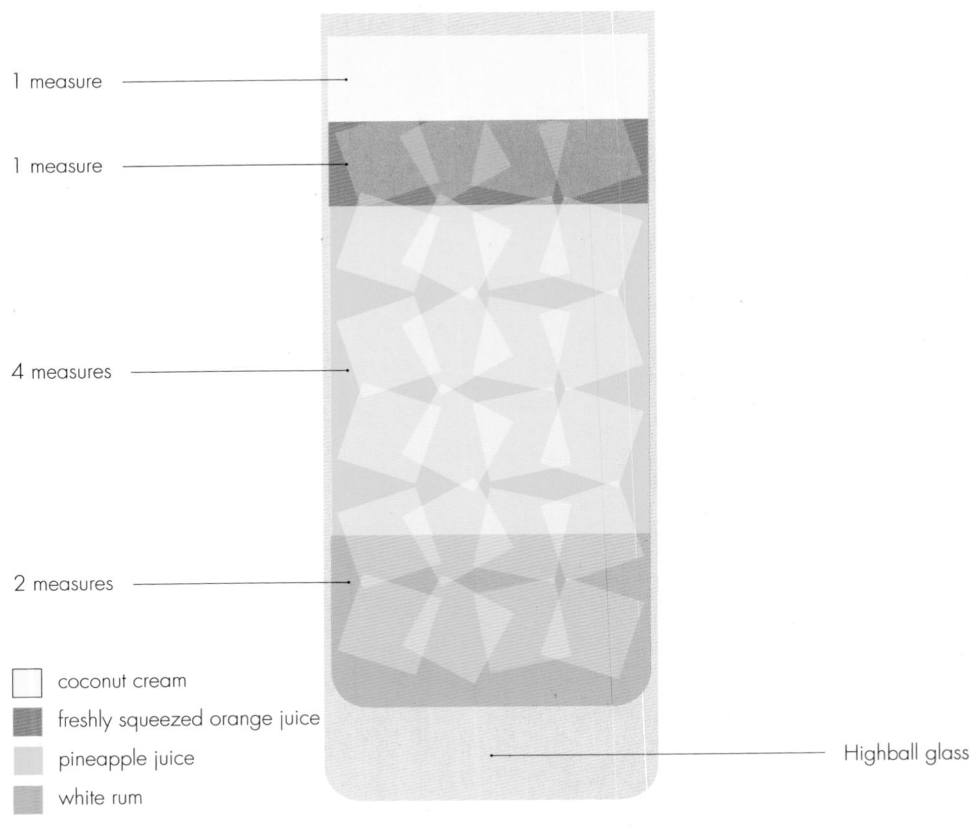

1 measure
1 measure
4 measures
2 measures
coconut cream
freshly squeezed orange juice
pineapple juice
white rum
Highball glass

Instructions

1. Shake all the ingredients together and strain into a highball glass filled with ice.

Piña Colada

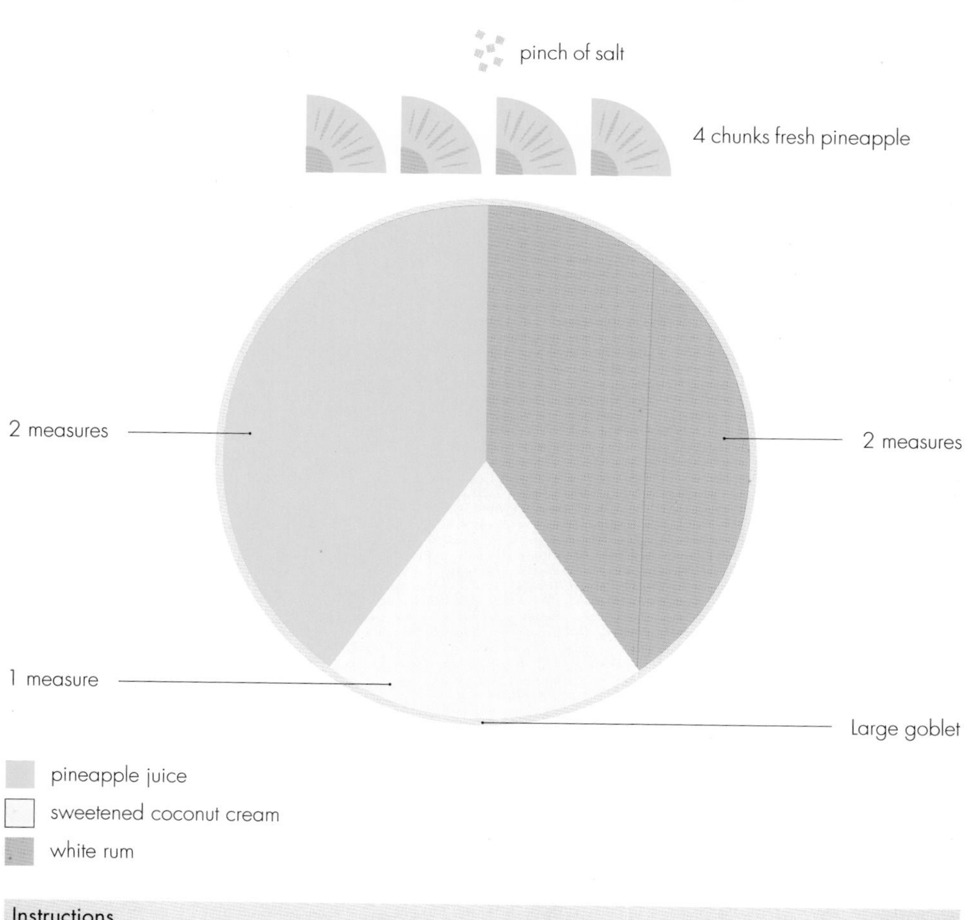
pinch of salt
4 chunks fresh pineapple
2 measures
2 measures
1 measure
Large goblet

pineapple juice

sweetened coconut cream

white rum

Instructions

1. Blend all the ingredients together until smooth, then pour into a large goblet.

Pussy Foot

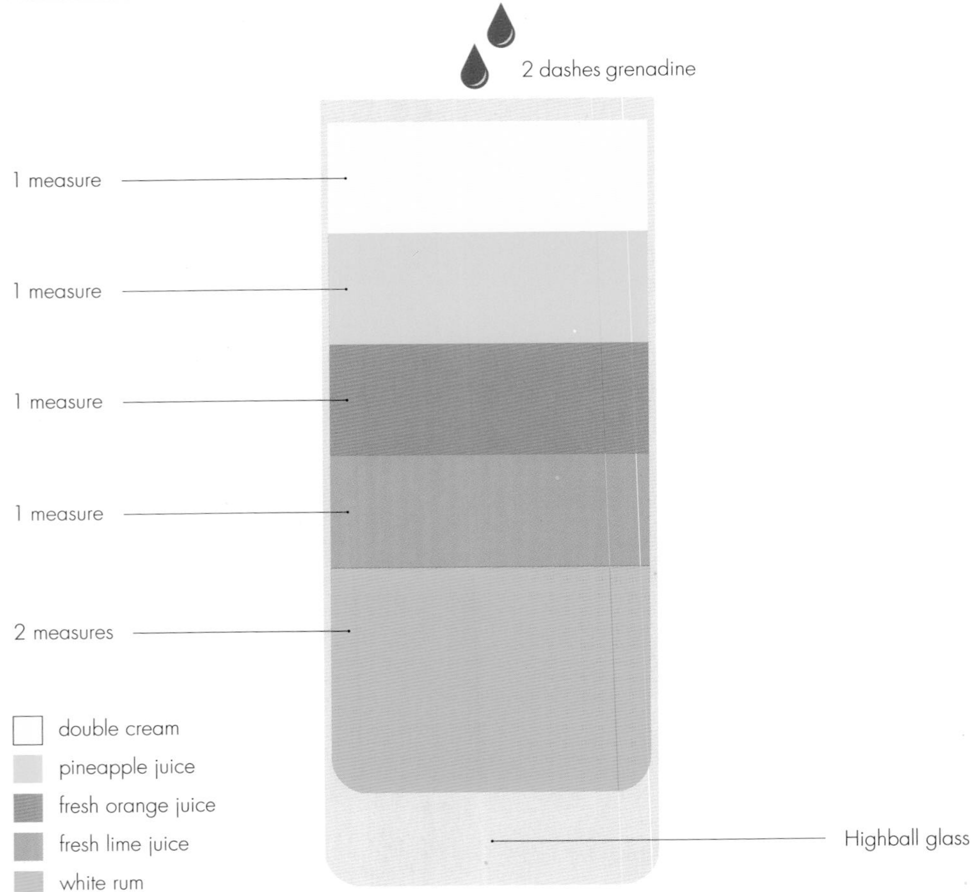

2 dashes grenadine
1 measure
1 measure
1 measure
1 measure
2 measures
double cream
pineapple juice
fresh orange juice
fresh lime juice
white rum
Highball glass

Instructions

1 Mix all the ingredients together in a shaker, then pour into a highball glass and serve.

Zombie

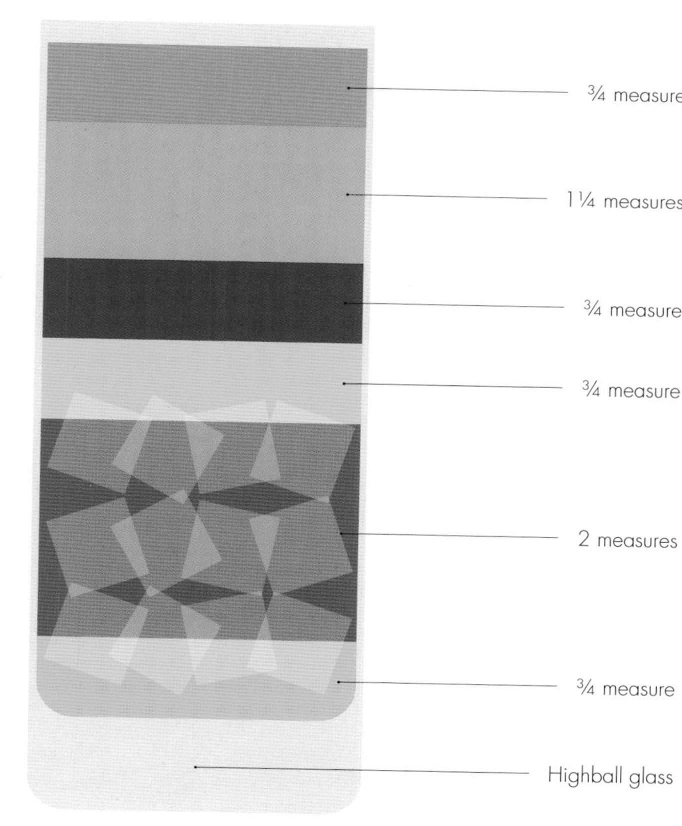

dash of grenadine
¾ measure
1¼ measures
¾ measure
¾ measure
2 measures
¾ measure
Highball glass

- orange juice
- lime juice
- Cherry Heering
- overproof rum
- dark rum
- gold rum

Instructions

1. Shake all the ingredients together and strain into a large highball glass half-filled with ice.

WHISKY

Algonquin

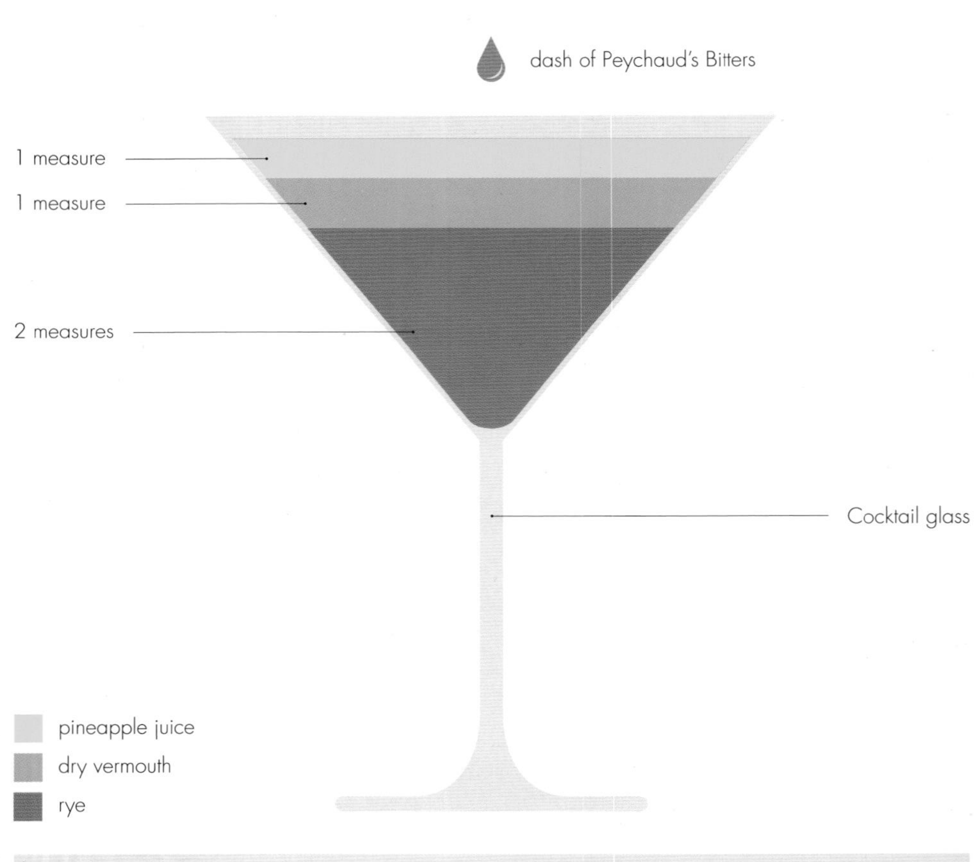
dash of Peychaud's Bitters
1 measure
1 measure
2 measures
Cocktail glass
pineapple juice
dry vermouth
rye

Instructions

1 Shake all the ingredients together and strain into a cocktail glass.

Angelic

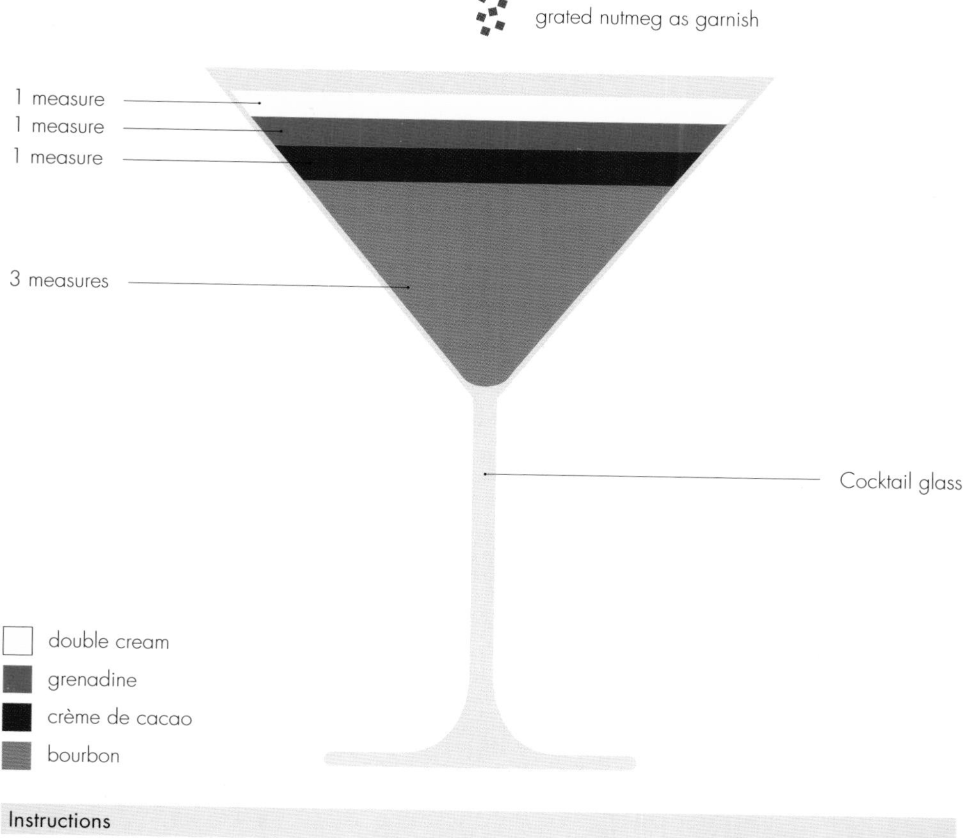

grated nutmeg as garnish
1 measure
1 measure
1 measure
3 measures
Cocktail glass
double cream
grenadine
crème de cacao
bourbon

Instructions

1 Mix the ingredients together in a shaker, then strain into a cocktail glass. **2** Sprinkle on the nutmeg and serve.

Ballantine's

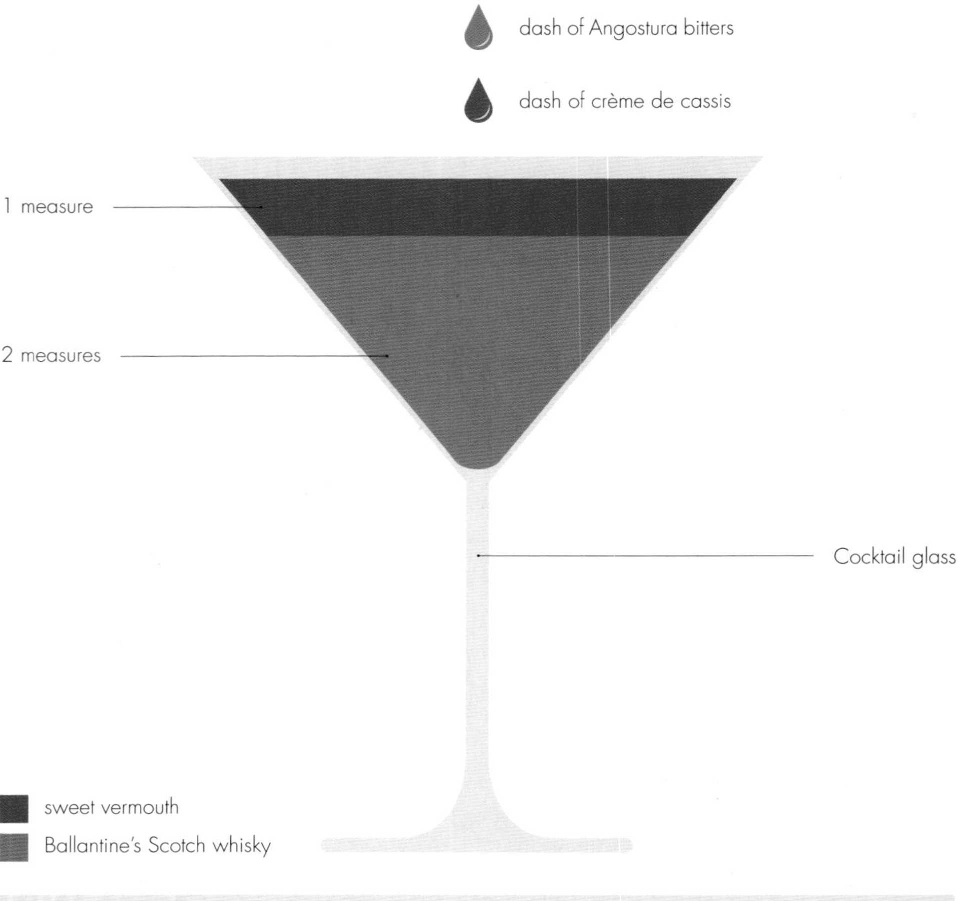

dash of Angostura bitters
dash of crème de cassis
1 measure
2 measures
Cocktail glass
sweet vermouth
Ballantine's Scotch whisky

Instructions

1 Pour all the ingredients into a shaker and shake. **2** Strain into a cocktail glass and serve.

Blood and Sand

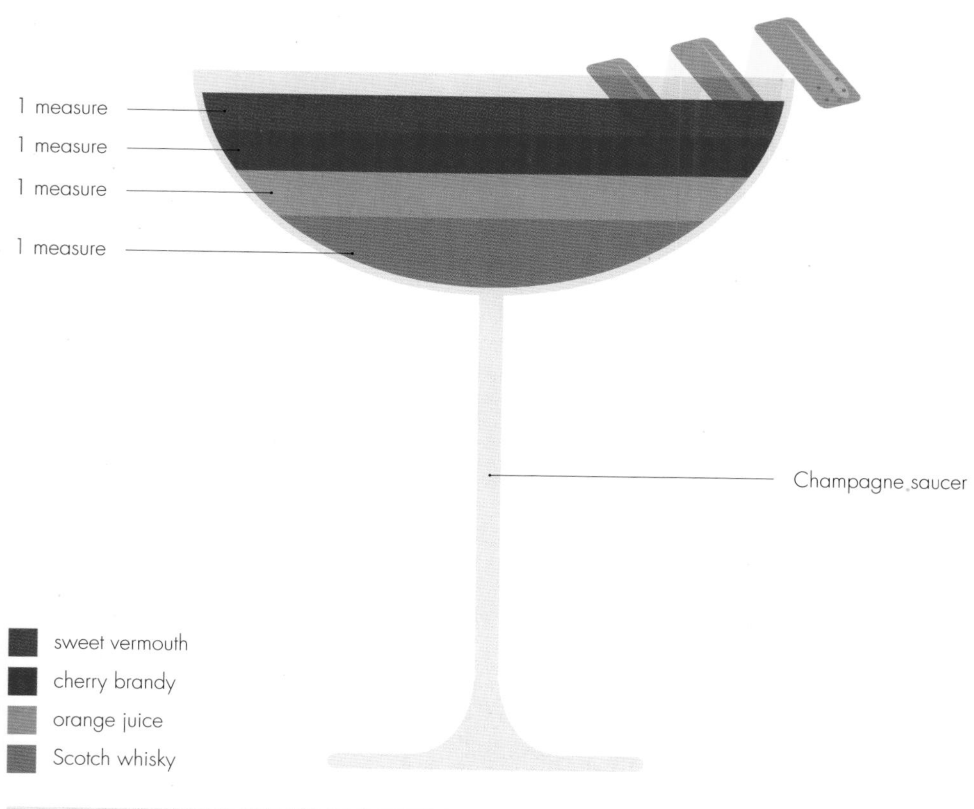

1 measure
1 measure
1 measure
1 measure
Champagne saucer
sweet vermouth
cherry brandy
orange juice
Scotch whisky

Instructions

1 Mix ingredients with ice in a mixing glass, then strain into a champagne saucer. **2** Garnish with an orange twist.

Brooklyn

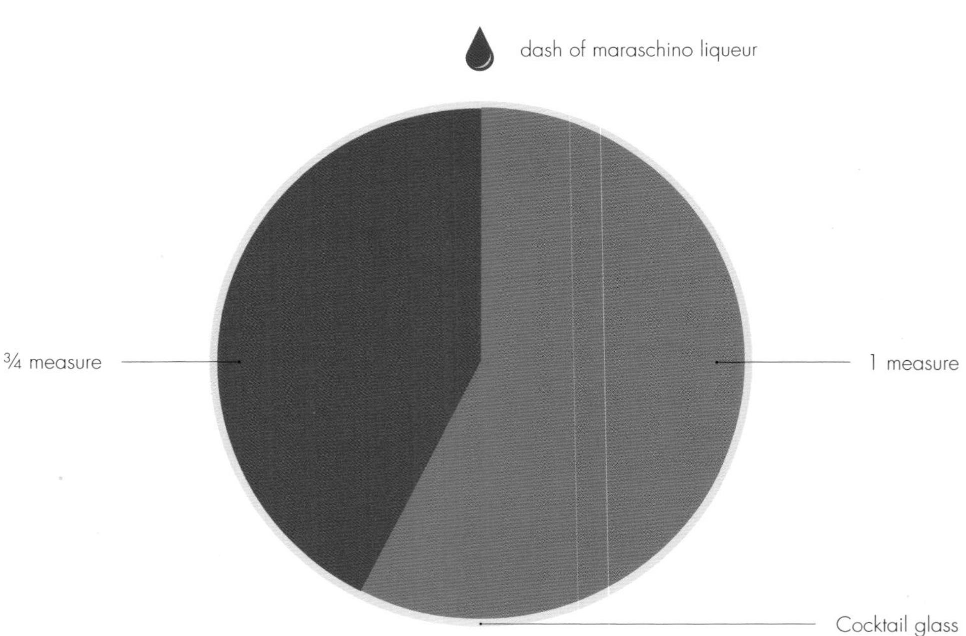
dash of maraschino liqueur
¾ measure
1 measure
Cocktail glass

vermouth rosso

rye

Instructions

1 Stir all the ingredients together, then strain into a cocktail glass.

Canadian Sherbet

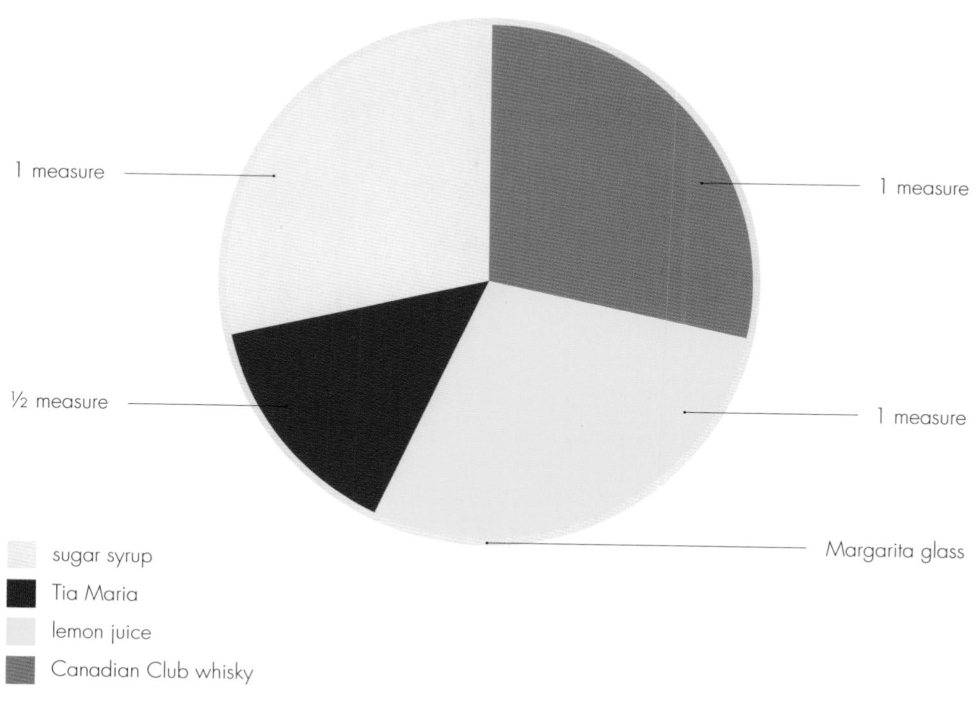
1 measure
1 measure
½ measure
1 measure
Margarita glass
sugar syrup
Tia Maria
lemon juice
Canadian Club whisky

Instructions

1 Blend ingredients with ice and pour into a margarita glass.

Chapel Hill

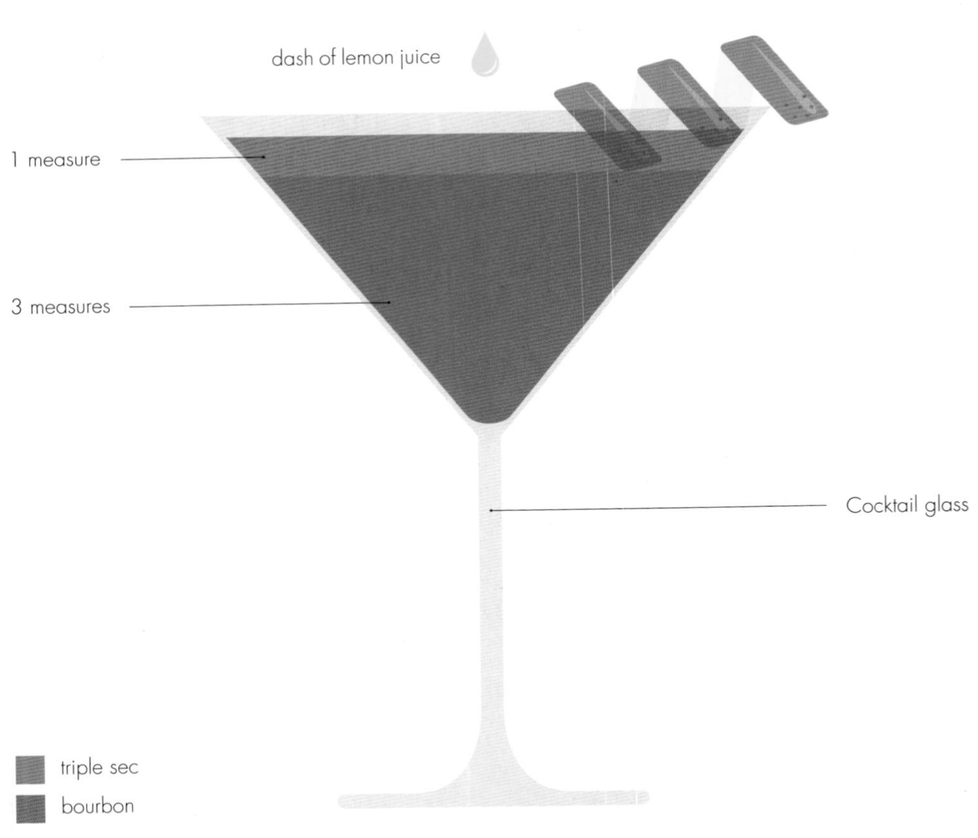

dash of lemon juice
1 measure
3 measures
Cocktail glass
triple sec
bourbon

Instructions

1. Shake all the liquids together, then strain into a cocktail glass and serve with an orange twist.

Colonel Fizz

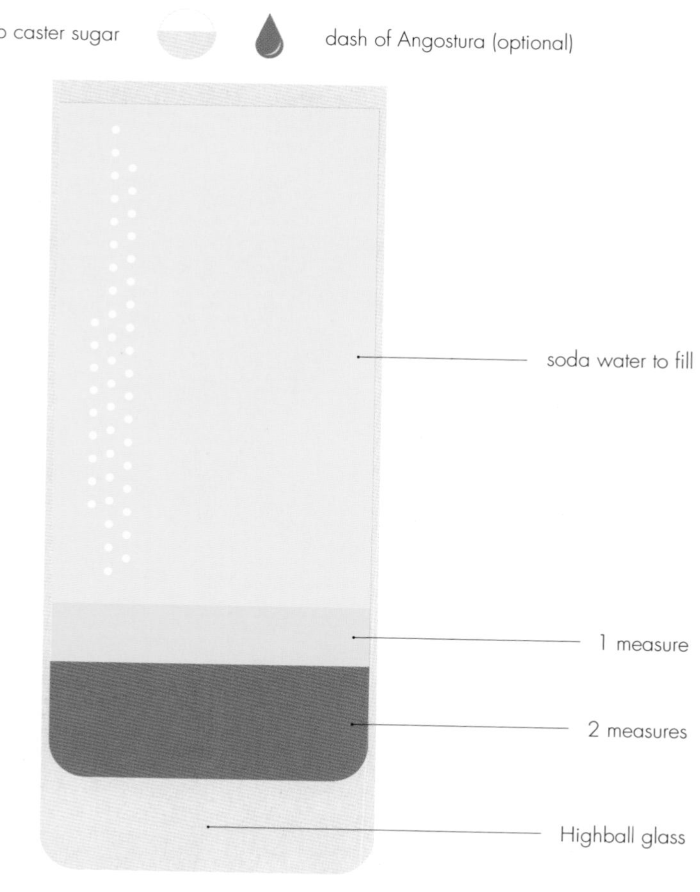
1 tsp caster sugar
dash of Angostura (optional)
soda water to fill
1 measure
2 measures
Highball glass
soda water
lemon juice
bourbon

Instructions

■ Shake the juice, bourbon, sugar and Angostura and strain into a tall glass. ■ Top up with soda.

Frisco

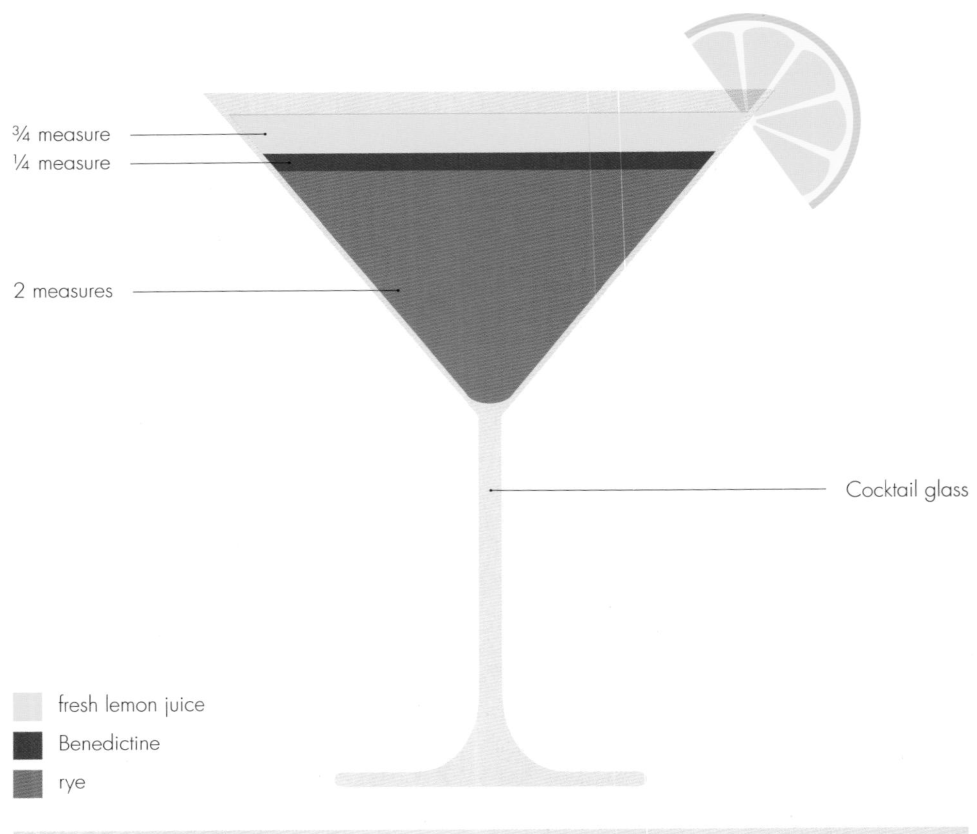

¾ measure
¼ measure
2 measures
Cocktail glass
fresh lemon juice
Benedictine
rye

Instructions

1 Shake all ingredients with ice and strain into a cocktail glass. **2** Garnish with a slice of lemon.

Godfather

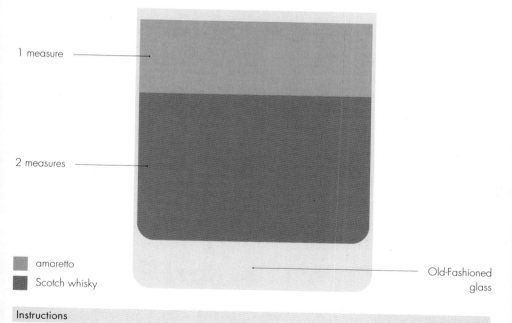

1 measure
2 measures
amaretto
Scotch whisky
Old-Fashioned glass

Instructions

1. Pour the Scotch and amaretto into an Old-Fashioned glass and serve.

Gumdrop

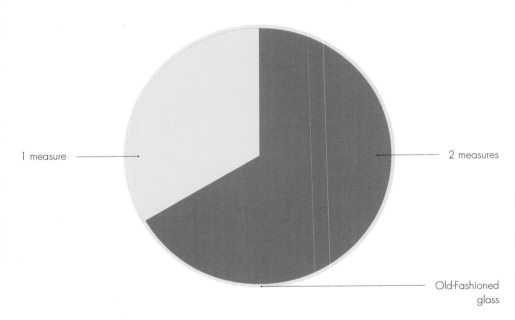

1 measure

2 measures

Old-Fashioned glass

Galliano

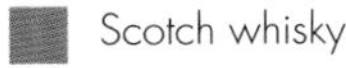
Scotch whisky

Instructions

1. Pour the Scotch and Galliano into an Old-Fashioned glass and serve.

Kentucky Sunset

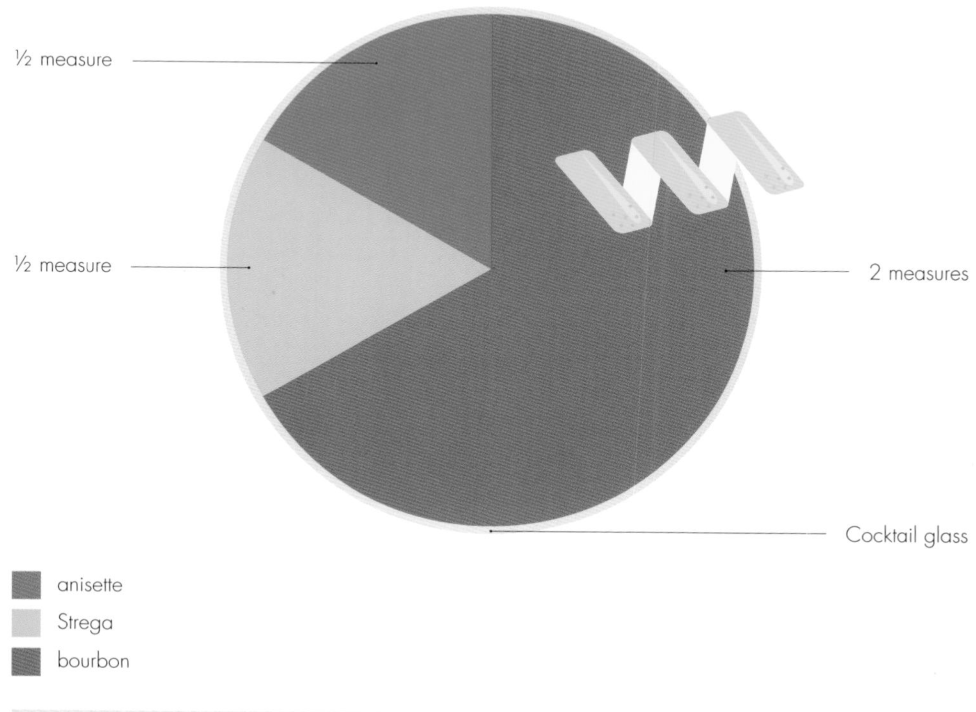

½ measure
½ measure
2 measures
Cocktail glass
anisette
Strega
bourbon

Instructions

1 Stir the bourbon, Strega, and anisette together, then strain into a cocktail glass. **2** Serve, garnished with a lemon twist.

Last Emperor

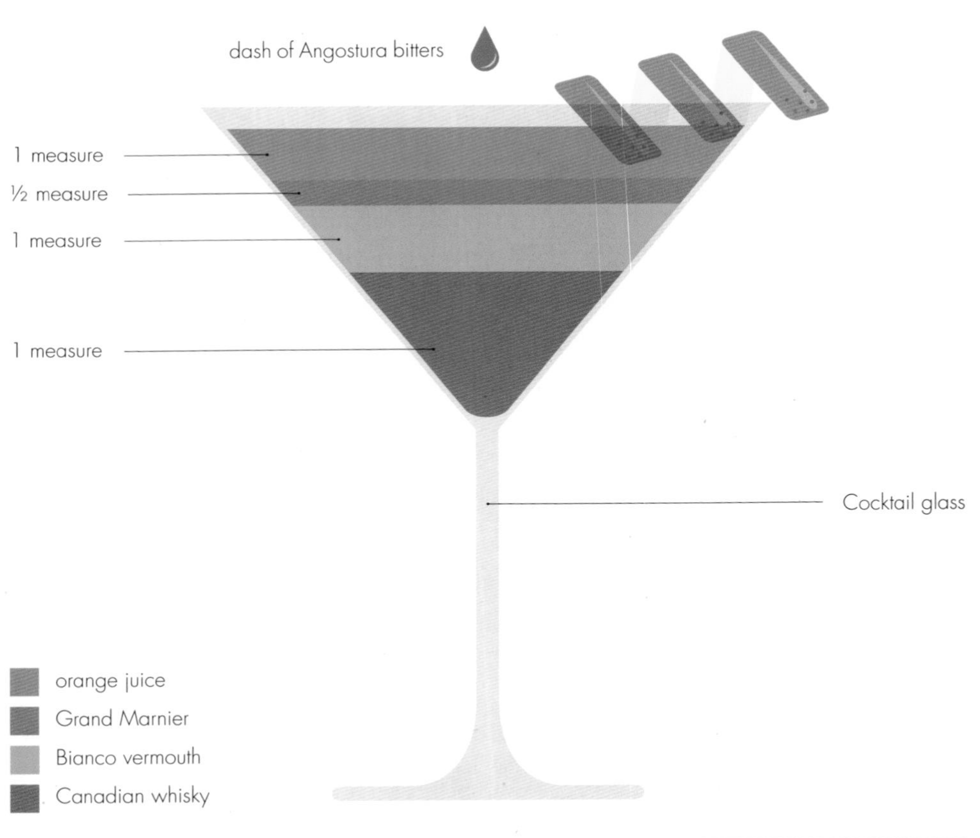

dash of Angostura bitters
1 measure
½ measure
1 measure
1 measure
Cocktail glass
orange juice
Grand Marnier
Bianco vermouth
Canadian whisky

Instructions

1 Place ingredients in mixing glass with ice and stir well. **2** Strain into a cocktail glass and stir again.
3 Add a strip of orange peel.

Liberty Bell

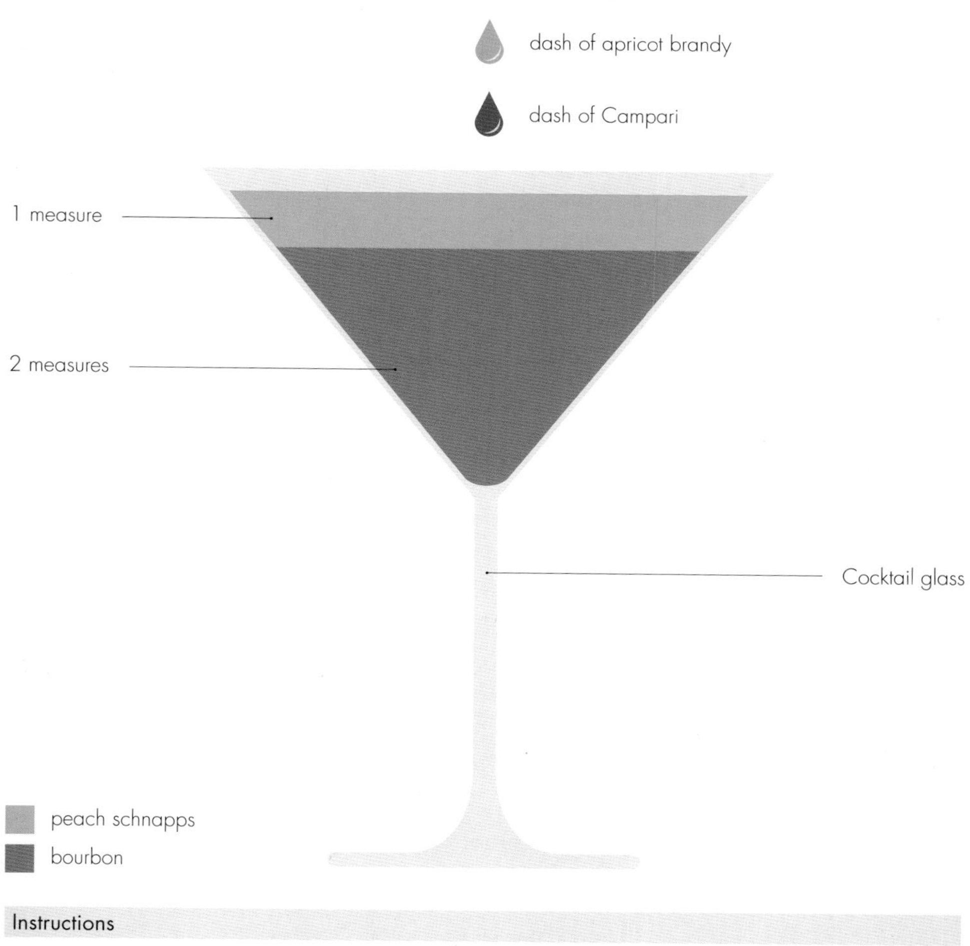

dash of apricot brandy
dash of Campari
1 measure
2 measures
Cocktail glass
peach schnapps
bourbon

Instructions

1. Stir all the ingredients together, then strain into a cocktail glass and serve.

Milk Punch

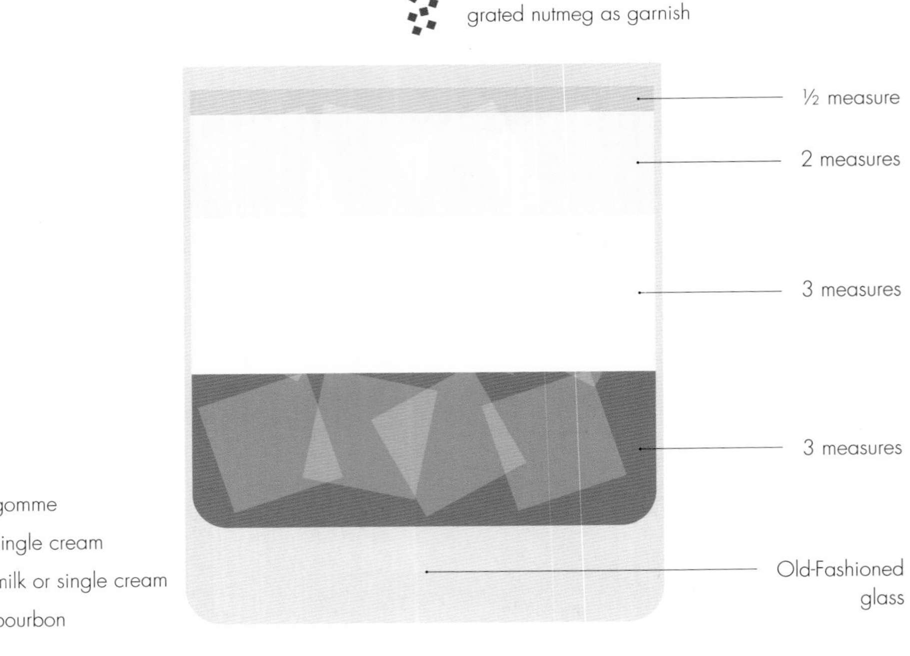
grated nutmeg as garnish
½ measure
2 measures
3 measures
3 measures
Old-Fashioned glass
gomme
single cream
milk or single cream
bourbon

Instructions

1 Shake all the liquid ingredients with ice and strain into a ice-filled Old-Fashioned glass. **2** Shake grated nutmeg over the drink.

Rob Roy

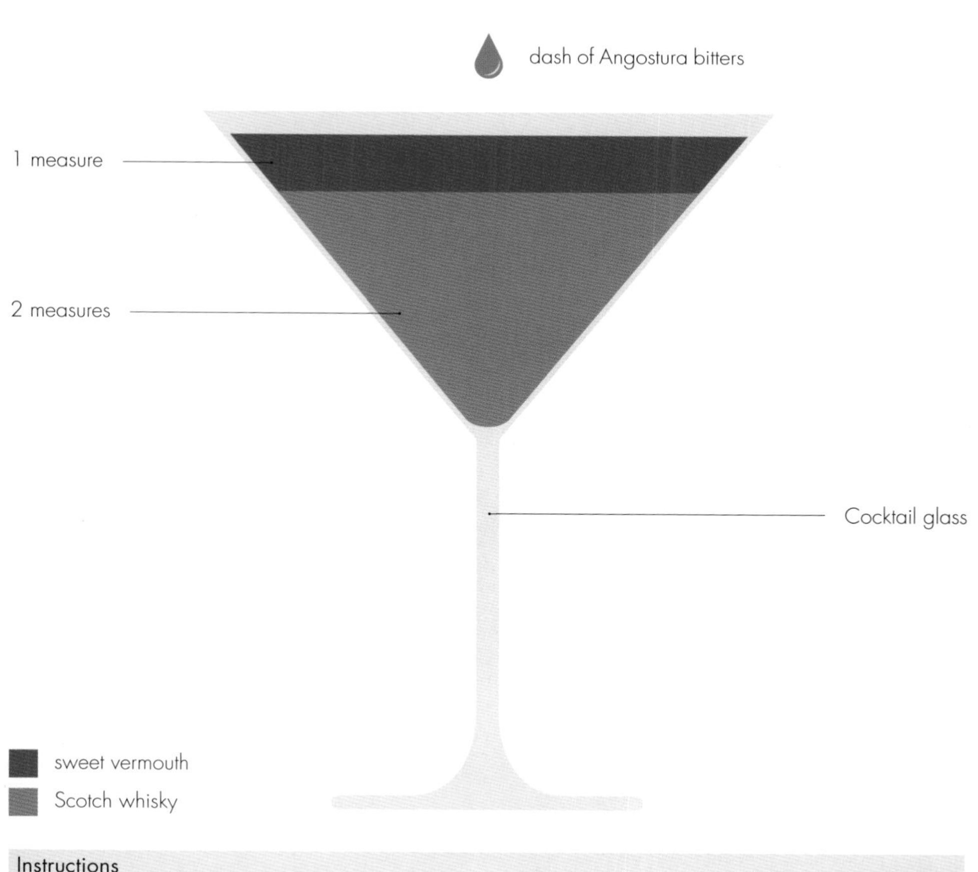

dash of Angostura bitters
1 measure
2 measures
Cocktail glass
sweet vermouth
Scotch whisky

Instructions

1. Stir all the ingredients together, then strain into a cocktail glass and serve.

Rusty Nail

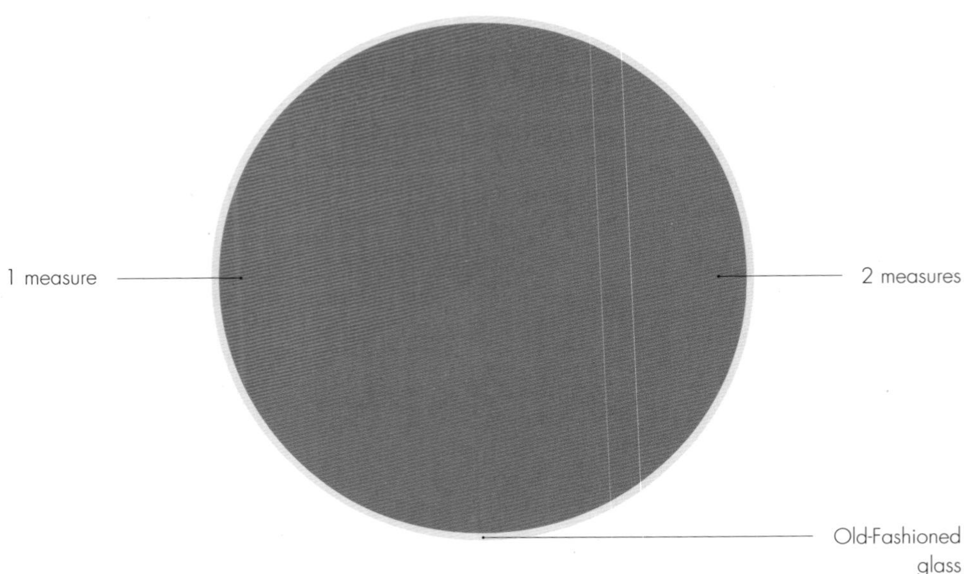
1 measure
2 measures
Old-Fashioned glass

Drambuie

Scotch whisky

Instructions

1 Pour the Scotch and Drambuie into an Old-Fashioned glass and serve.

Sazerac

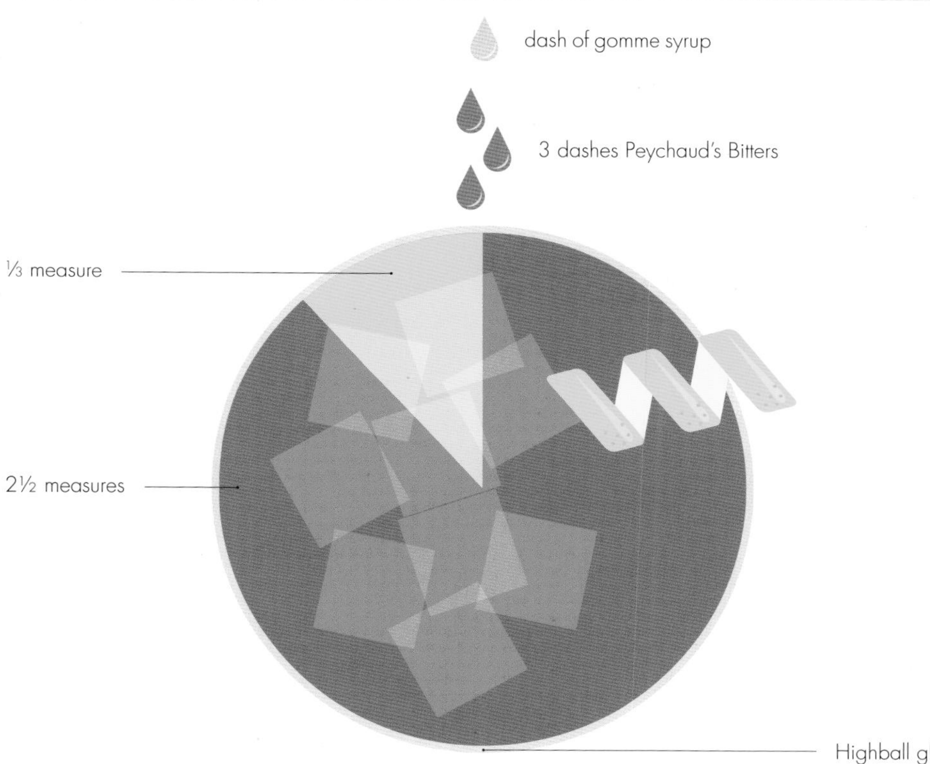
dash of gomme syrup
3 dashes Peychaud's Bitters
⅓ measure
2½ measures
Highball glass

absinthe or Pernod

bourbon

Instructions

1 Pour the absinthe (Pernod) into a highball glass, coat and discard the excess. 2 Shake the other ingredients and pour over ice into the glass.

Shamrock

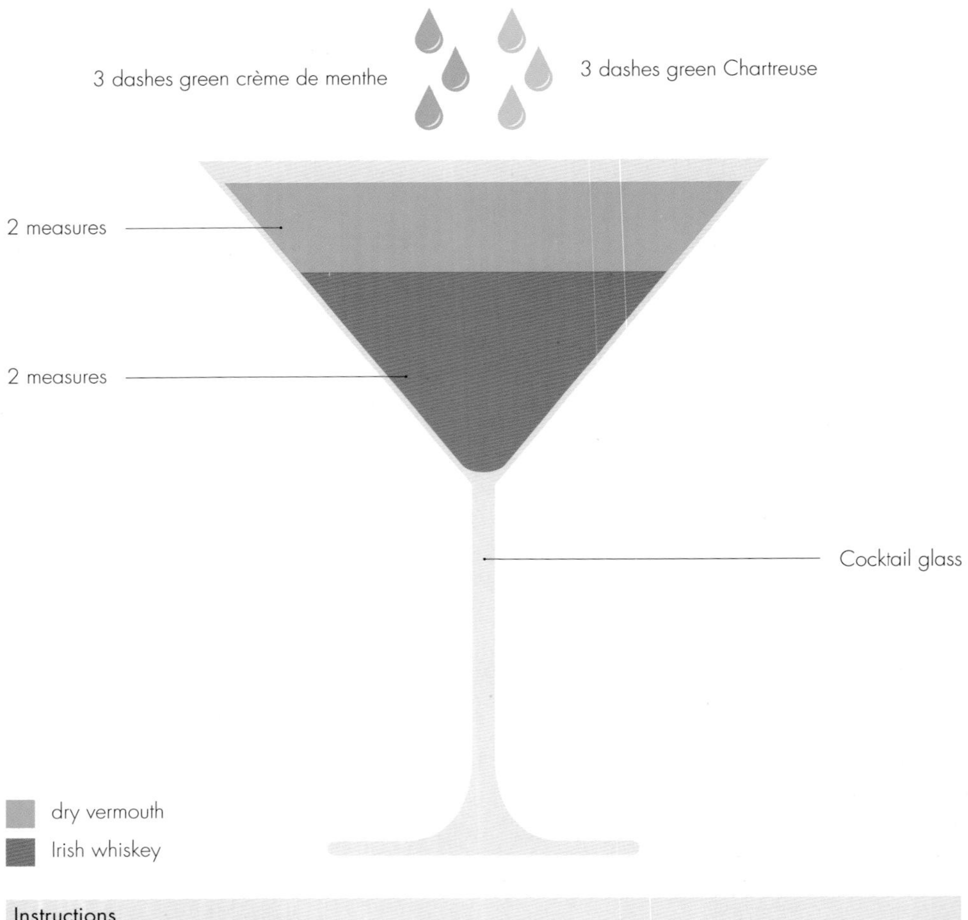
3 dashes green crème de menthe
3 dashes green Chartreuse
2 measures
2 measures
Cocktail glass
dry vermouth
Irish whiskey

Instructions

1. Mix all the ingredients together in a shaker, strain, and serve in a cocktail glass.

VIP

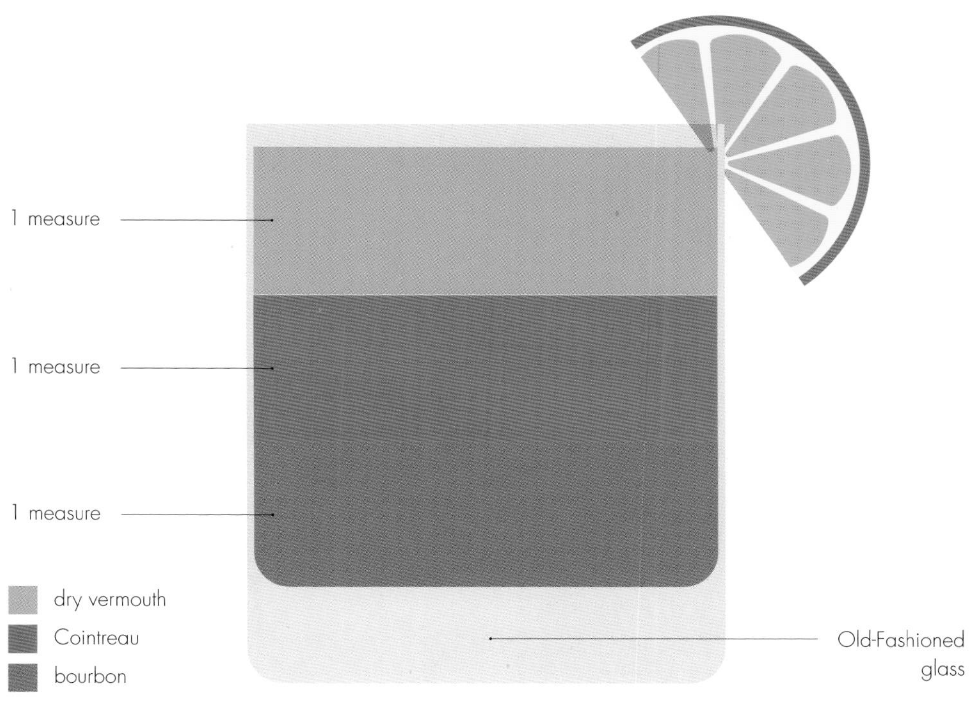

1 measure
1 measure
1 measure
dry vermouth
Cointreau
bourbon
Old-Fashioned glass

Instructions

1 Pour the ingredients into an Old-Fashioned glass, garnish with the orange slice and serve.

Whisky Mac

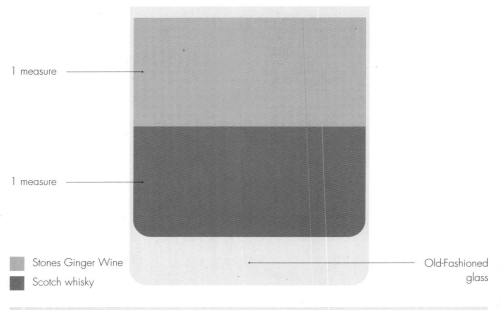

1 measure
1 measure
Stones Ginger Wine
Scotch whisky
Old-Fashioned glass

Instructions

1. Pour the Scotch and ginger wine into an Old-Fashioned glass, stir, and serve.

Whizz Doodle

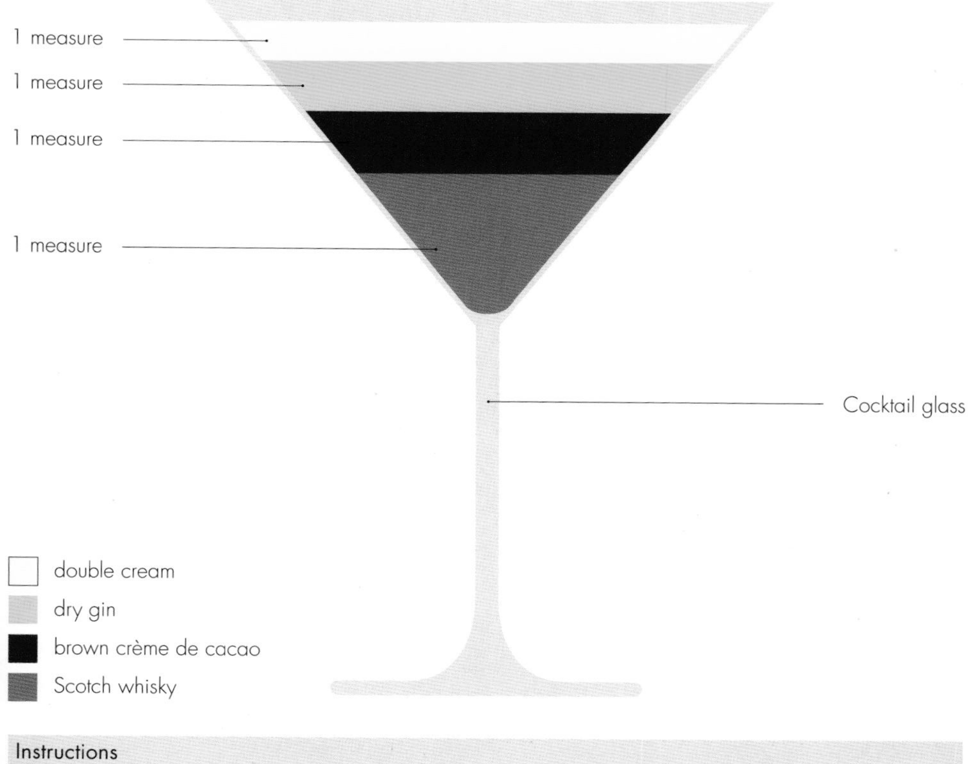

1 measure
1 measure
1 measure
1 measure
Cocktail glass
double cream
dry gin
brown crème de cacao
Scotch whisky

Instructions

1 Mix all the ingredients together in a shaker with ice, strain and pour into a cocktail glass.

TEQUILA

Acapulco

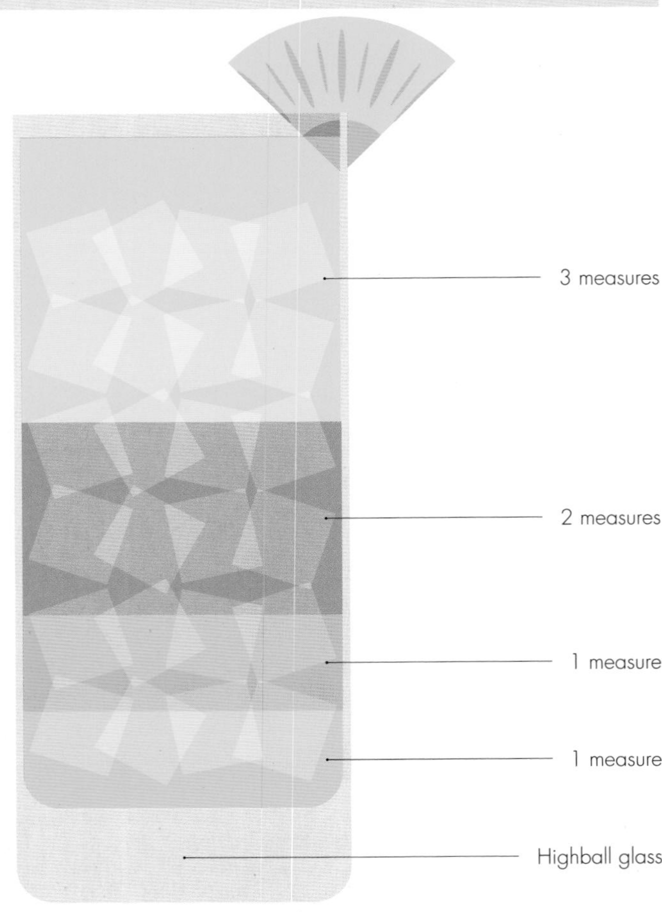
3 measures
2 measures
1 measure
1 measure
Highball glass

pineapple juice
grapefruit juice
gold rum
gold tequila

Instructions

1 Shake all the ingredients and strain into a highball filled with ice. **2** Garnish with a pineapple wedge.

All Night

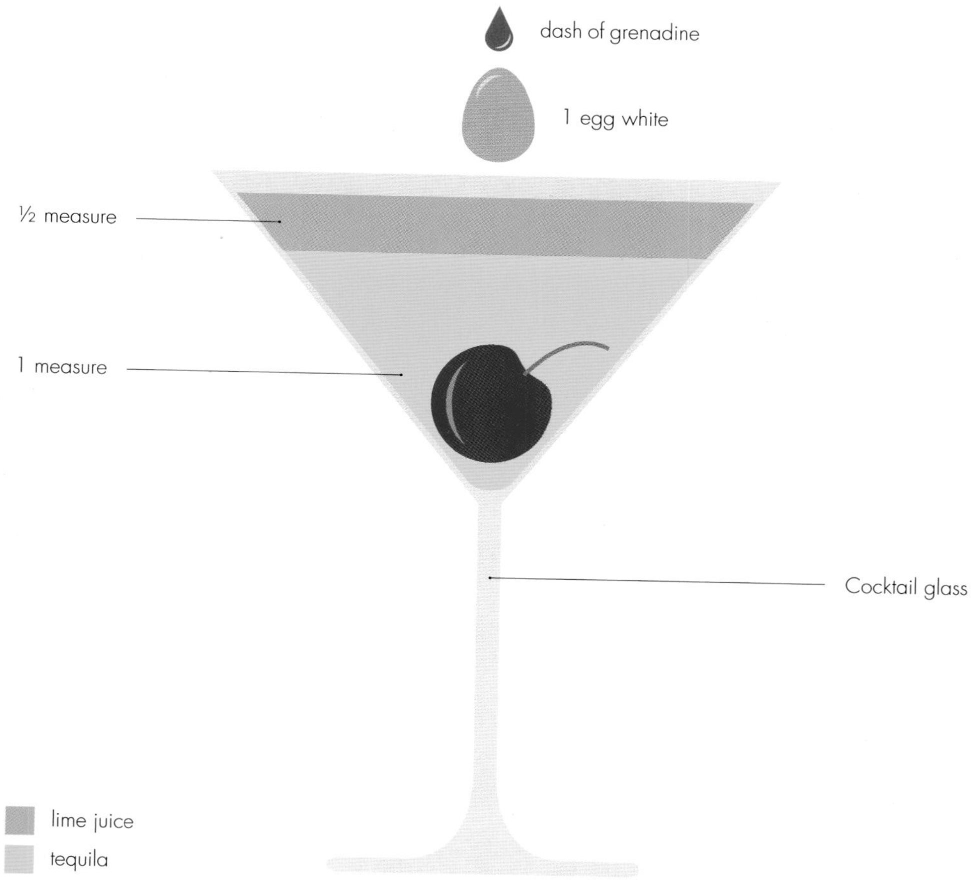

dash of grenadine

1 egg white

½ measure

1 measure

Cocktail glass

lime juice

tequila

Instructions

1 Shake all ingredients with ice and strain into a chilled cocktail glass. **2** Garnish with a maraschino cherry.

Chapala

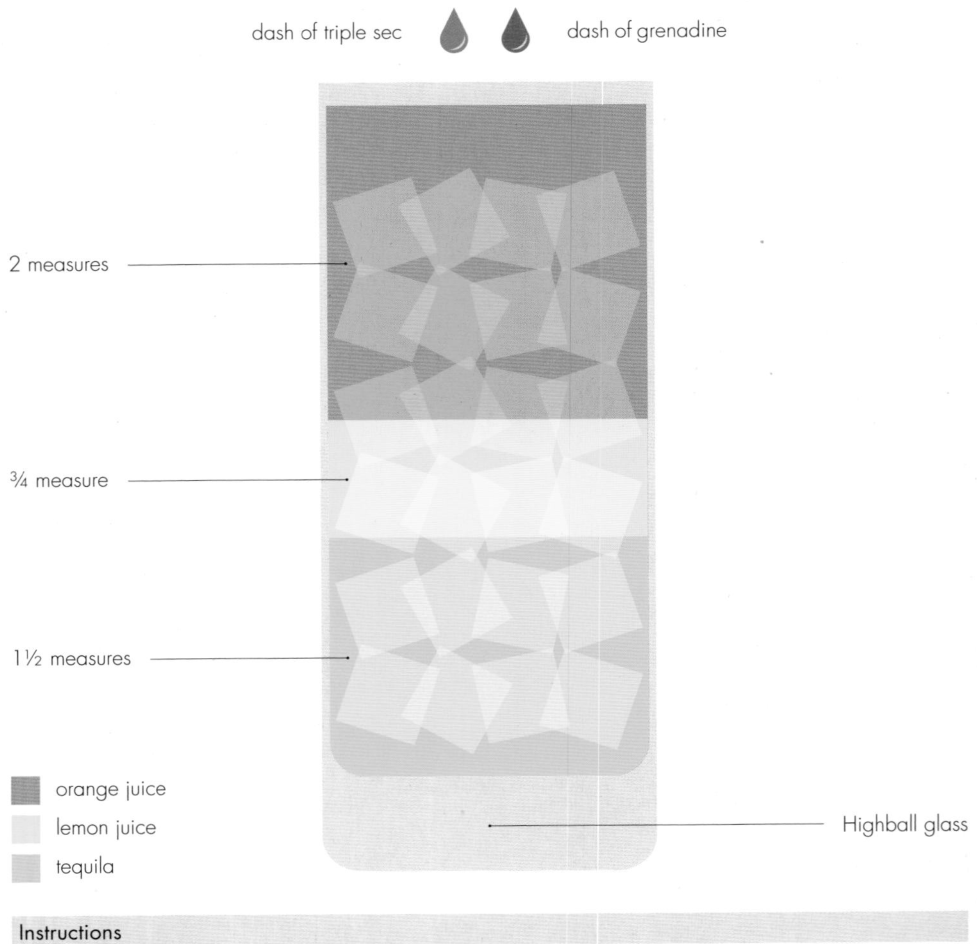

dash of triple sec
dash of grenadine
2 measures
¾ measure
1½ measures
orange juice
lemon juice
tequila
Highball glass

Instructions

1. Stir all the ingredients together over ice in a highball glass.

Clam Digger

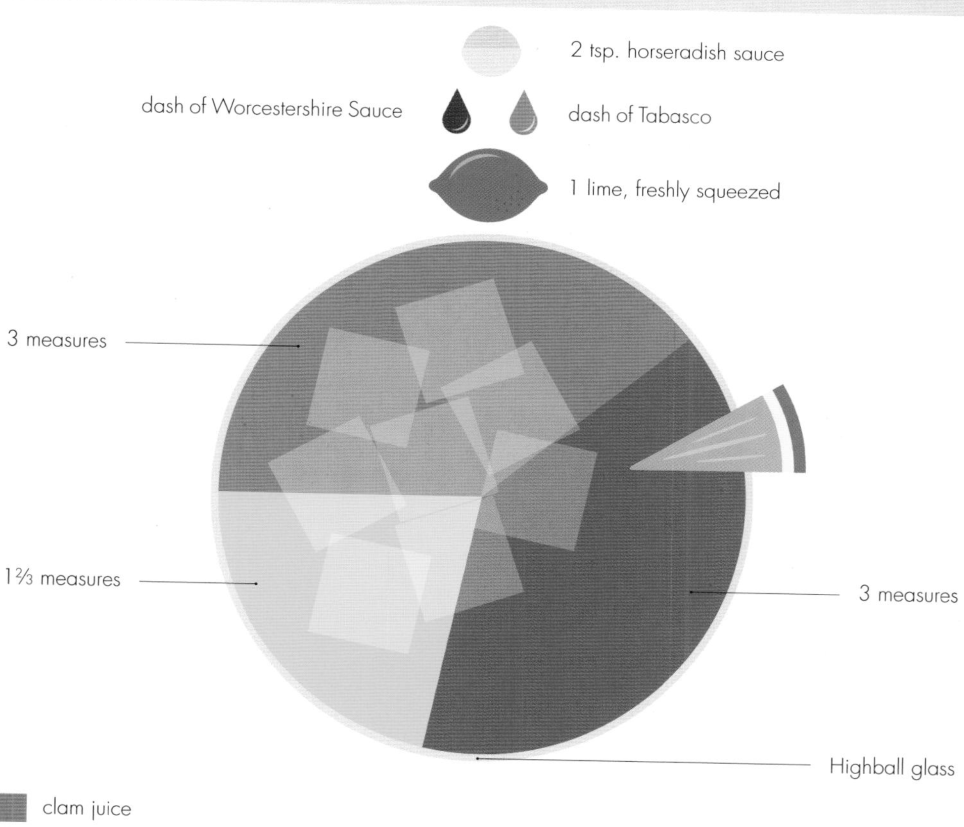

2 tsp. horseradish sauce
dash of Worcestershire Sauce
dash of Tabasco
1 lime, freshly squeezed
3 measures
1⅔ measures
3 measures
Highball glass

- clam juice
- tomato juice
- silver tequila

Instructions

1 Shake all the liquid ingredients together and strain into a highball with ice. **2** Garnish with a lime wedge.

Cool Gold

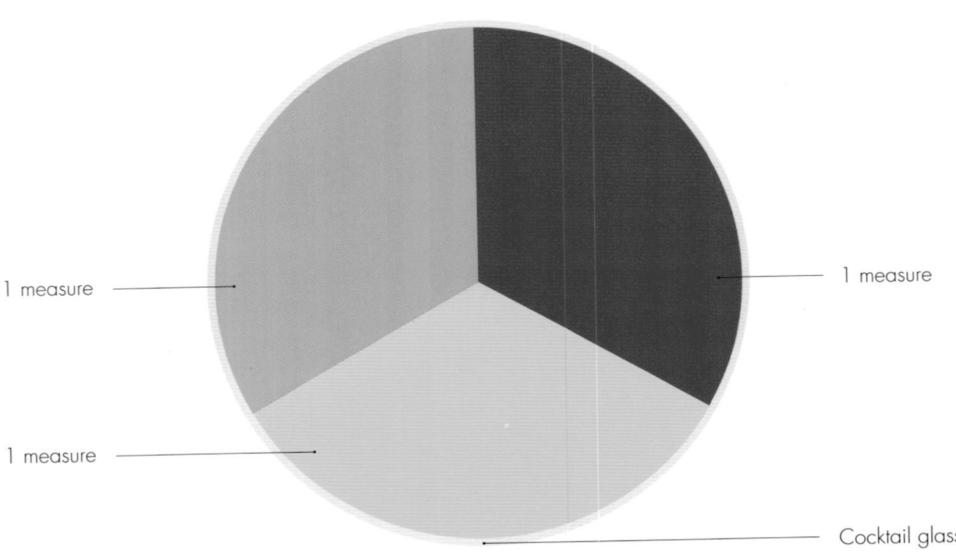

1 measure
1 measure
1 measure
Cocktail glass

cranberry juice
melon liqueur
gold tequila

Instructions

1. Shake all the ingredients together and strain into a cocktail glass.

El Diablo

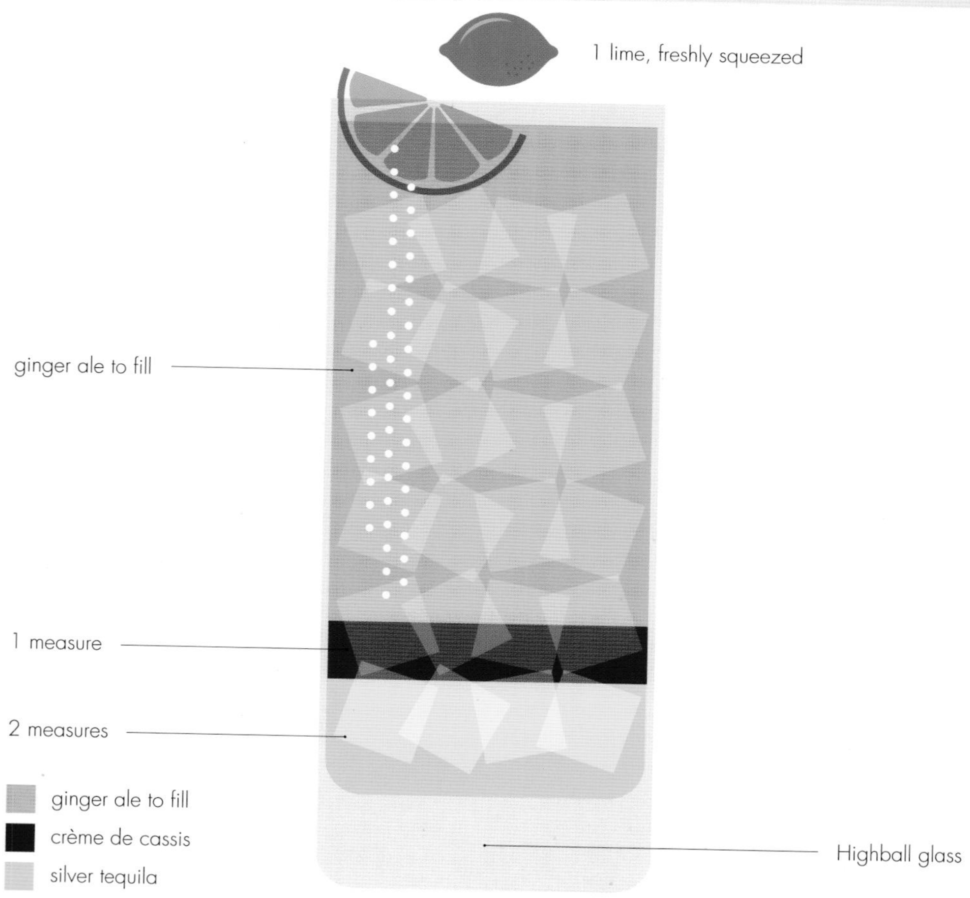
1 lime, freshly squeezed
ginger ale to fill
1 measure
2 measures
Highball glass
ginger ale to fill
crème de cassis
silver tequila

Instructions

1 Pour lime juice into a highball with crushed ice. 2 Add tequila and crème de cassis. 3 Fill with ginger ale. Stir. 4 Drop in a lime wedge and serve with a straw.

Eldorado

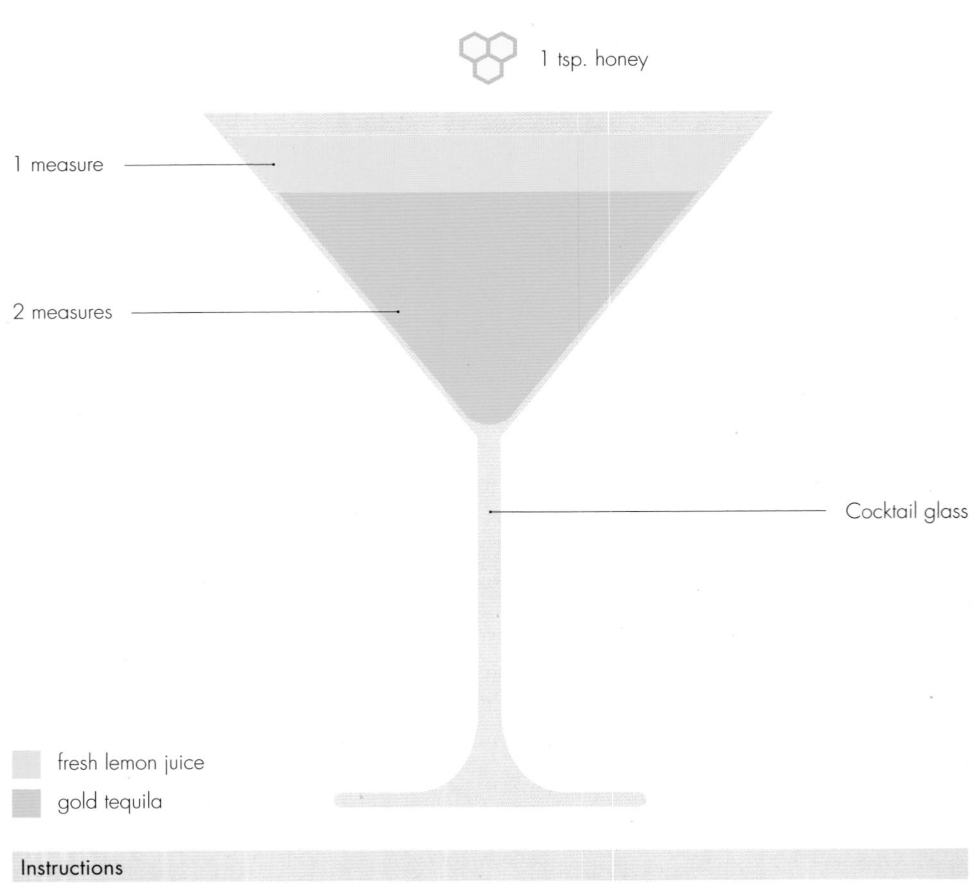

1 tsp. honey
1 measure
2 measures
Cocktail glass
fresh lemon juice
gold tequila

Instructions

1. Shake all the ingredients together, then strain into a cocktail glass and serve.

Frostbite

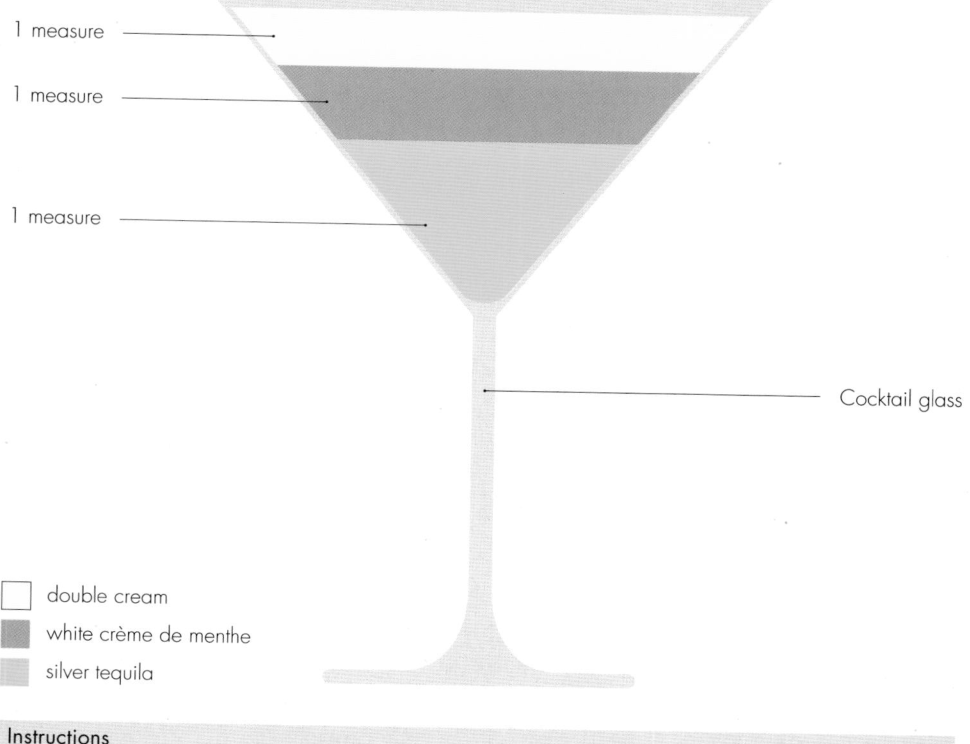

1 measure
1 measure
1 measure
Cocktail glass
double cream
white crème de menthe
silver tequila

Instructions

1. Mix the ingredients together in a shaker, then strain into a cocktail glass and serve.

La Bomba

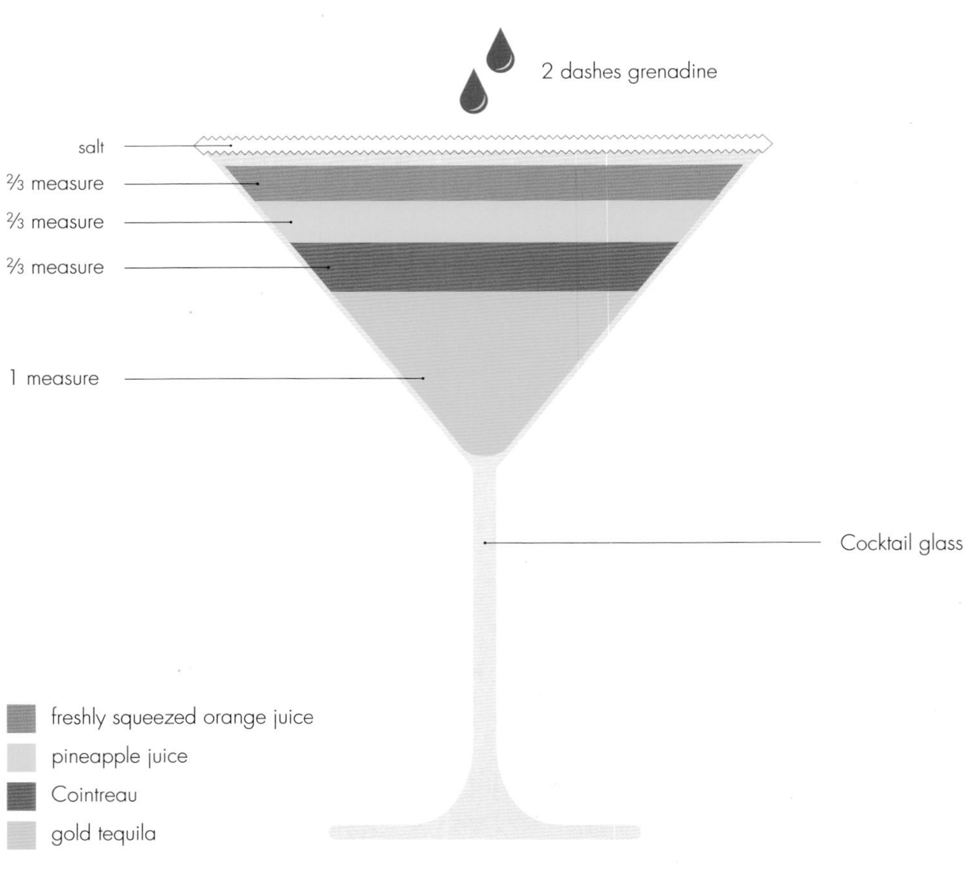

2 dashes grenadine
salt
⅔ measure
⅔ measure
⅔ measure
1 measure
Cocktail glass
freshly squeezed orange juice
pineapple juice
Cointreau
gold tequila

Instructions

1 Shake the tequila, Cointreau, pineapple and oranges juices, then strain into a cocktail glass with a salted rim. **2** Add the grenadine.

Laser Beam

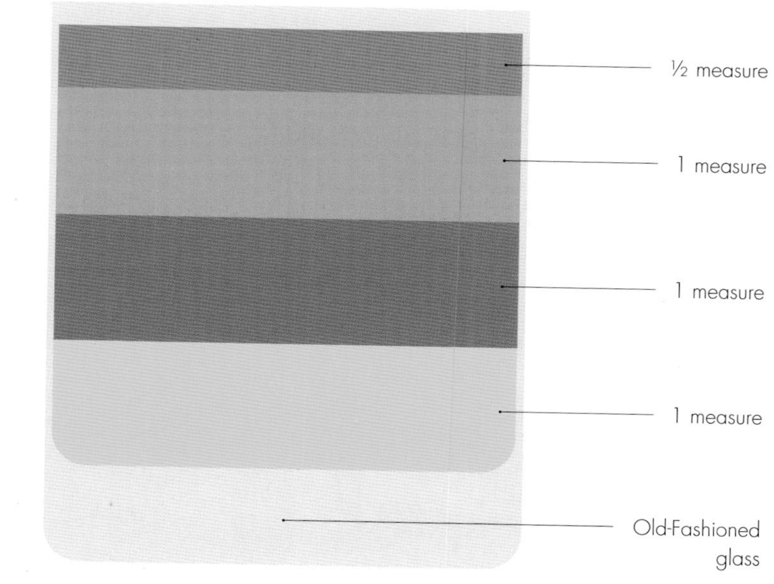

½ measure
1 measure
1 measure
1 measure
triple sec
amaretto
Jack Daniels
tequila
Old-Fashioned glass

Instructions

1. Shake all the ingredients together, pour into an Old-Fashioned glass, and serve.

Matador

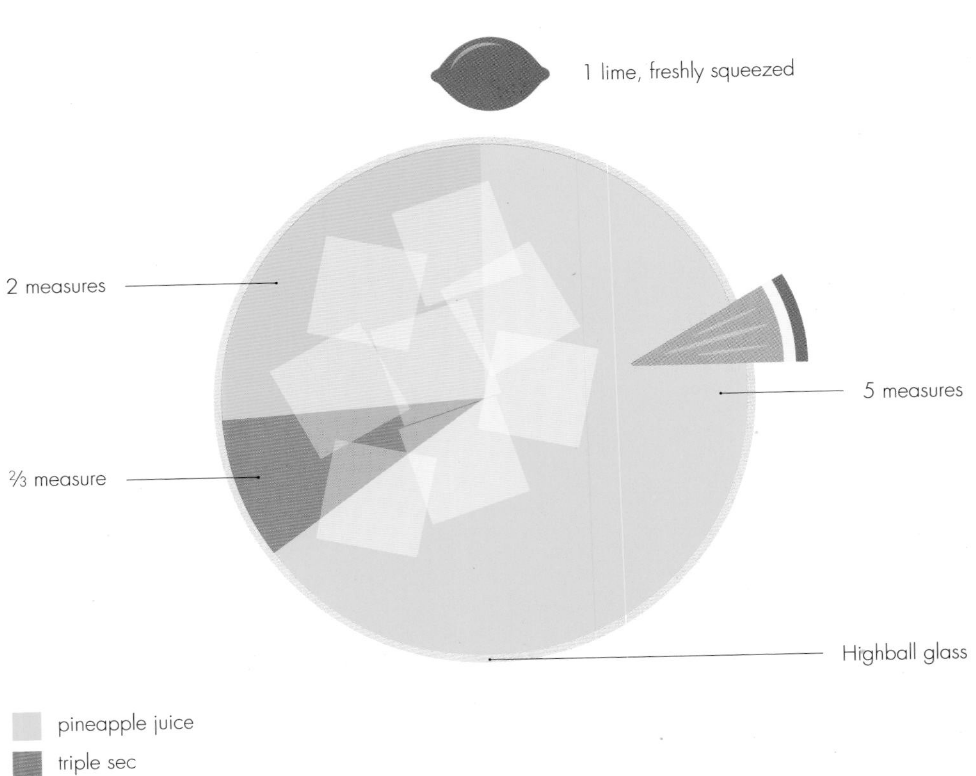
1 lime, freshly squeezed
2 measures
5 measures
⅔ measure
Highball glass

pineapple juice

triple sec

gold tequila

Instructions

1 Shake all the liquid ingredients, then strain into a highball with ice. 2 Add a lime wedge.

Mexican Mule

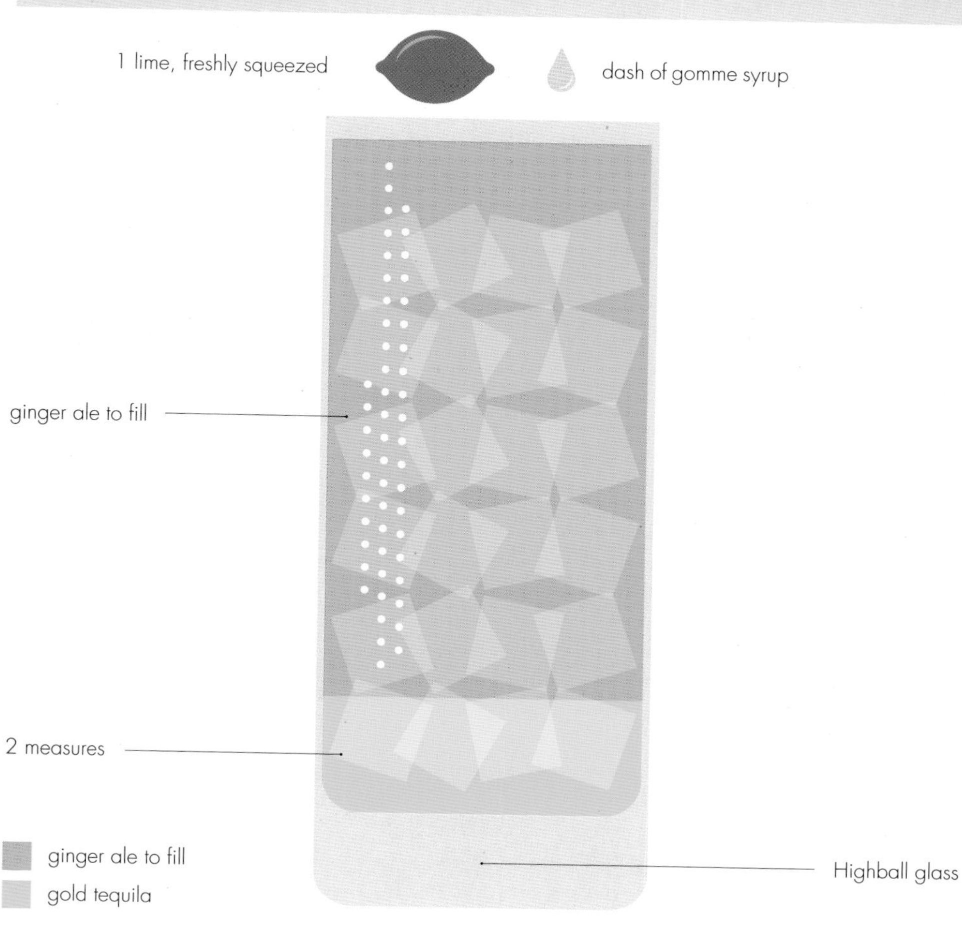

1 lime, freshly squeezed
dash of gomme syrup
ginger ale to fill
2 measures
ginger ale to fill
gold tequila
Highball glass

Instructions

1 Shake the tequila, lime juice, and gomme, and strain into a highball with ice. **2** Top up with ginger ale.

Mexicana

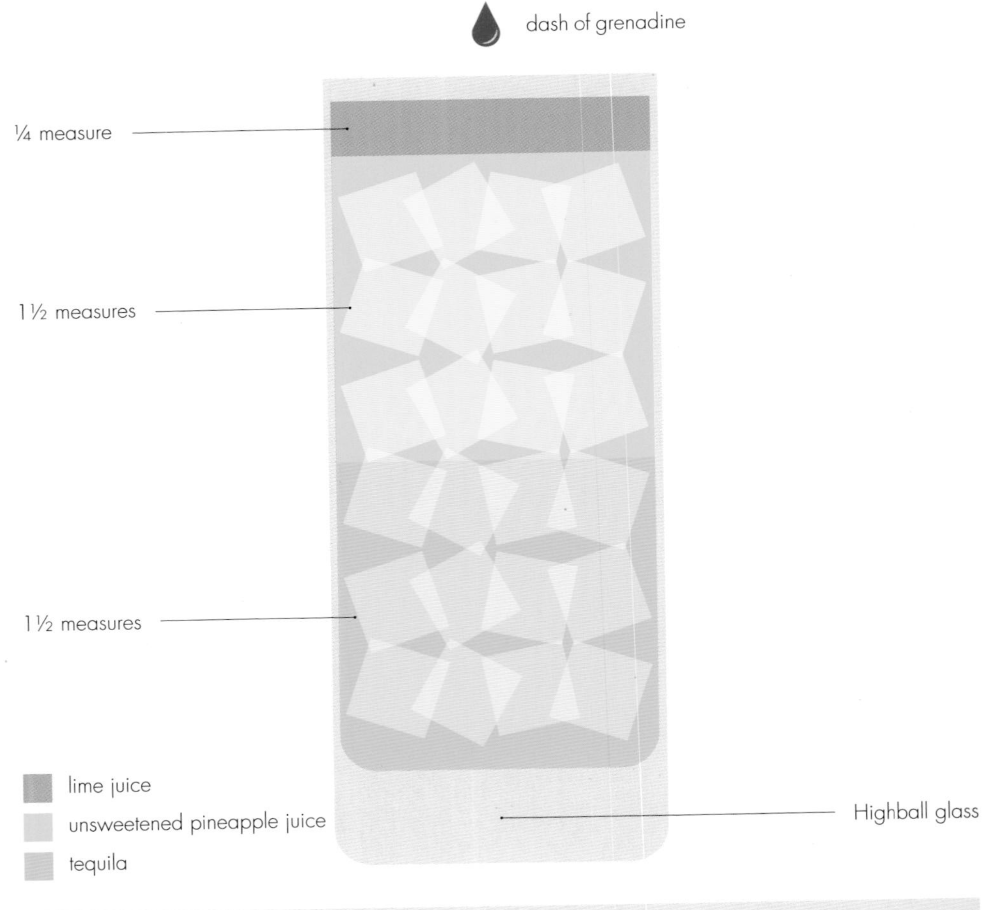
dash of grenadine
¼ measure
1½ measures
1½ measures
lime juice
unsweetened pineapple juice
tequila
Highball glass

Instructions

1. Shake all the ingredients together and strain into a highball glass filled with ice.

Red Desert

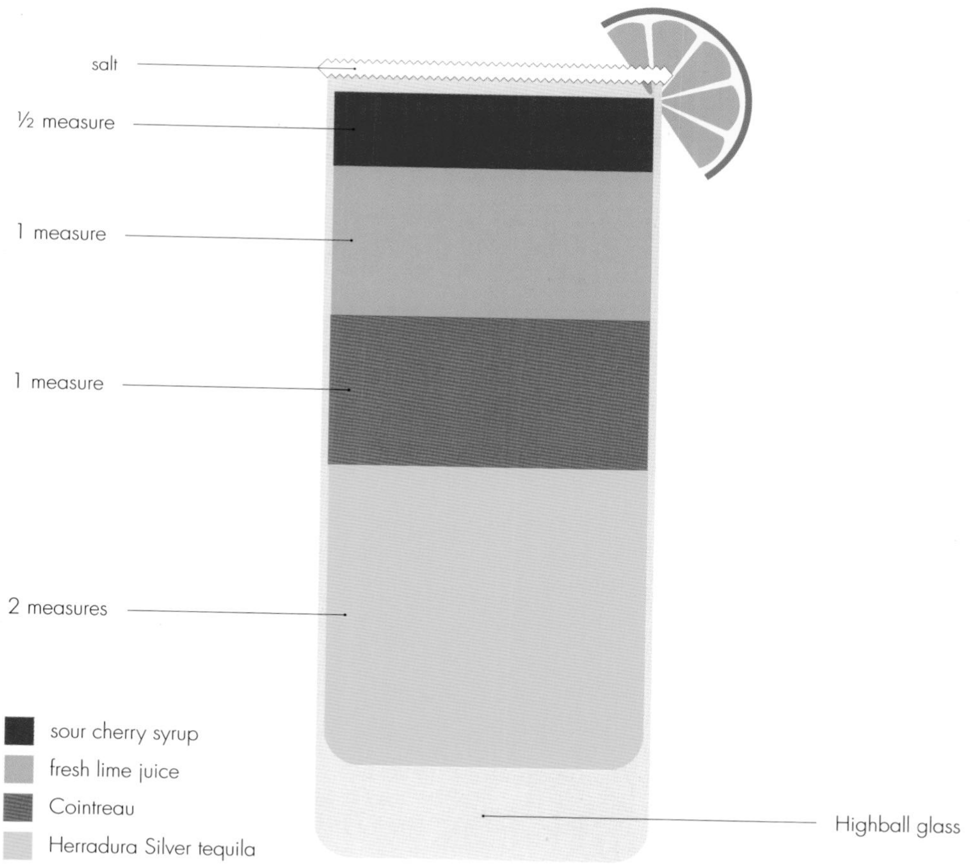

salt
½ measure
1 measure
1 measure
2 measures
sour cherry syrup
fresh lime juice
Cointreau
Herradura Silver tequila
Highball glass

Instructions

1 Shake all the ingredients and strain into a salt-rimmed highball glass. **2** Garnish with a lime wedge.

Rosalita

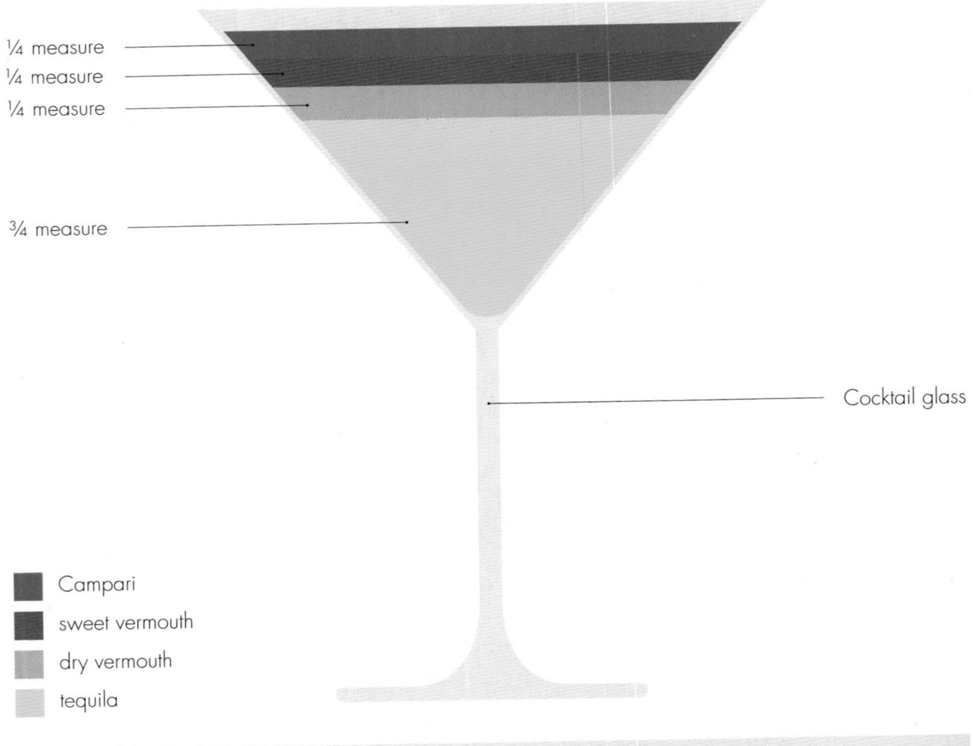

¼ measure
¼ measure
¼ measure
¾ measure
Cocktail glass
Campari
sweet vermouth
dry vermouth
tequila

Instructions

1. Shake all the ingredients together and strain into a cocktail glass.

Short Fuse

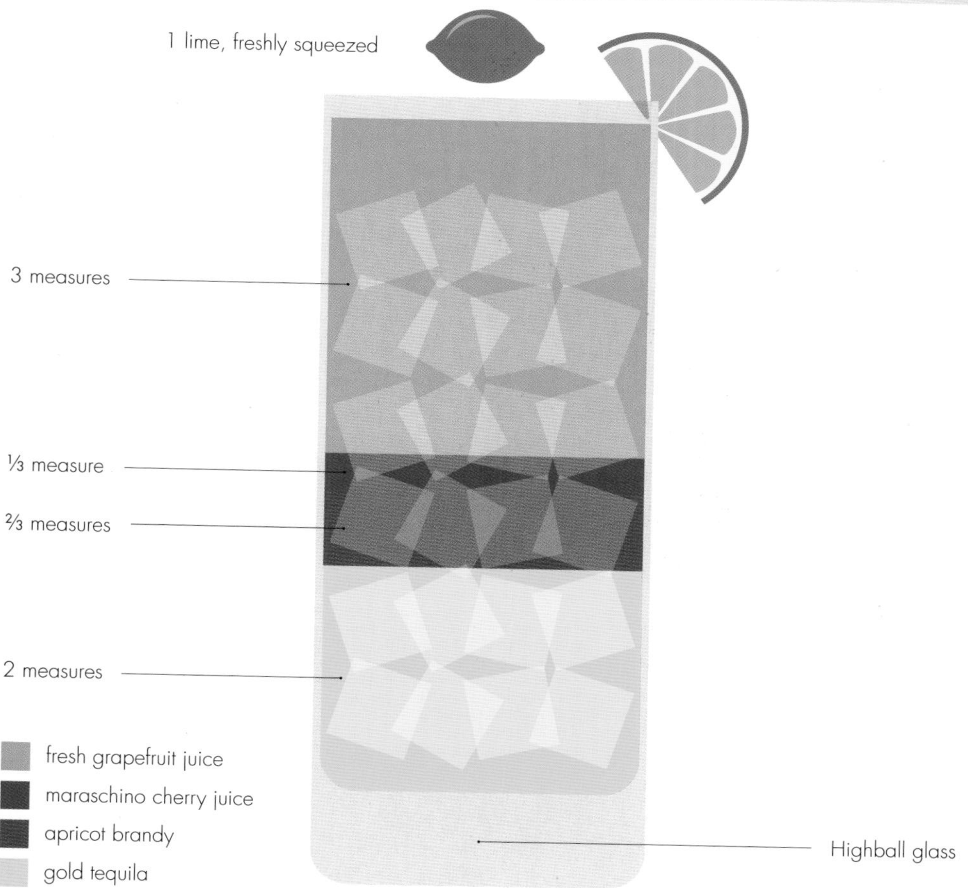

1 lime, freshly squeezed
3 measures
⅓ measure
⅔ measures
2 measures
fresh grapefruit juice
maraschino cherry juice
apricot brandy
gold tequila
Highball glass

Instructions

1 Shake all the liquid ingredients together and strain into an ice-filled highball glass. 2 Add a lime wedge.

Silk Stocking

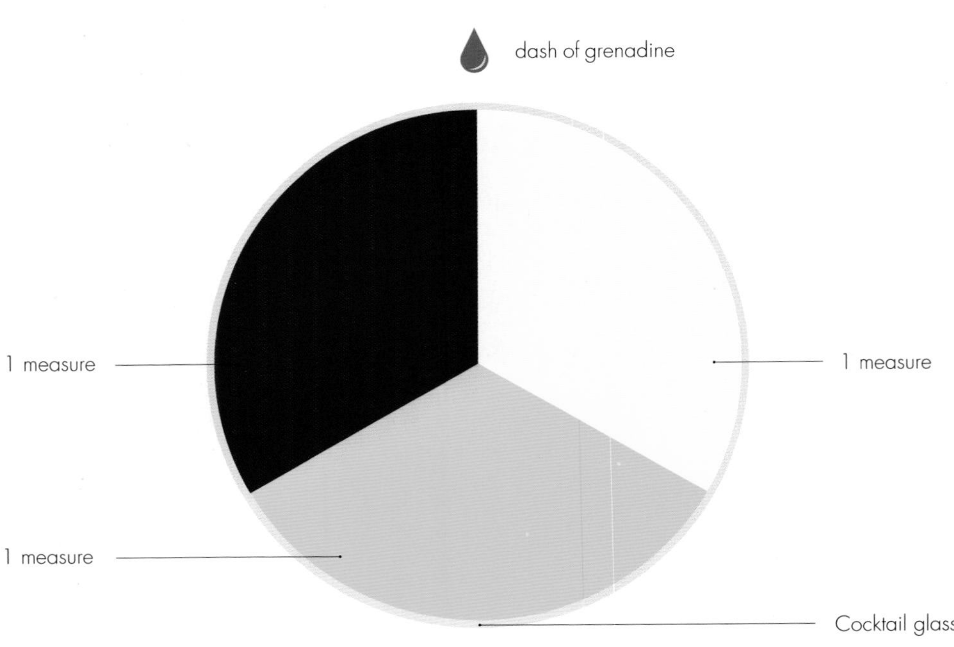
dash of grenadine
1 measure
1 measure
1 measure
Cocktail glass

- double cream
- white crème de cacao
- tequila

Instructions

1. Mix the ingredients together in a shaker, then strain into a cocktail glass and serve.

South of the Border

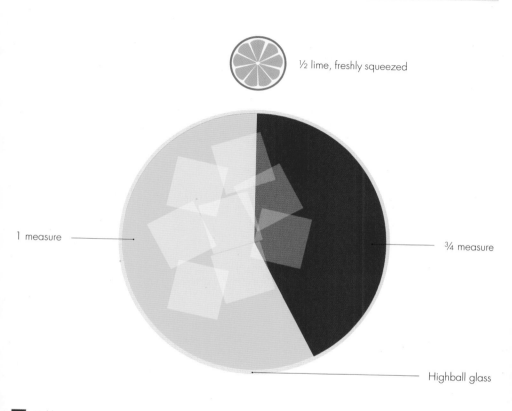

½ lime, freshly squeezed

1 measure

¾ measure

Highball glass

 Kahlua

 tequila

Instructions

1 Squeeze the lime over ice in a highball glass and stir before adding the spirits. **2** Stir again to mix.

Tequila Sunrise

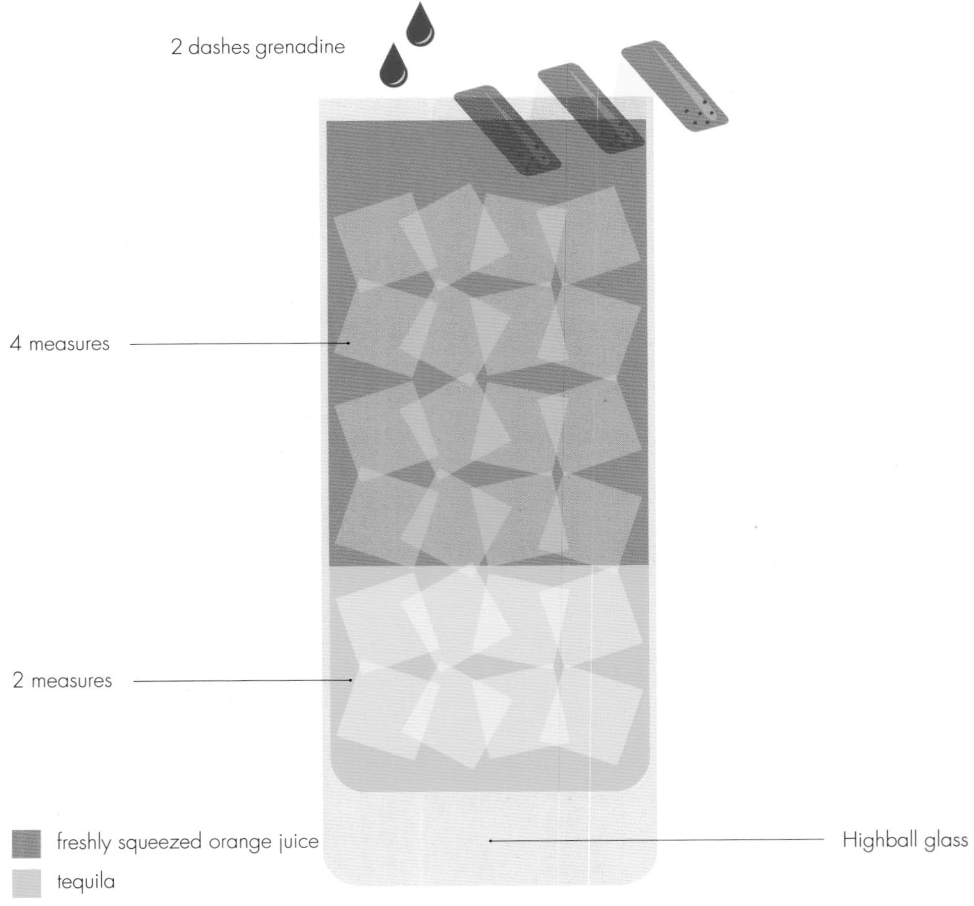
2 dashes grenadine
4 measures
2 measures
freshly squeezed orange juice
tequila
Highball glass

Instructions

1 Pour the tequila and orange juice into a highball glass filled with ice. **2** Stir, then slowly add the grenadine. **3** Add an orange spiral as garnish and serve with a stirrer.

Tijuana Taxi

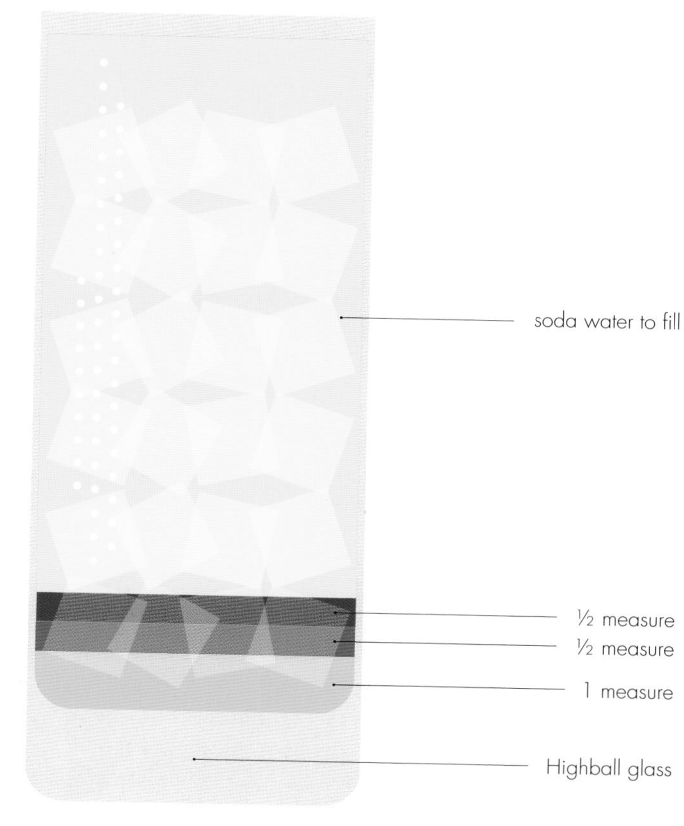
soda water to fill
½ measure
½ measure
1 measure
Highball glass

soda water to fill

tropical fruit schnapps

blue curaçao

gold tequila

Instructions

1 Pour the tequila, curaçao, and schnapps into a highball glass filled with ice. **2** Top up with soda.

Tomahawk

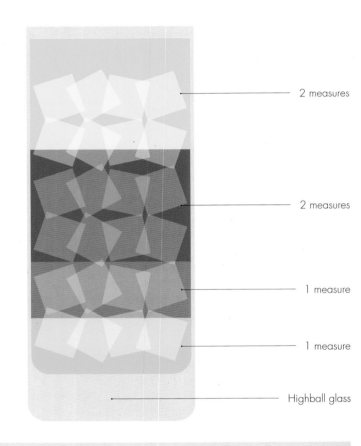

2 measures

2 measures

1 measure

1 measure

Highball glass

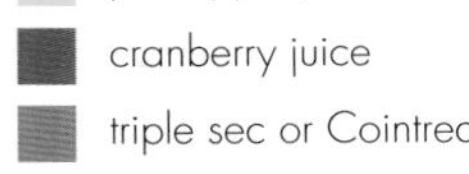

pineapple juice

cranberry juice

triple sec or Cointreau

tequila

Instructions

1. Shake all the ingredients together and strain into a highball glass filled with ice.

Vampiro

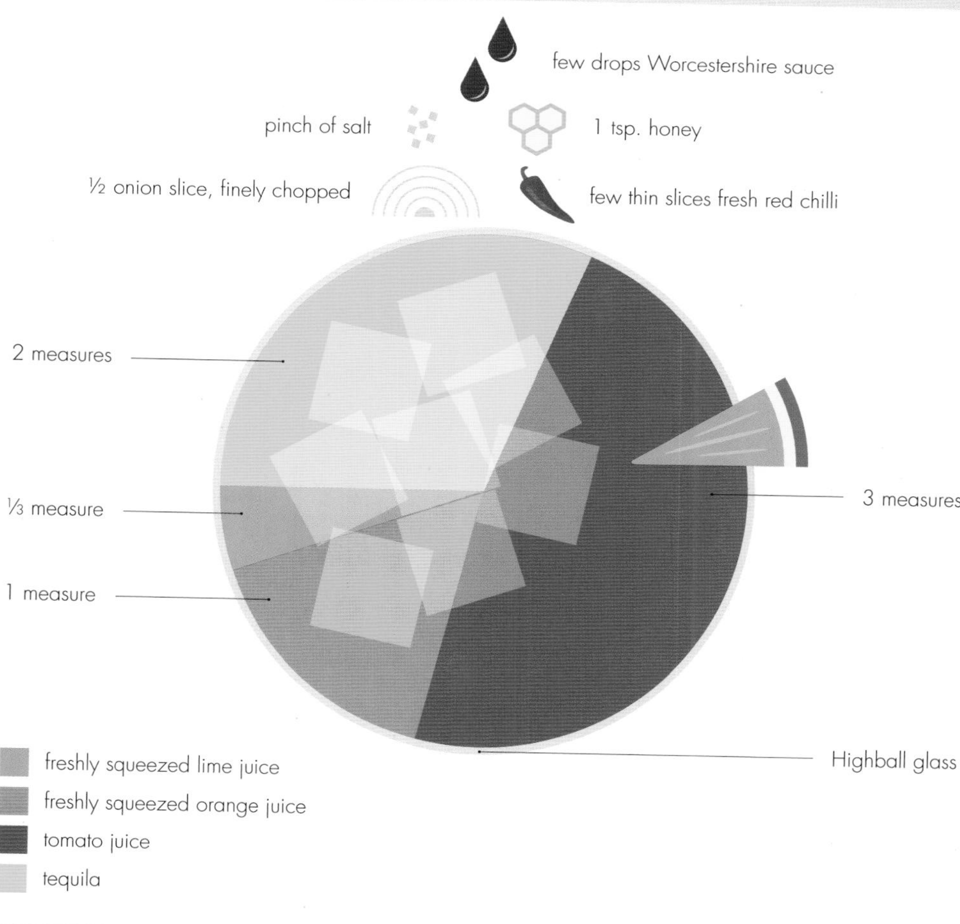
few drops Worcestershire sauce
pinch of salt
1 tsp. honey
½ onion slice, finely chopped
few thin slices fresh red chilli
2 measures
⅓ measure
1 measure
3 measures
Highball glass
freshly squeezed lime juice
freshly squeezed orange juice
tomato juice
tequila

Instructions

1. Shake all the ingredients, except the lime wedge, and strain into an ice-filled highball glass.
2. Garnish with a lime wedge.

CHAMPAGNE

Bastile

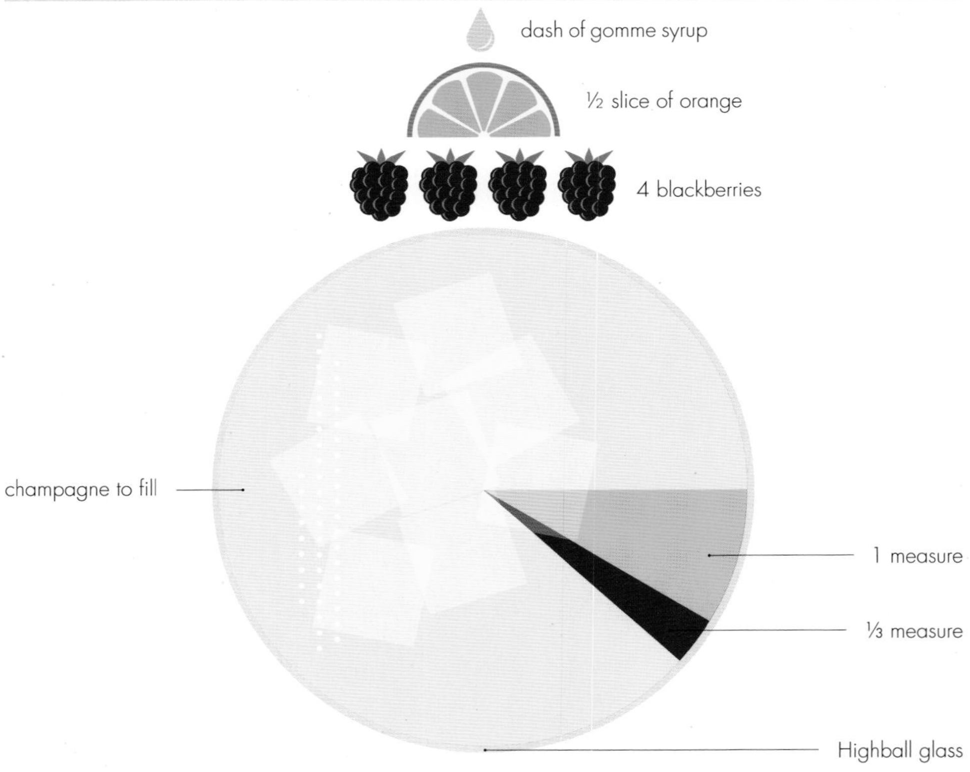

dash of gomme syrup
½ slice of orange
4 blackberries
champagne to fill
1 measure
⅓ measure
Highball glass

champagne
crème de mure
white rum

Instructions

1 Muddle the blackberries with the gomme and the crème de mure in a shaker. **2** Add the rum and squeeze a half-slice of orange over the mixture. **3** Add ice cubes, shake, and strain into a highball glass with crushed ice, then top up with champagne and stir gently.

Black Velvet

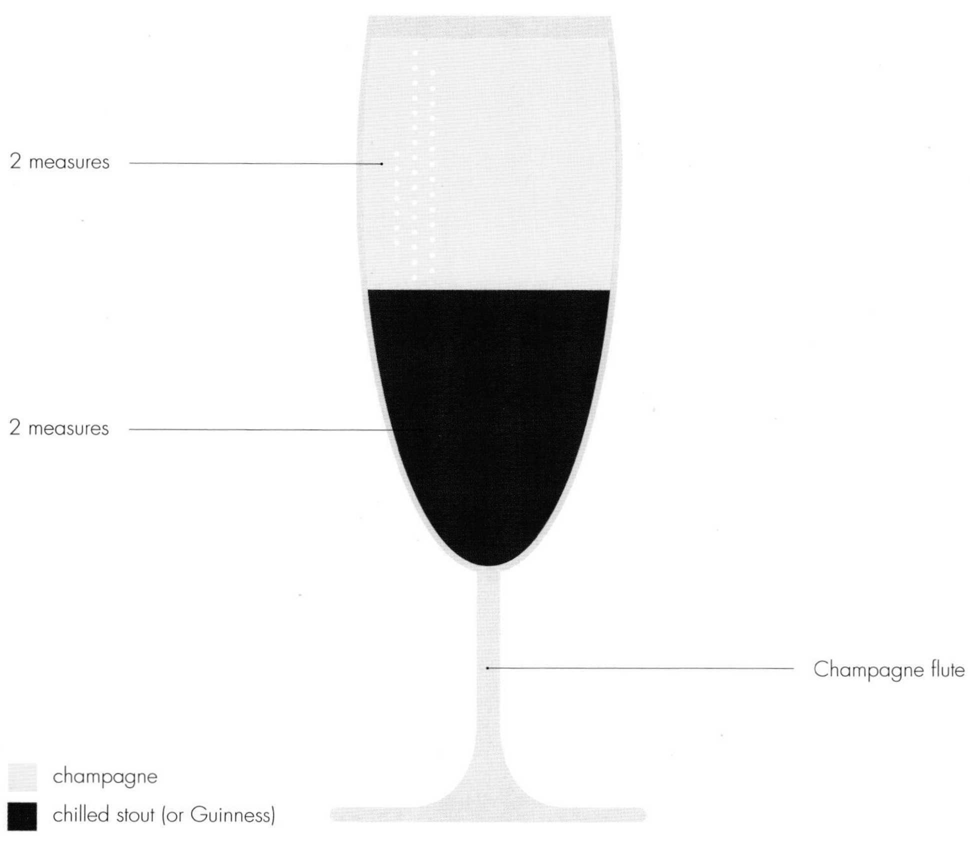
2 measures
2 measures
Champagne flute
champagne
chilled stout (or Guinness)

Instructions

1 Pour the stout and then the champagne into a champagne flute and serve.

Casanova

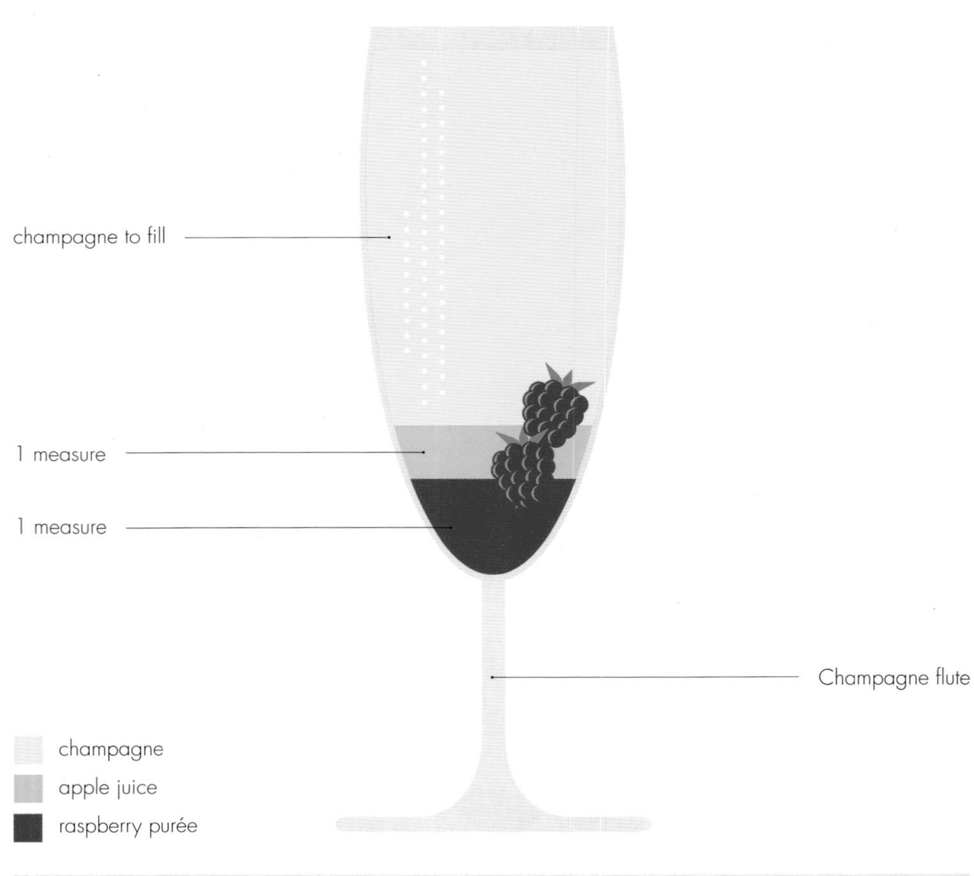
champagne to fill
1 measure
1 measure
Champagne flute
champagne
apple juice
raspberry purée

Instructions

1 Pour the raspberry purée into a champagne flute. **2** Add the apple juice and stir, then top up with champagne and stir gently. **3** Drop two small raspberries into the glass and serve.

Champagne Cobbler

4 dashes Cointreau
champagne to fill
Large goblet
champagne

Instructions

1 Fill a large goblet with crushed ice, then pour the champagne until it is three-quarters full. 2 Stir in the Cointreau and garnish with fruit and mint.

Champagne Cocktail

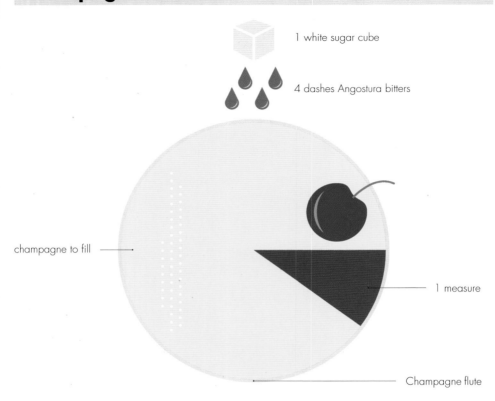

1 white sugar cube

4 dashes Angostura bitters

champagne to fill

1 measure

Champagne flute

 champagne

 Cognac

Instructions

1 Place the sugar cube in a champagne flute and soak with the Angostura bitters. **2** Pour on the Cognac and top up with champagne. **3** Garnish with the maraschino cherry and serve.

Champagne Cooler

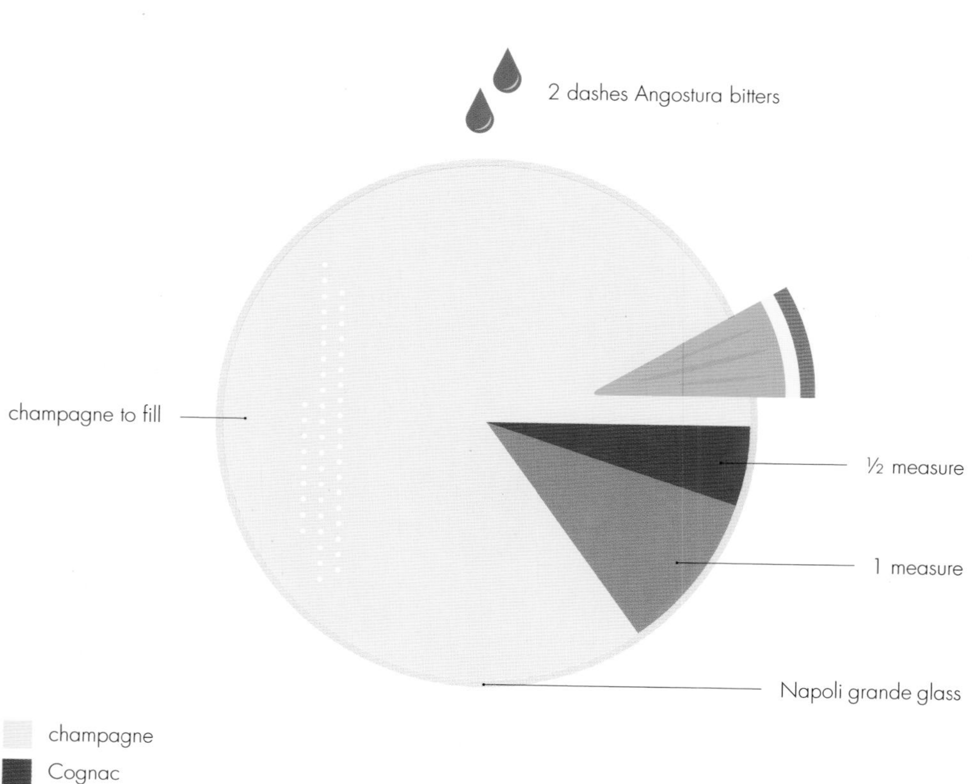

2 dashes Angostura bitters
champagne to fill
½ measure
1 measure
Napoli grande glass
champagne
Cognac
Grand Marnier

Instructions

1 Pour the Grand Marnier, Cognac and bitters into a napoli grande glass. **2** Top up with champagne and garnish with an orange slice.

Cool Cucumber

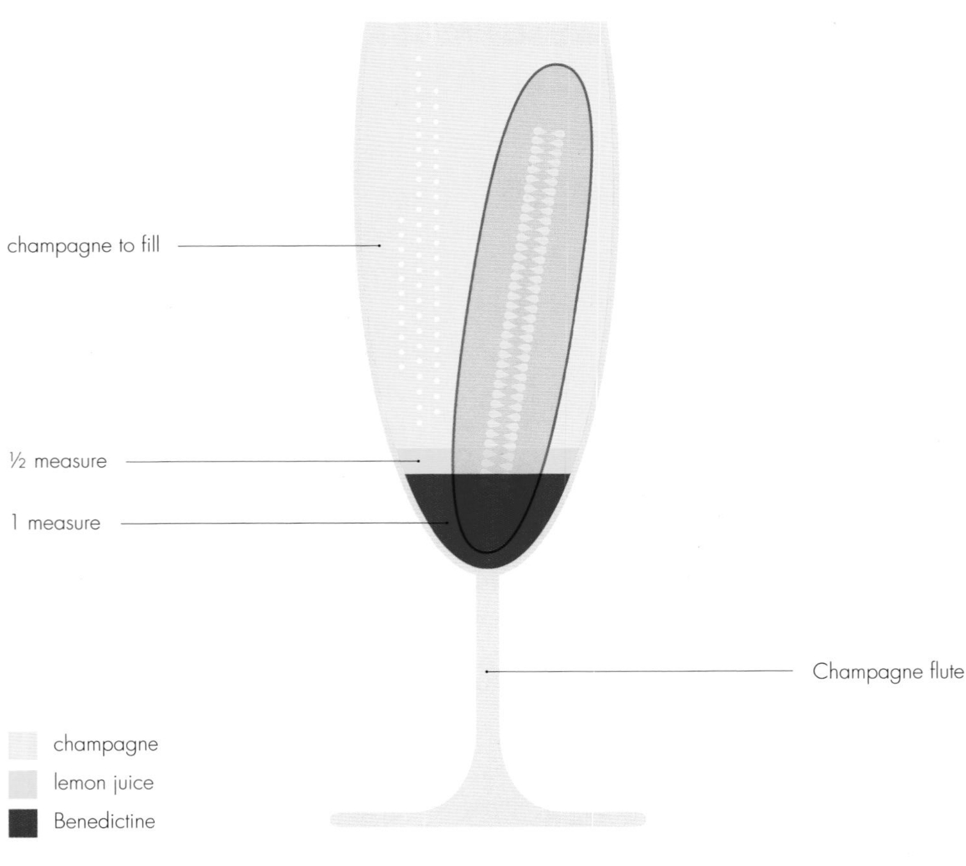
champagne to fill
½ measure
1 measure
Champagne flute
champagne
lemon juice
Benedictine

Instructions

1. Pour the Benedictine and lemon juice into a chilled champagne flute and top up with champagne.
2. Add a strip of cucumber as a garnish.

Death in the Afternoon

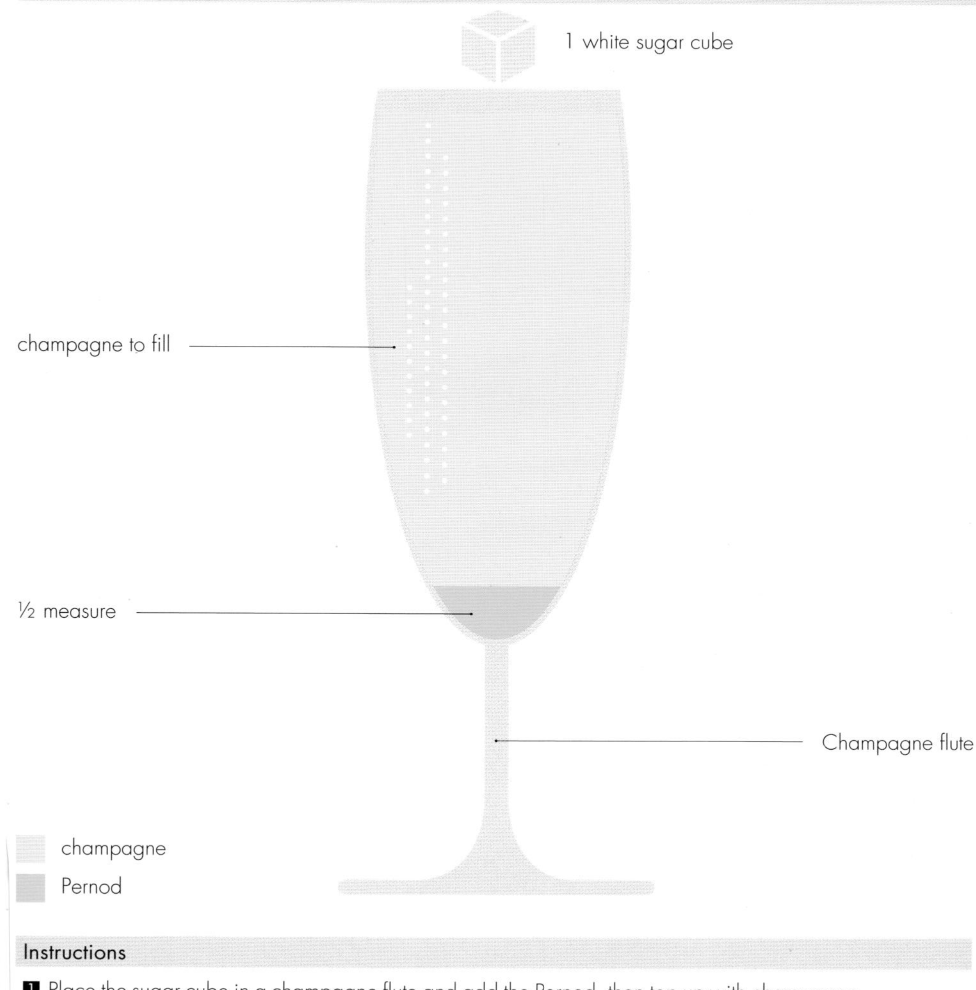
1 white sugar cube
champagne to fill
½ measure
Champagne flute
champagne
Pernod

Instructions

1 Place the sugar cube in a champagne flute and add the Pernod, then top up with champagne.

French Sherbet

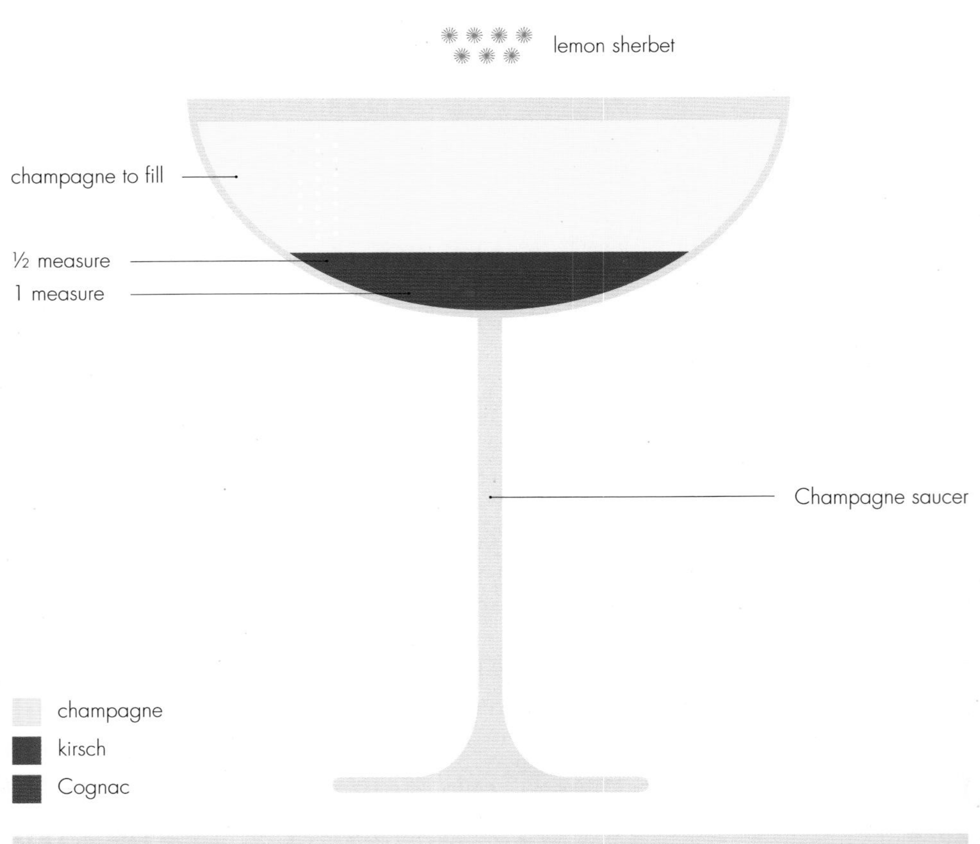

lemon sherbet
champagne to fill
½ measure
1 measure
Champagne saucer
champagne
kirsch
Cognac

Instructions

1. Stir the sherbert, kirsch and Cognac in a deep champagne saucer, and fill with champagne.

Honeymoon Paradise

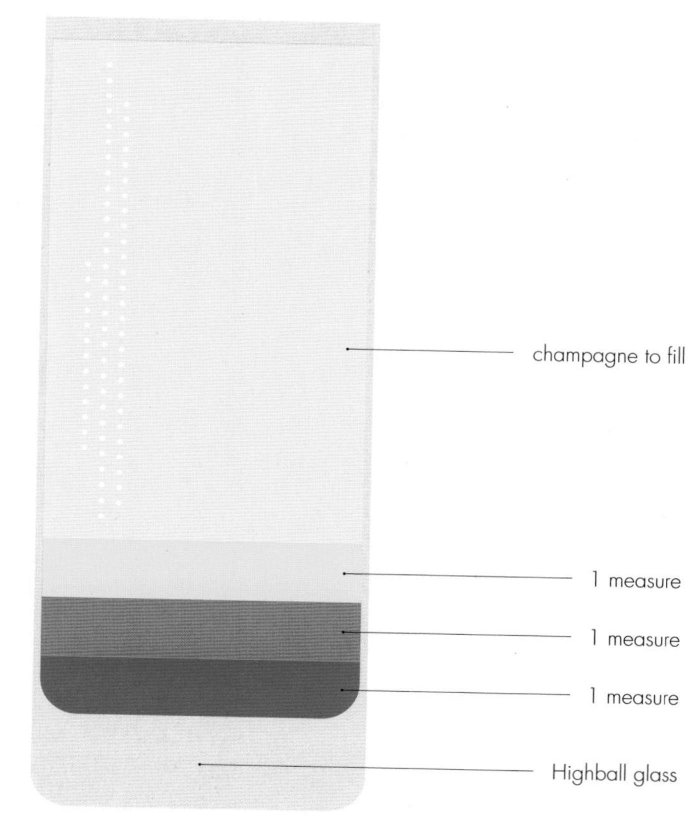

champagne to fill
1 measure
1 measure
1 measure
Highball glass

champagne
fresh lemon juice
Cointreau
blue curaçao

Instructions

1 Pour the blue curaçao and Cointreau into a highball glass, then top up with champagne and serve.

James Bond

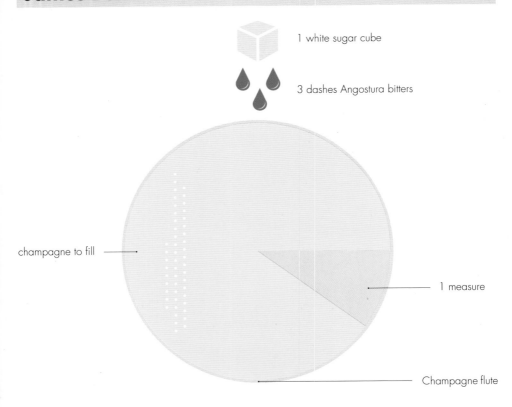

1 white sugar cube

3 dashes Angostura bitters

champagne to fill

1 measure

Champagne flute

champagne

vodka

Instructions

1 In a champagne flute soak the sugar cube in the bitters, then pour on the vodka. **2** Top up with champagne and serve.

Kir Royale

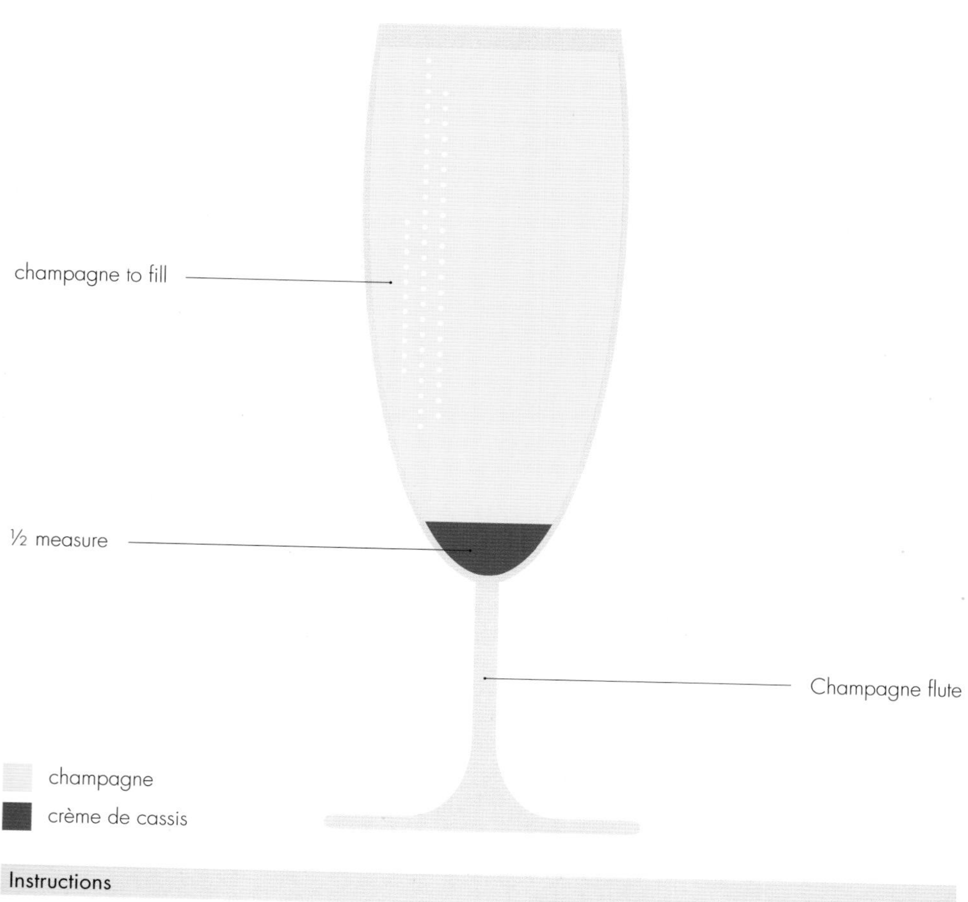
champagne to fill
½ measure
Champagne flute
champagne
crème de cassis

Instructions

1. Put the crème de cassis in a champagne flute, then pour on the champagne and serve.

La Dolce Vita

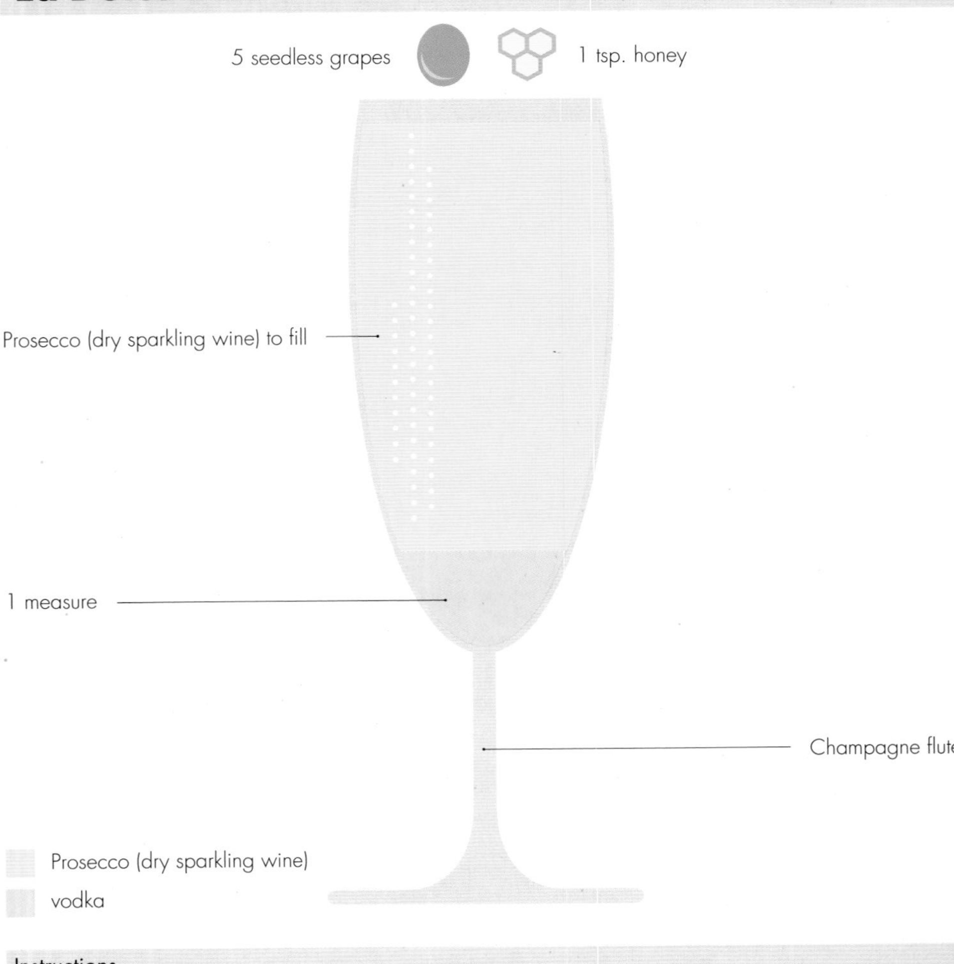

5 seedless grapes
1 tsp. honey
Prosecco (dry sparkling wine) to fill
1 measure
Champagne flute
Prosecco (dry sparkling wine)
vodka

Instructions

1 Muddle the grapes in a shaker, then add the vodka and honey. **2** Shake and strain into a champagne glass, then top up with Prosecco.

Mimosa

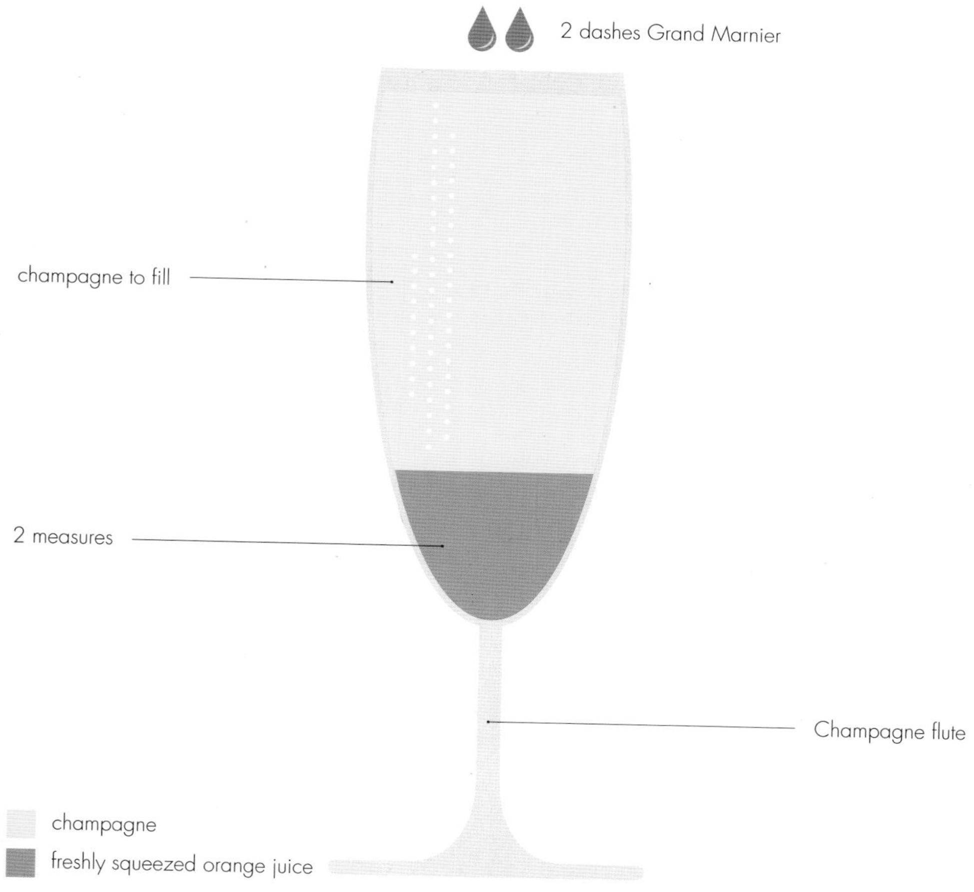

2 dashes Grand Marnier

champagne to fill

2 measures

Champagne flute

champagne

freshly squeezed orange juice

Instructions

1 Fill a champagne glass to a quarter-full with orange juice. **2** Add the Grand Marnier, then top up with champagne.

Poinsettia

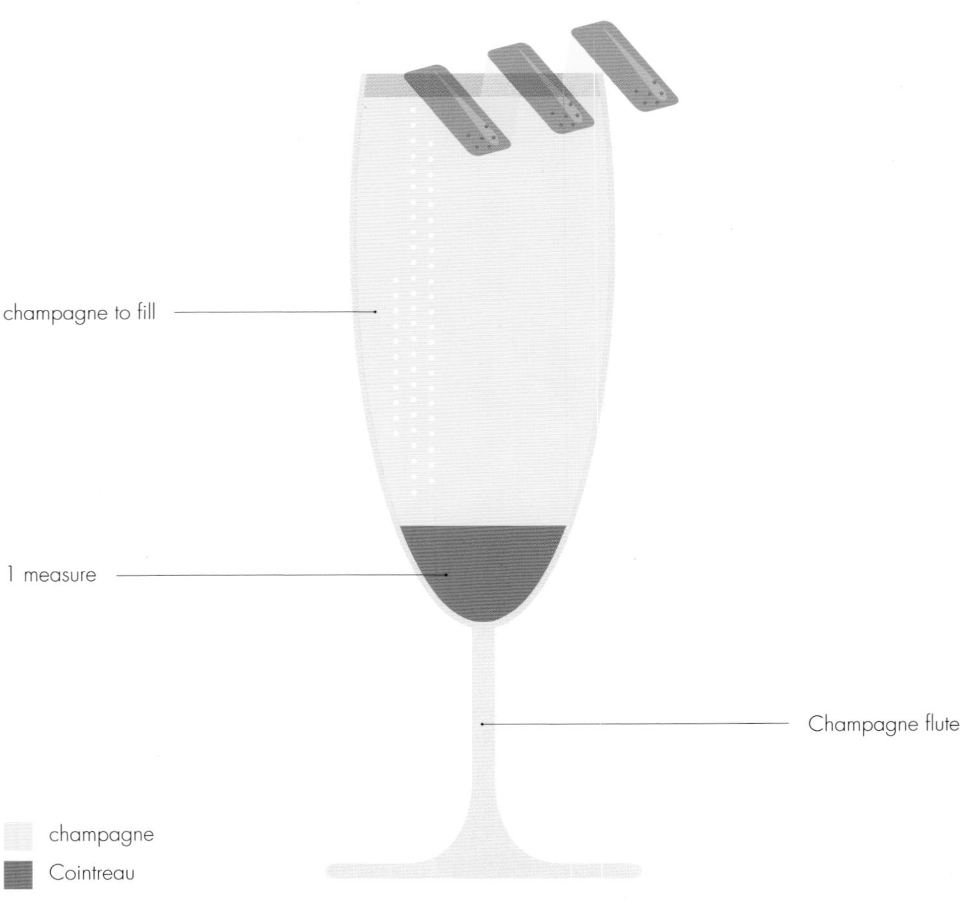
champagne to fill
1 measure
Champagne flute
champagne
Cointreau

Instructions

1 Pour the Cointreau into a champagne flute and top up with champagne. 2 Add an orange twist and serve.

Raspberry Sip

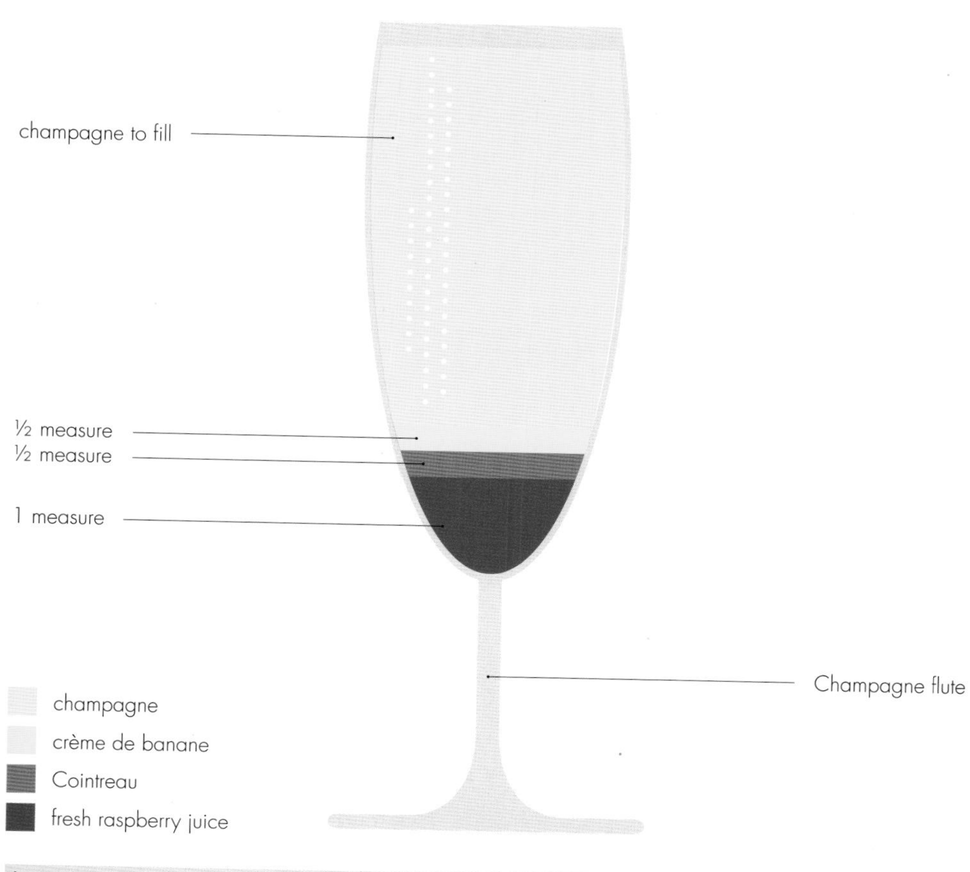

champagne to fill
½ measure
½ measure
1 measure
Champagne flute
champagne
crème de banane
Cointreau
fresh raspberry juice

Instructions

1 Pour ingredients, except champagne, into a shaker with ice. **2** Strain into a champagne flute, and top up with champagne.

Ritz Fizz

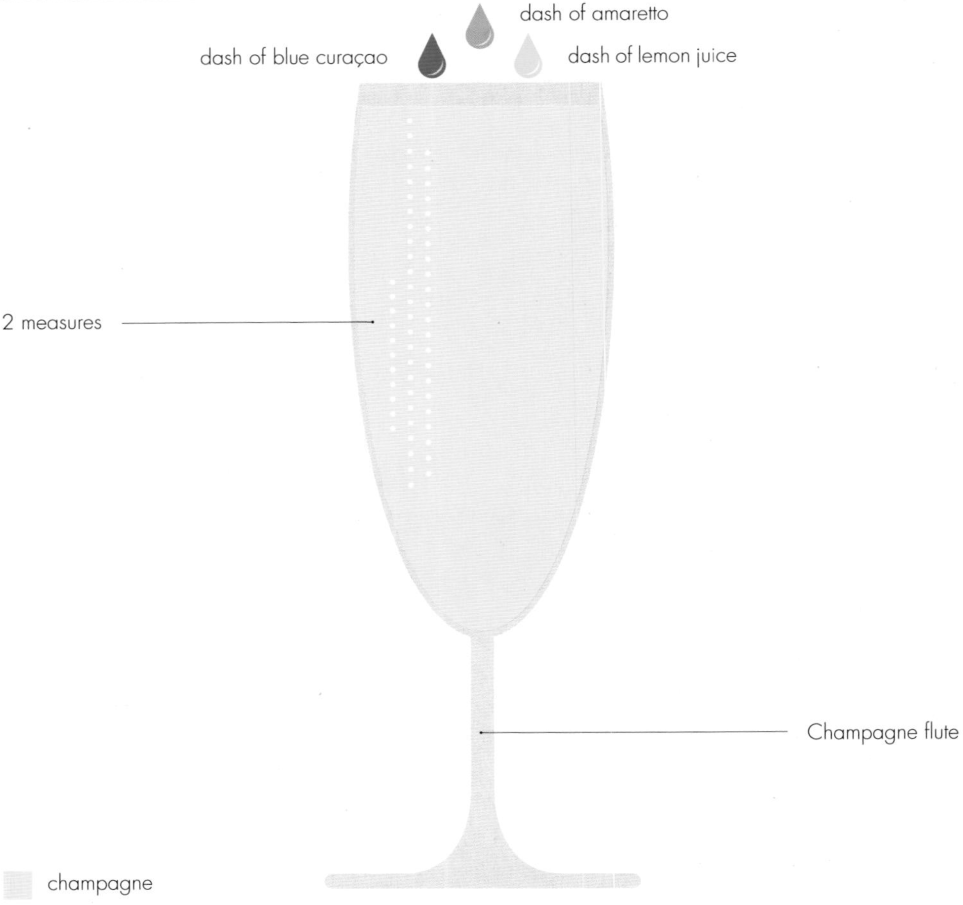

dash of amaretto

dash of blue curaçao

dash of lemon juice

2 measures

Champagne flute

champagne

Instructions

1. Pour the amaretto, curaçao and lemon juice into a champagne flute, top up with champagne, and serve.

Soixante-Neuf

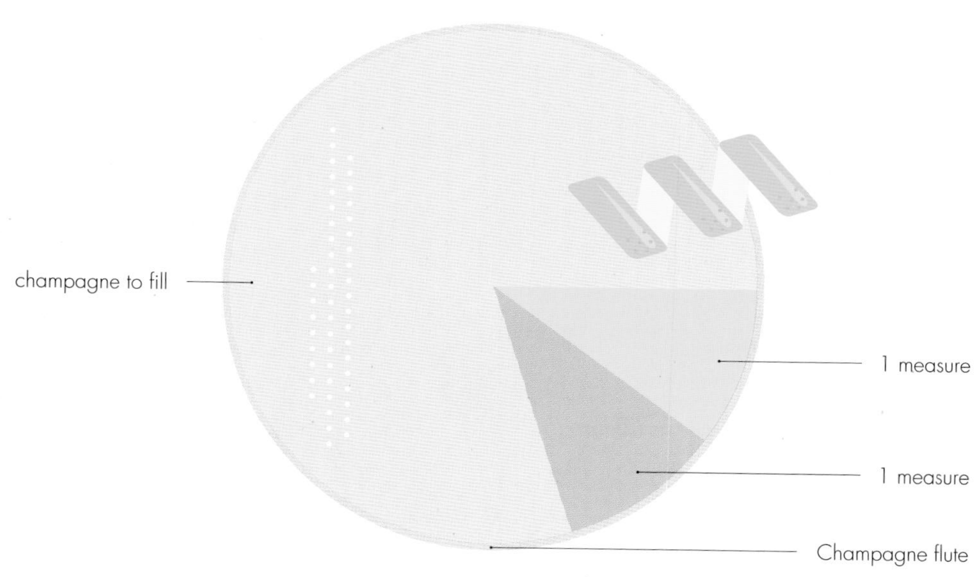
champagne to fill
1 measure
1 measure
Champagne flute

champagne
fresh lemon juice
gin

Instructions

1 Shake the gin and lemon juice together, then strain into a champagne flute. 2 Top up with champagne, garnish with a lemon twist and serve.

Sweet Surrender

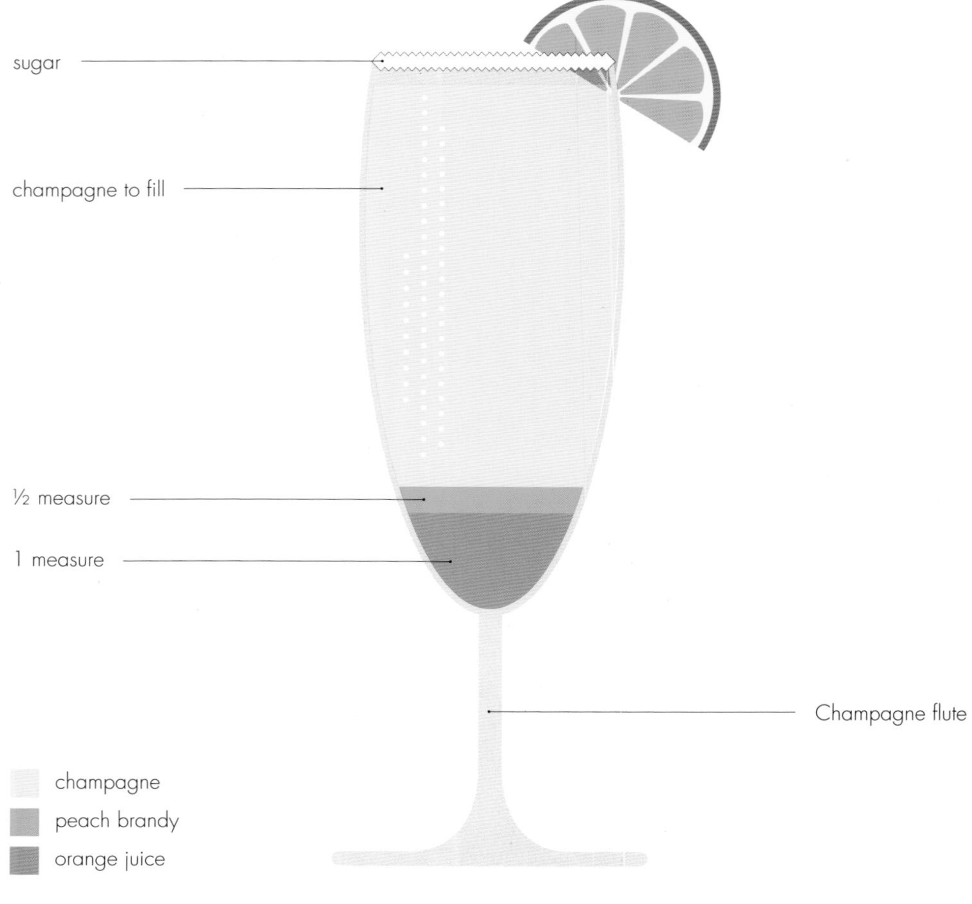
sugar
champagne to fill
½ measure
1 measure
Champagne flute
champagne
peach brandy
orange juice

Instructions

1 Rub an orange slice around the rim of a champage flute, then coat the rim in sugar. 2 Mix the orange juice and peach brandy together in an ice-filled shaker, strain, and pour into the glass. 3 Top up with champagne.

Typhoon

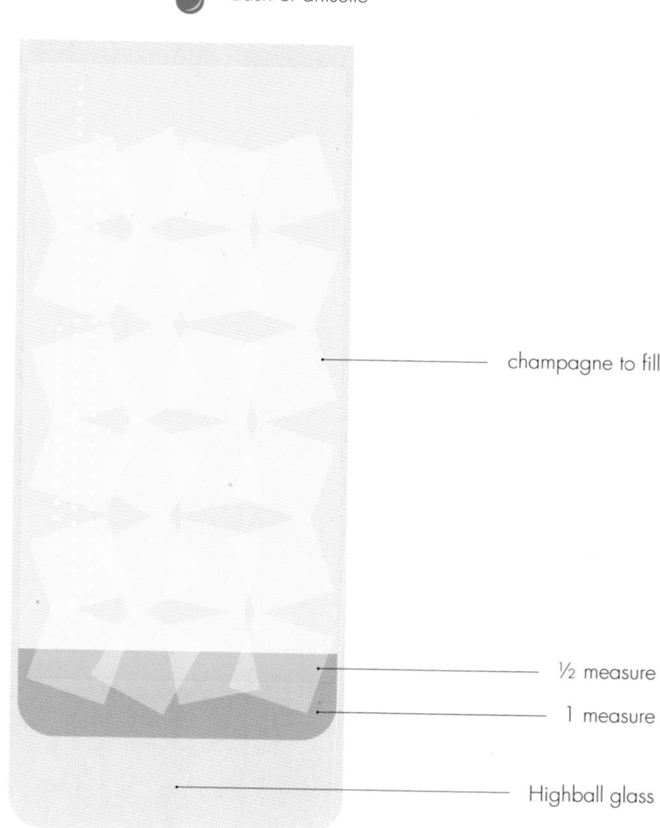
dash of anisette
champagne to fill
½ measure
1 measure
Highball glass

champagne
fresh lime juice
gin

Instructions

1. In a shaker mix together the gin, anisette and lime juice, then strain into an ice-filled highball glass.
2. Top up with champagne and serve.

LIQUEUR

After Eight

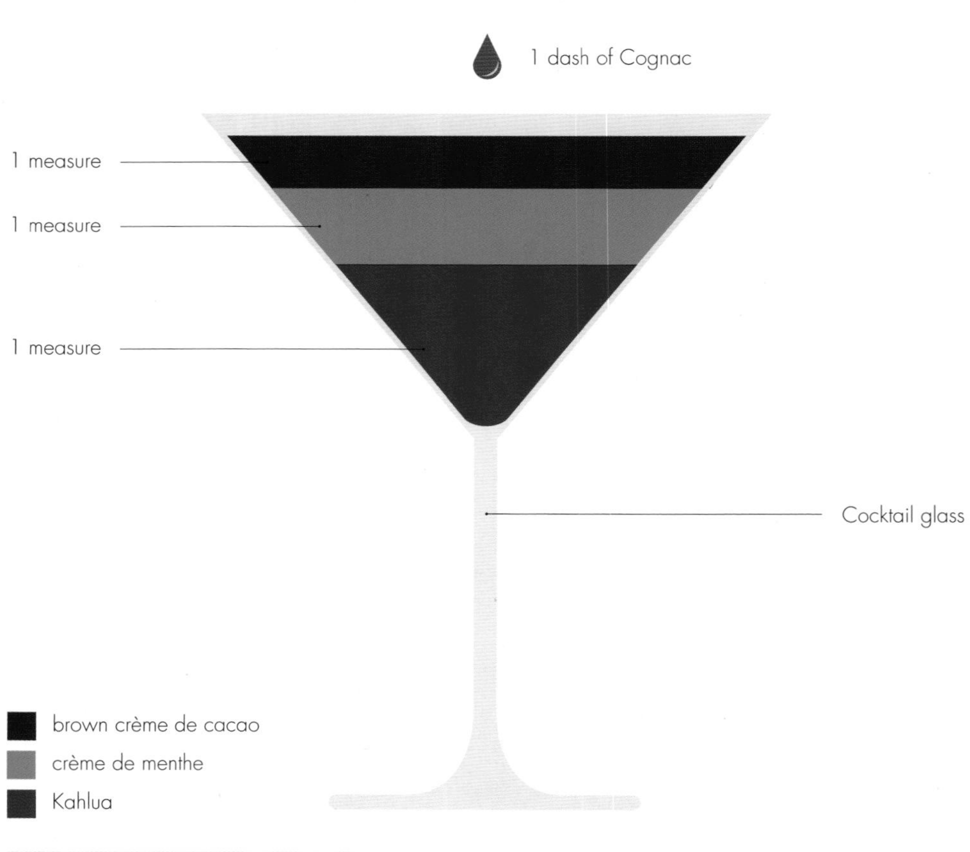

1 dash of Cognac
1 measure
1 measure
1 measure
Cocktail glass
brown crème de cacao
crème de menthe
Kahlua

Instructions

1 Shake all the ingredients together, then strain into a cocktail glass and serve.

Amaretto Comfort

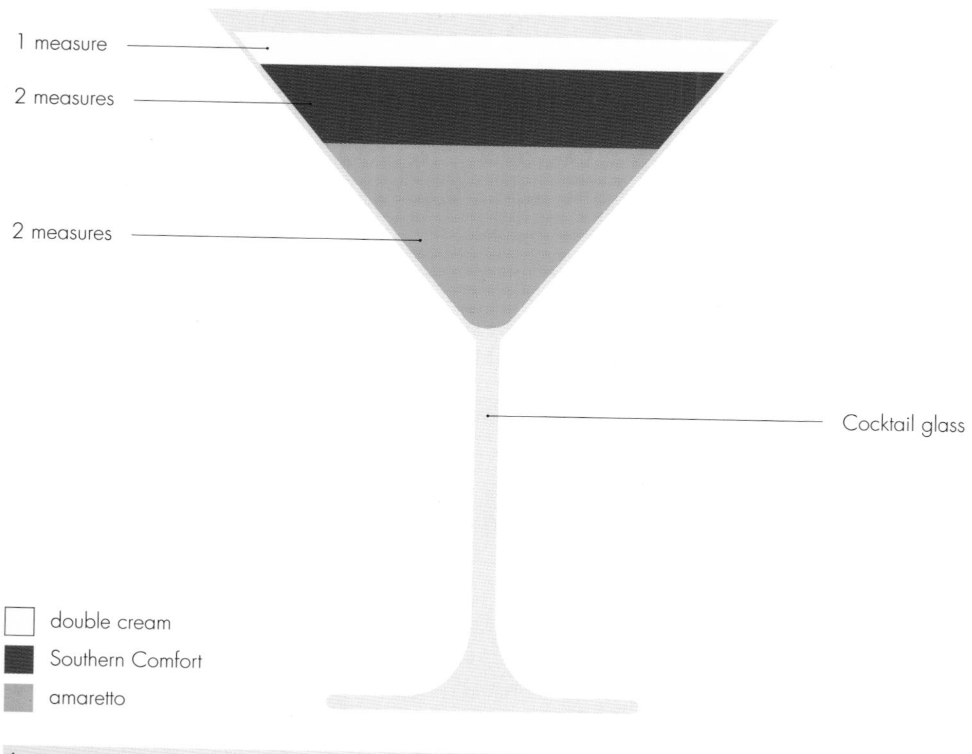

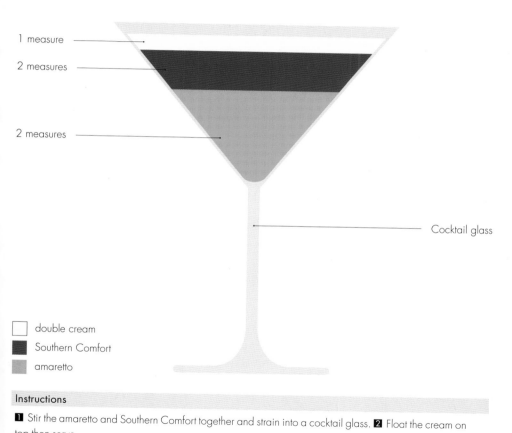

1 measure
2 measures
2 measures
Cocktail glass
double cream
Southern Comfort
amaretto

Instructions

1 Stir the amaretto and Southern Comfort together and strain into a cocktail glass. 2 Float the cream on top then serve.

Aristocrat

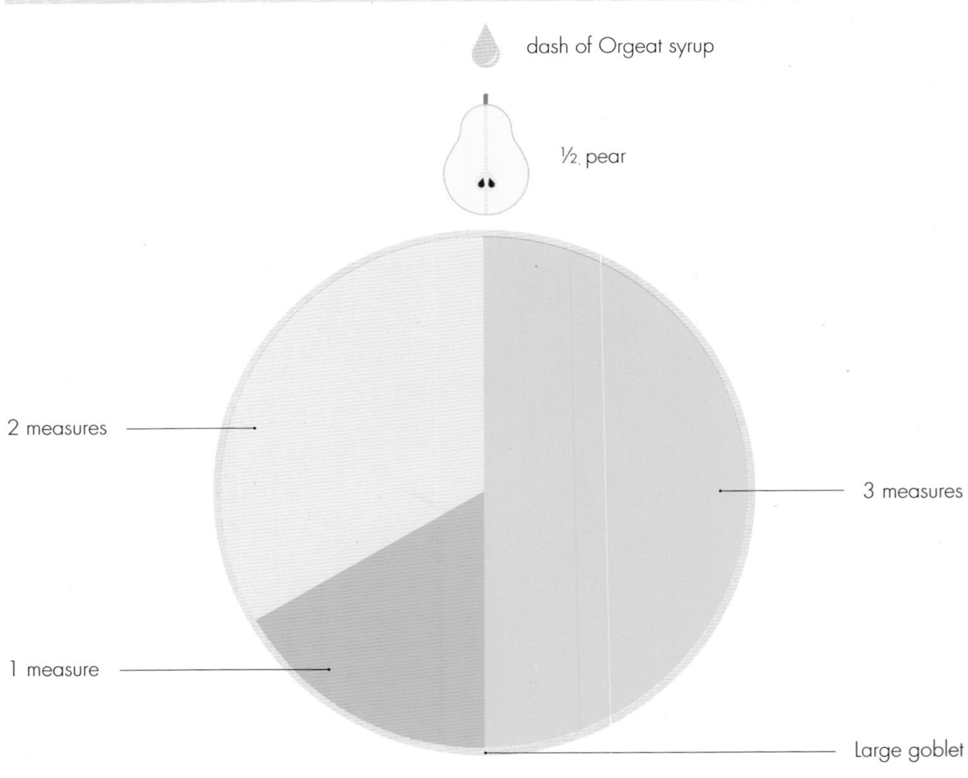

dash of Orgeat syrup
½ pear
2 measures
3 measures
1 measure
Large goblet

pineapple juice
white rum
Poire William

Instructions

1 Blend all the ingredients together and pour into a large goblet.

Bad Girl

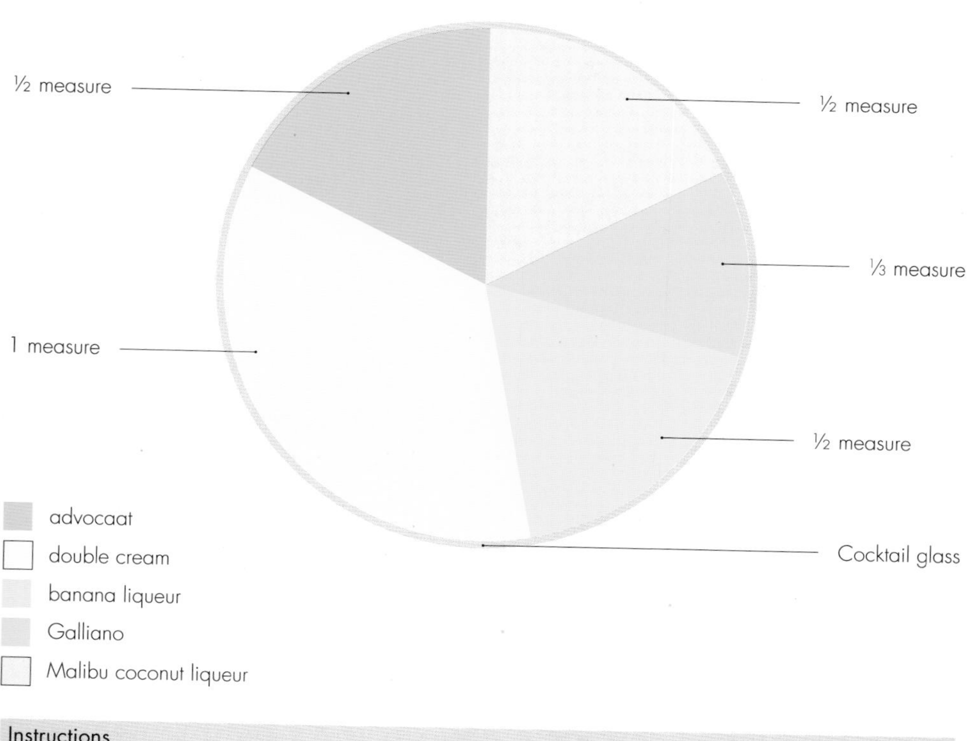

½ measure
½ measure
⅓ measure
1 measure
½ measure
Cocktail glass
advocaat
double cream
banana liqueur
Galliano
Malibu coconut liqueur

Instructions

1 Place all the ingredients in a blender with ice. **2** Blend, then pour into a cocktail glass.

Banshee

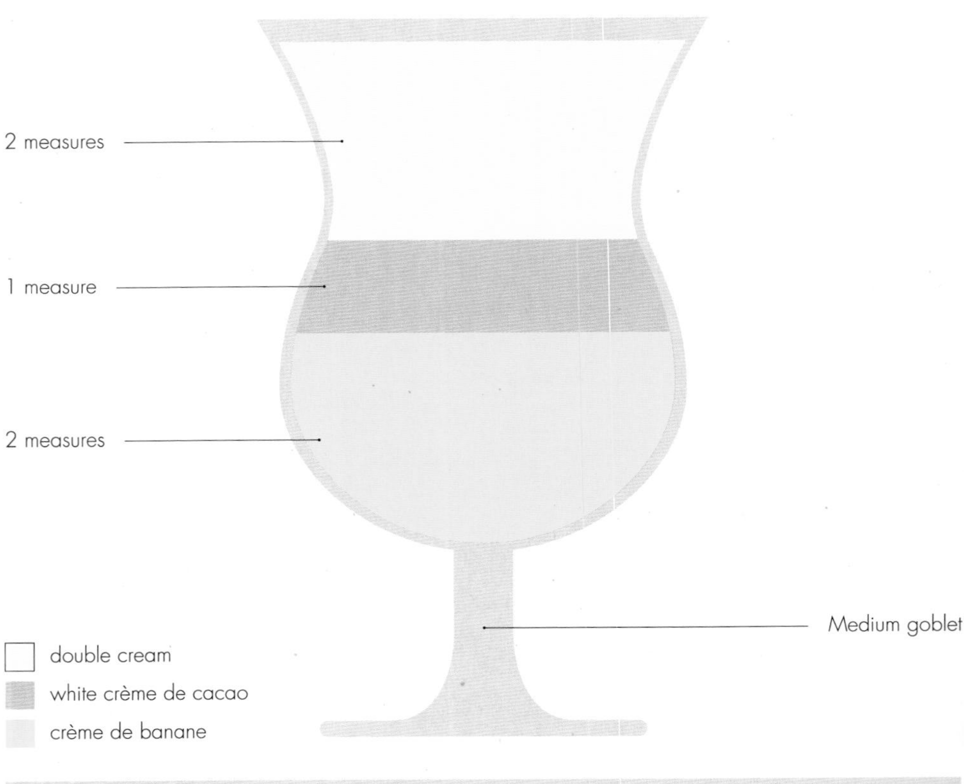
2 measures
1 measure
2 measures
Medium goblet
double cream
white crème de cacao
crème de banane

Instructions

1 Mix all the ingredients together in a shaker with ice, then strain into a medium goblet and serve.

Bee Stinger

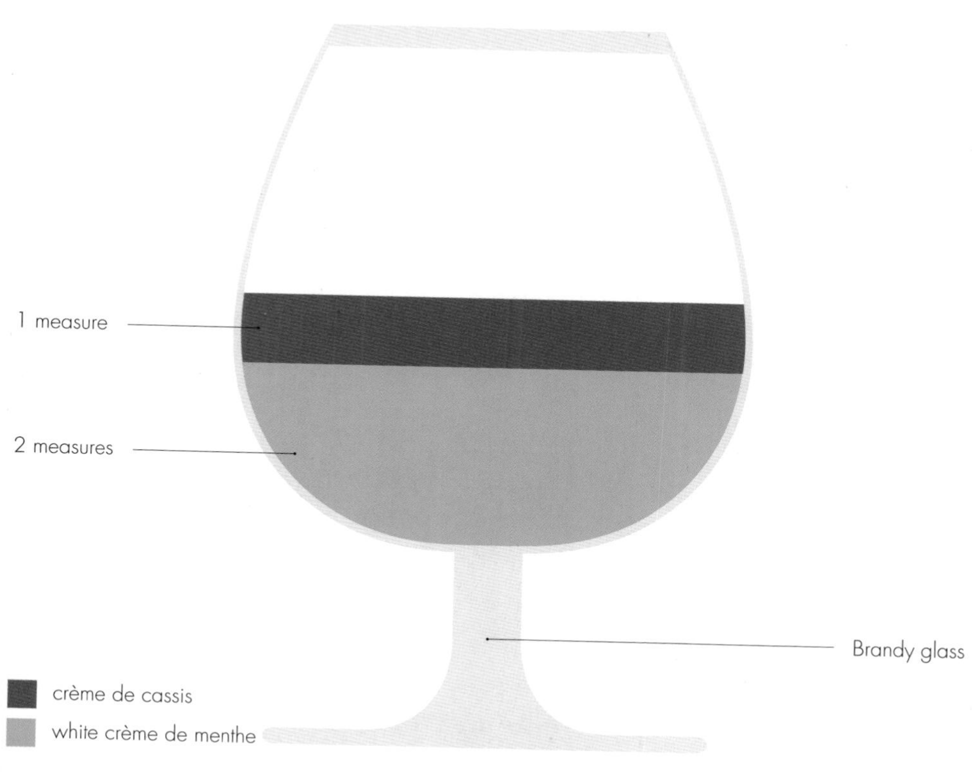

1 measure
2 measures
Brandy glass
crème de cassis
white crème de menthe

Instructions

1. Pour the crème de menthe and crème de cassis into a brandy glass. Stir and serve.

Black and Tan

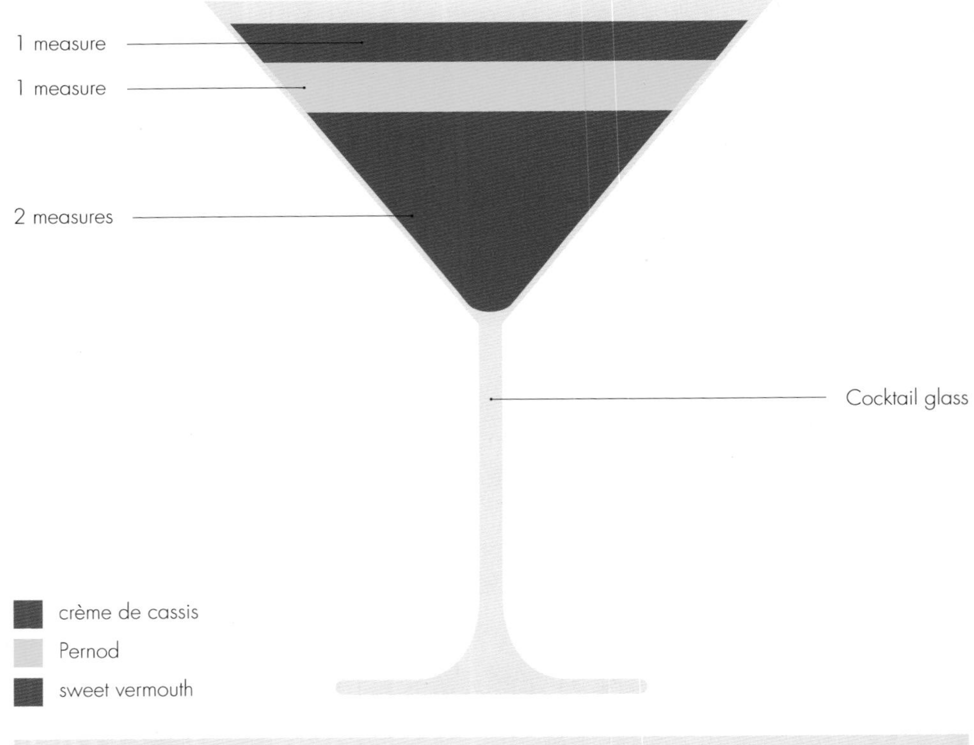
1 measure
1 measure
2 measures
Cocktail glass
crème de cassis
Pernod
sweet vermouth

Instructions

1. Shake all the ingredients together, then strain into a cocktail glass and serve.

Blackjack

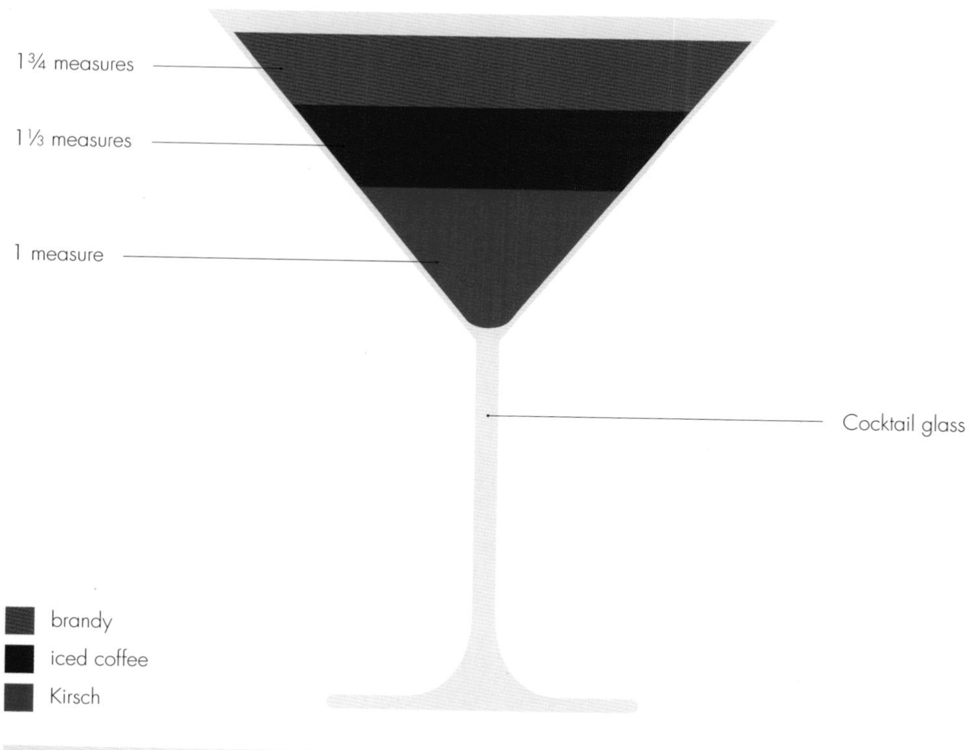
1 ¾ measures
1 ⅓ measures
1 measure
Cocktail glass
brandy
iced coffee
Kirsch

Instructions

1 Stir all ingredients over ice in a mixing glass. 2 Strain into a chilled cocktail glass.

Brighton Rock

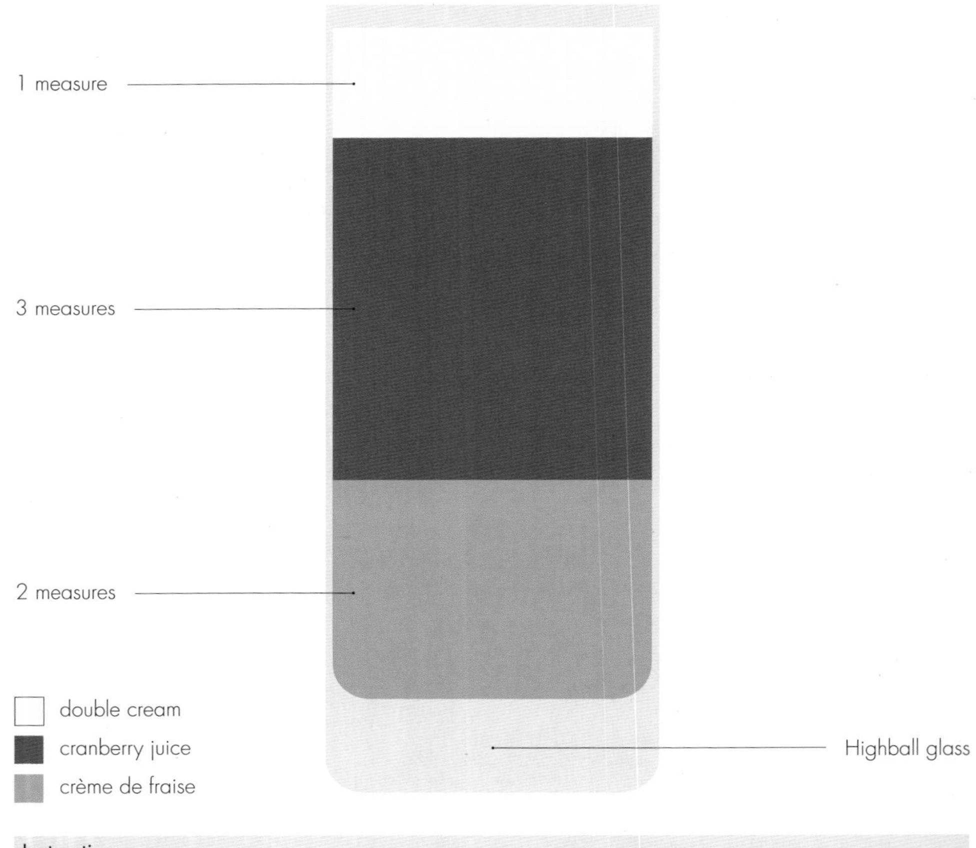

1 measure
3 measures
2 measures
double cream
cranberry juice
crème de fraise
Highball glass

Instructions

1. Mix all the ingredients together in a shaker with ice, then strain into a highball glass.

Death by Chocolate No. 1

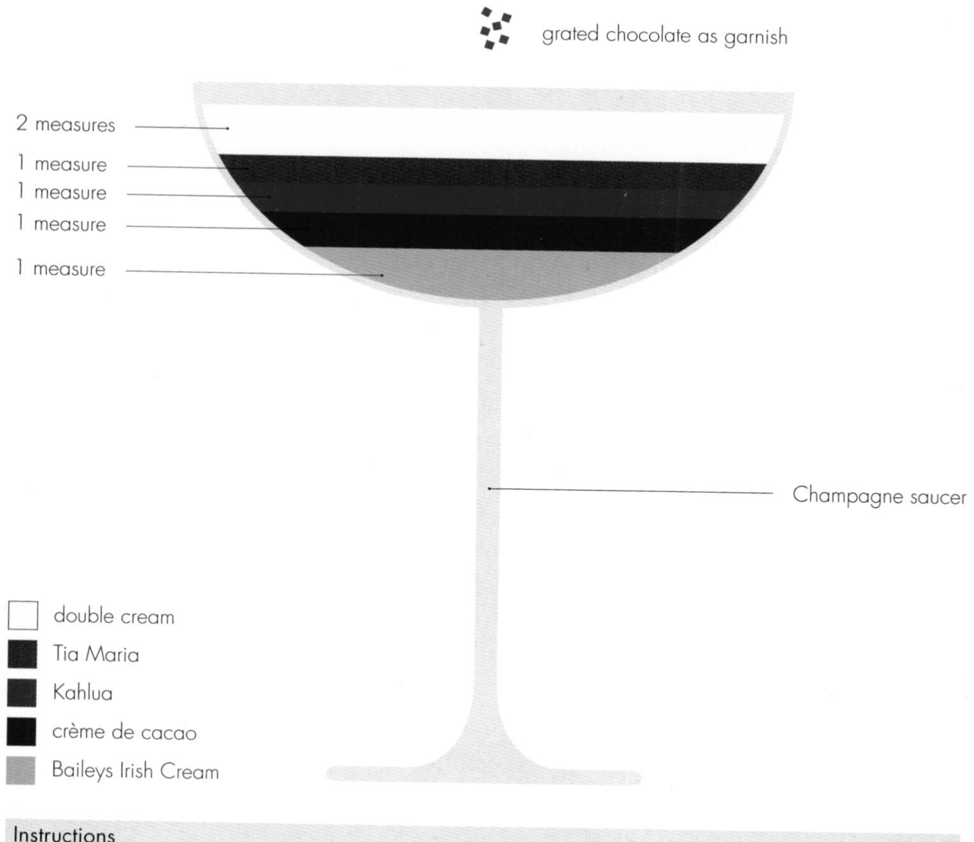
grated chocolate as garnish
2 measures
1 measure
1 measure
1 measure
1 measure
Champagne saucer
double cream
Tia Maria
Kahlua
crème de cacao
Baileys Irish Cream

Instructions

1 Shake all the ingredients together with ice and strain into a large champagne saucer. **2** Garnish with grated chocolate.

Fuzzy Navel

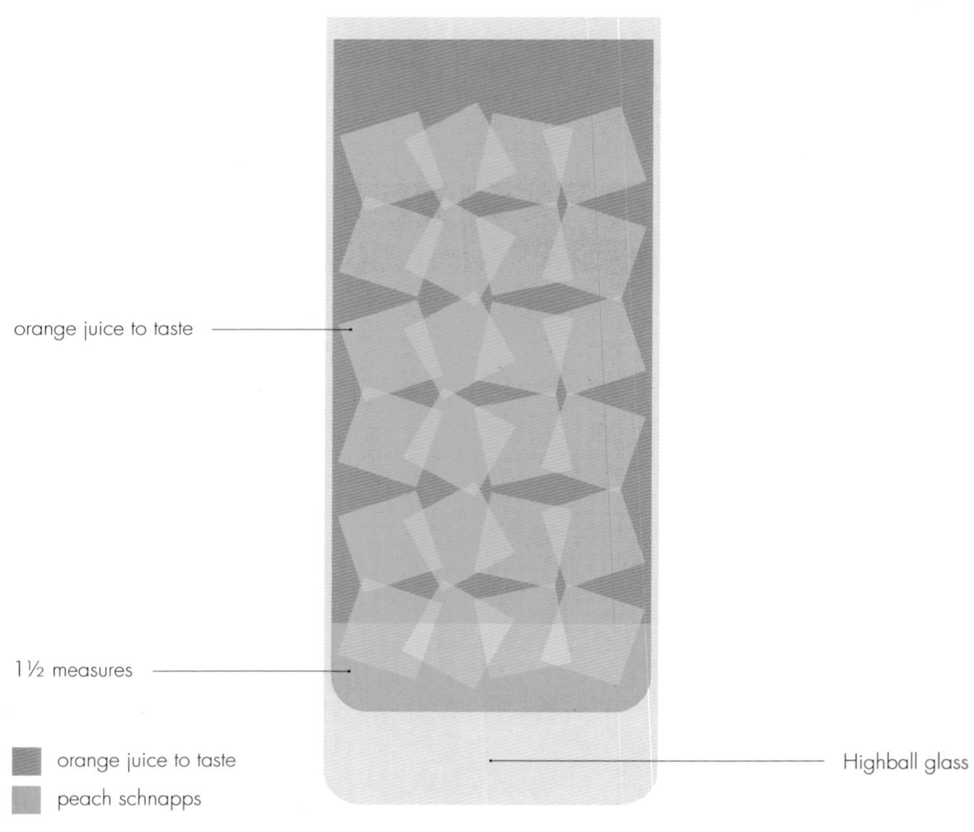
orange juice to taste
1 ½ measures
orange juice to taste
peach schnapps
Highball glass

Instructions

■1 Pour the peach schnapps into ice-filled highball glass. ■2 Fill with orange juice and stir to combine.

Grasshopper

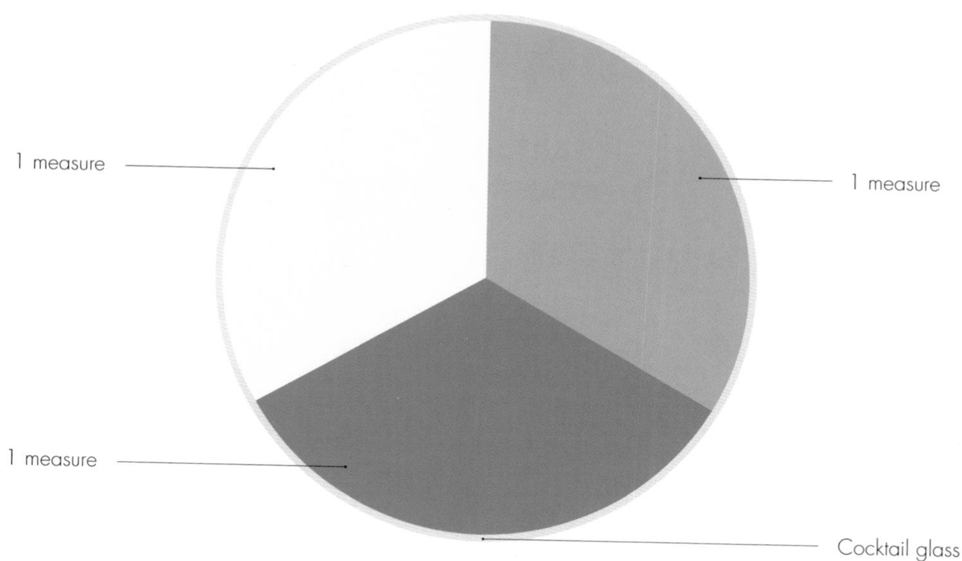

1 measure
1 measure
1 measure
Cocktail glass

double cream

white crème de menthe

crème de menthe

Instructions

1 Mix all the ingredients together in a shaker with ice, then strain into a cocktail glass.

Iron Lady

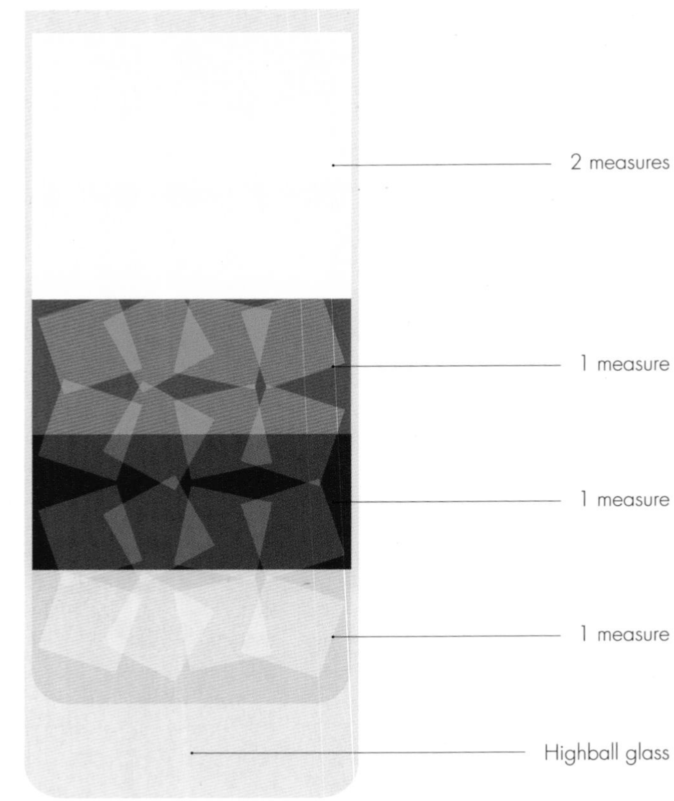

2 measures
1 measure
1 measure
1 measure
Highball glass

double cream

crème de cassis

noix de coco

white crème de cacao

Instructions

1. Mix all the ingredients together in a shaker filled with ice, then strain into an ice-filled highball glass.

Pink Cadillac

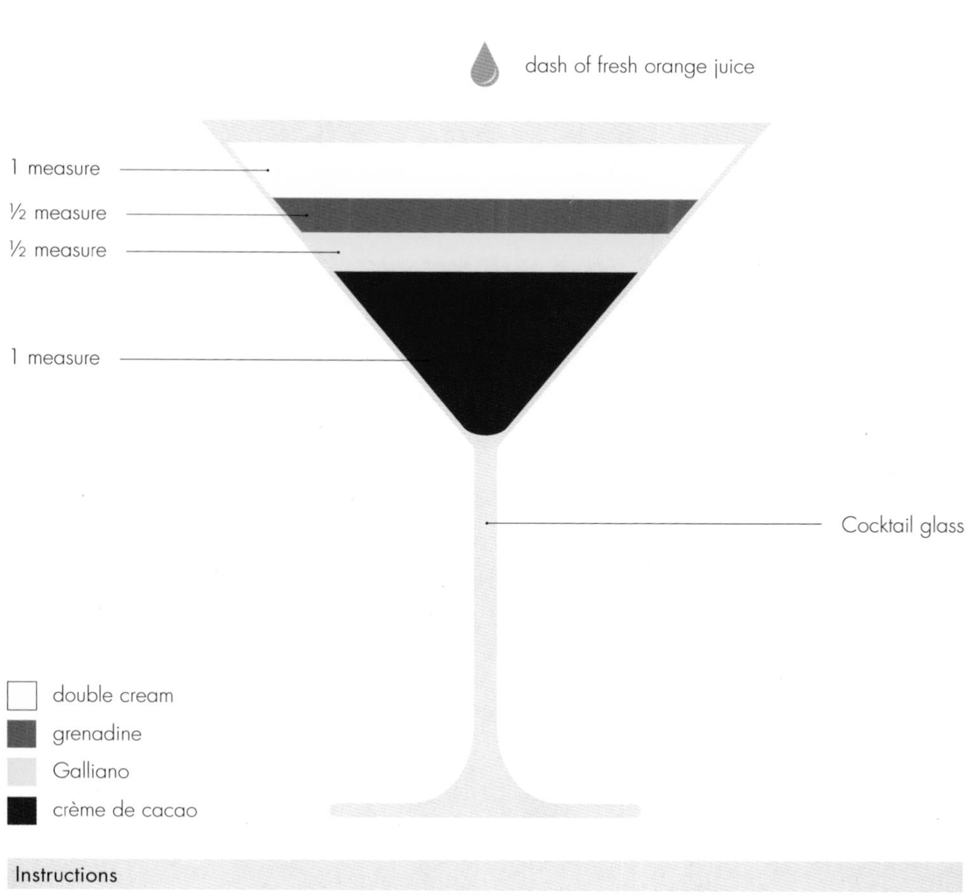

dash of fresh orange juice
1 measure
½ measure
½ measure
1 measure
Cocktail glass
double cream
grenadine
Galliano
crème de cacao

Instructions

1. Mix all the ingredients together in a shaker with ice, then strain into a cocktail glass.

Red Death

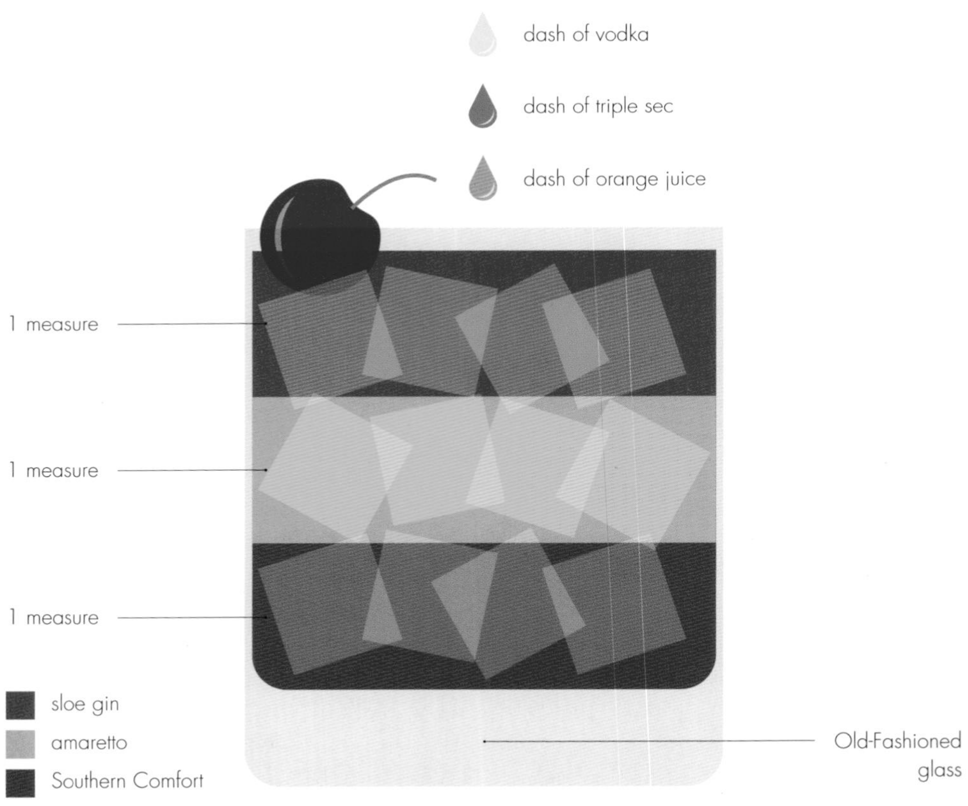

dash of vodka
dash of triple sec
dash of orange juice
1 measure
1 measure
1 measure
sloe gin
amaretto
Southern Comfort
Old-Fashioned glass

Instructions

1. Shake all the ingredients together with ice and strain into an Old-Fashioned glass filled with ice.
2. Garnish with a maraschino cherry.

Screaming Multiple Orgasm

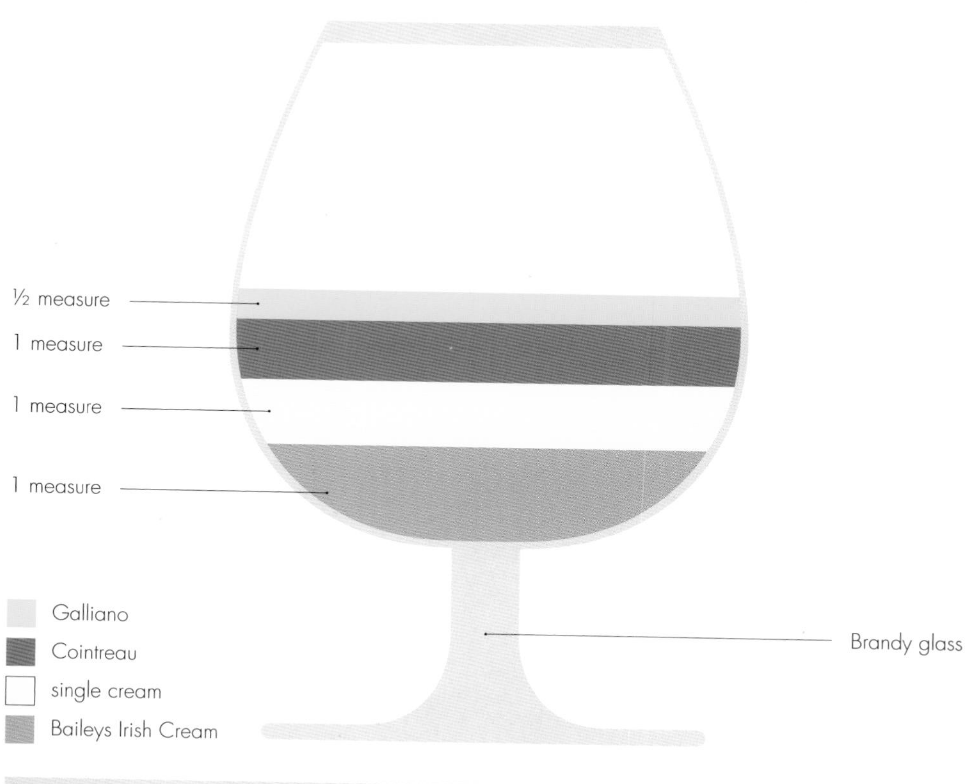
½ measure
1 measure
1 measure
1 measure
Galliano
Cointreau
single cream
Baileys Irish Cream
Brandy glass

Instructions

1. In the exact order layer in a brandy glass and serve.

Shooting Star

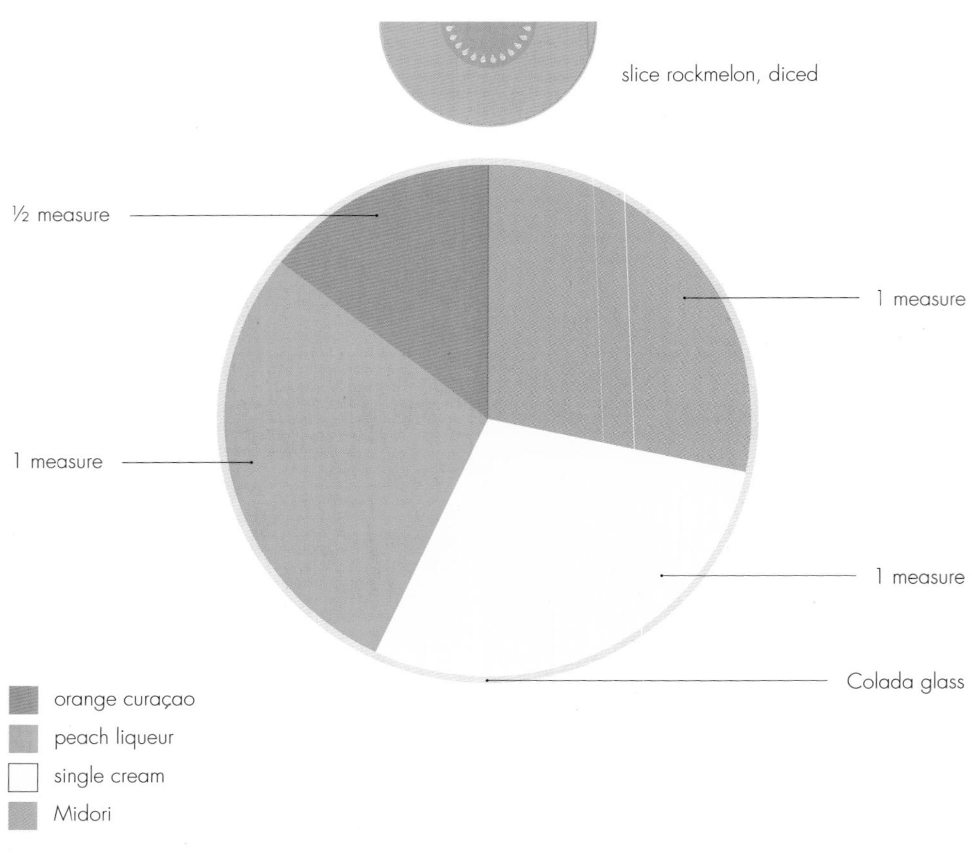

slice rockmelon, diced
½ measure
1 measure
1 measure
1 measure
Colada glass
orange curaçao
peach liqueur
single cream
Midori

Instructions

1 Blend all the ingredients together until smooth, then pour into a colada glass.

Swan Song

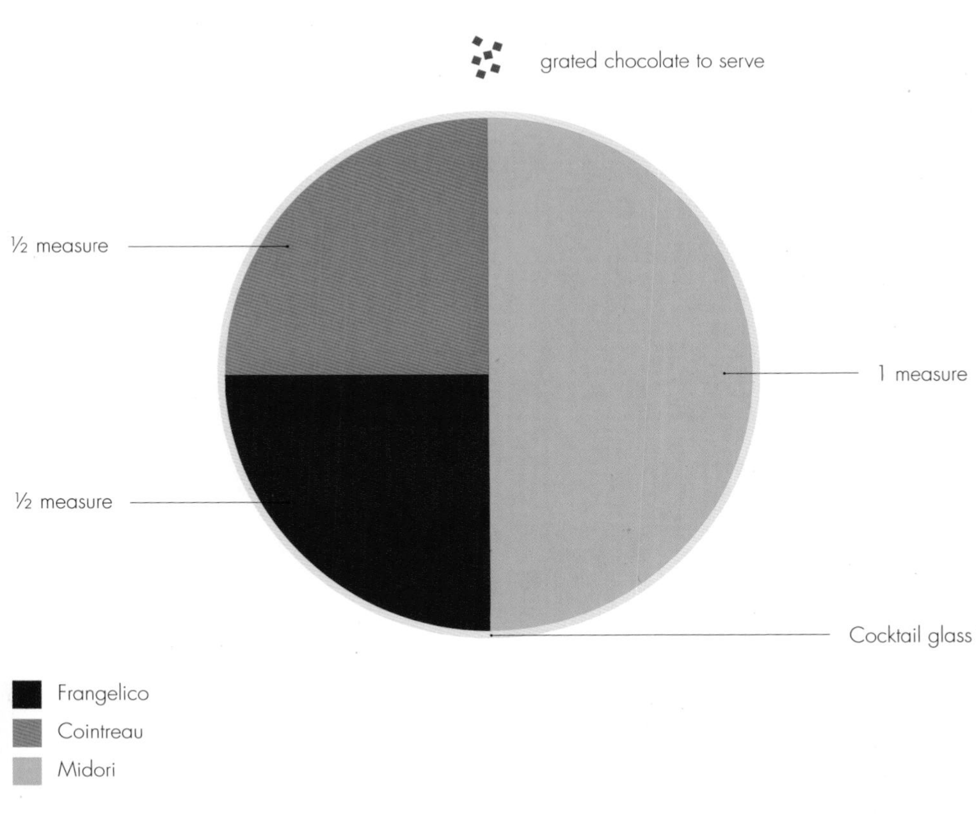

grated chocolate to serve
½ measure
1 measure
½ measure
Cocktail glass

Frangelico
Cointreau
Midori

Instructions

1 Mix all the ingredients together in a shaker, then strain into a cocktail glass. **2** Sprinkle with the chocolate and serve.

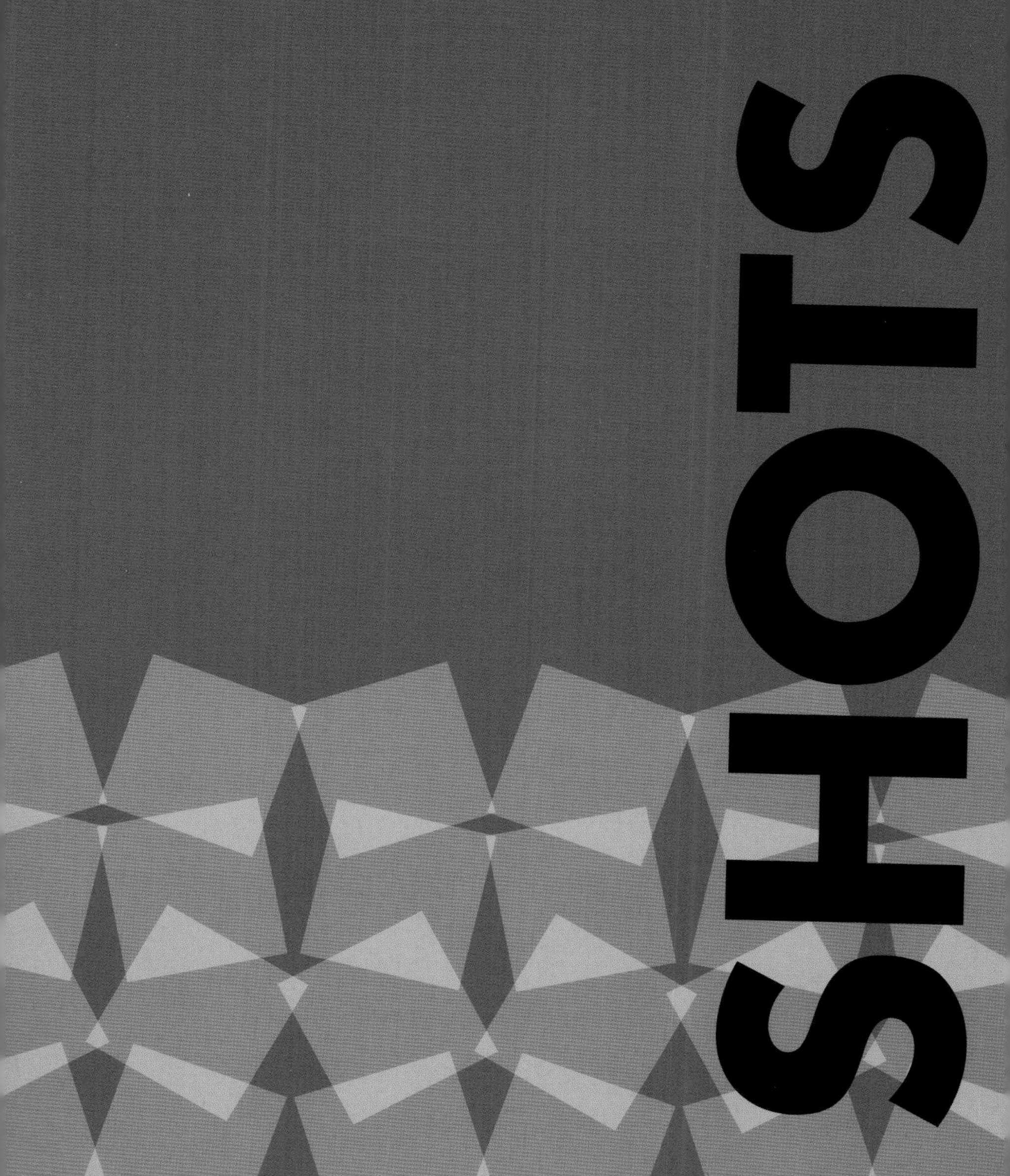
SHOTS

Alabama Slammer

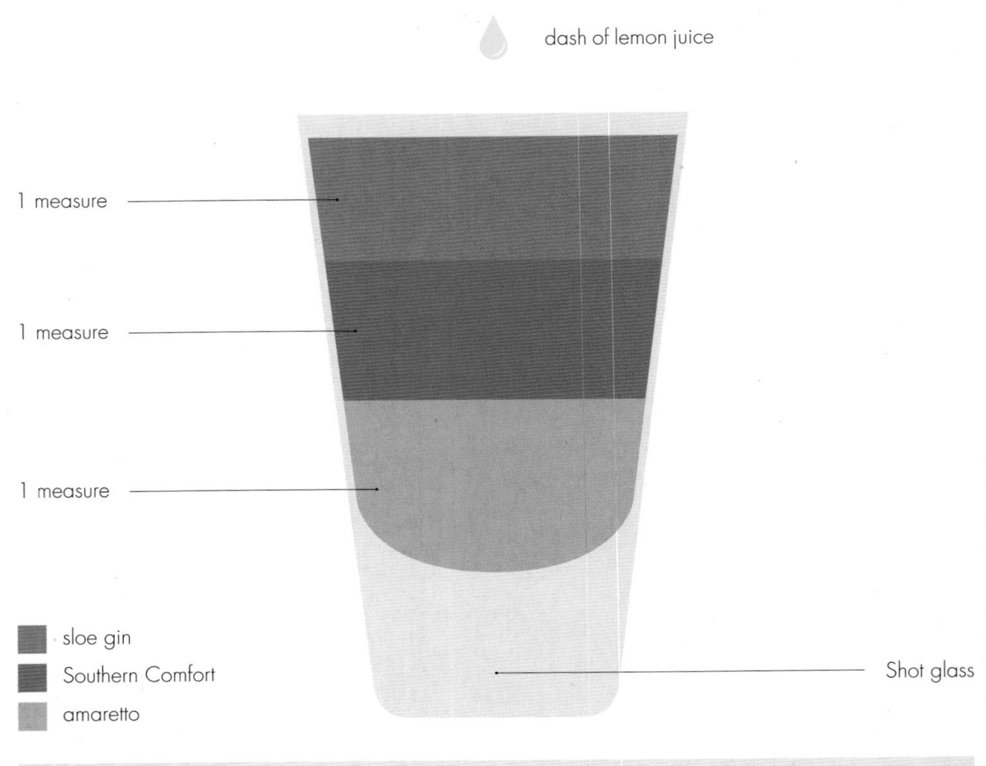

dash of lemon juice
1 measure
1 measure
1 measure
sloe gin
Southern Comfort
amaretto
Shot glass

Instructions

1 Stir the amaretto, Southern Comfort and gin together, then strain into a shot glass. **2** Add the lemon juice and serve.

Angel's Kiss No. 1

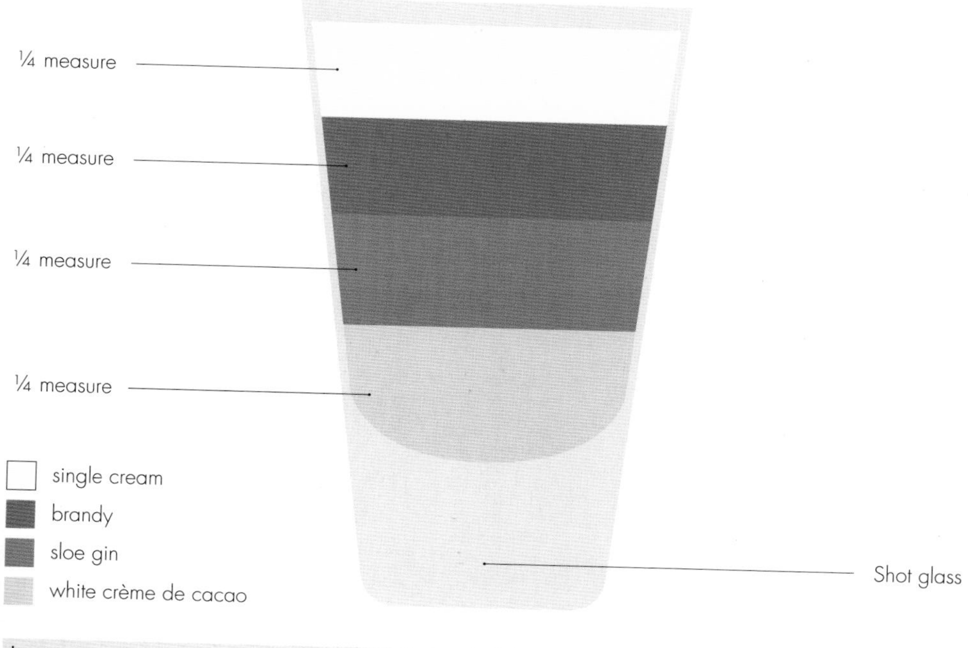
¼ measure
¼ measure
¼ measure
¼ measure
single cream
brandy
sloe gin
white crème de cacao
Shot glass

Instructions

1. In the exact order above, layer each of the ingredients in a shot glass and serve.

Angel Wing Shooter

½ measure
½ measure
½ measure
brandy
Baileys Irish Cream
crème de cacao
Shot glass

Instructions

1 In the exact order above, layer the ingredients in a liqueur glass.

B-52

⅔ measure
⅔ measure
⅔ measure
Cointreau
Baileys Irish Cream
Tia Maria
Shot glass

Instructions

1. In the exact order above, layer the ingredients in a shot glass and serve.

Black Jack Shooter

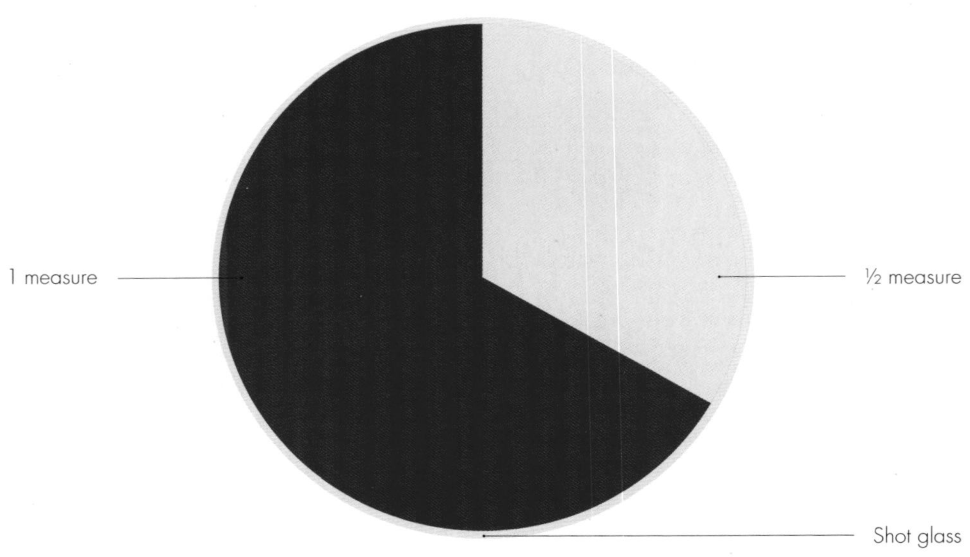
1 measure
½ measure
Shot glass

ouzo

Kahlua

Instructions

1. Layer the ingredients in a shot glass and serve.

Chastity Belt Shooter

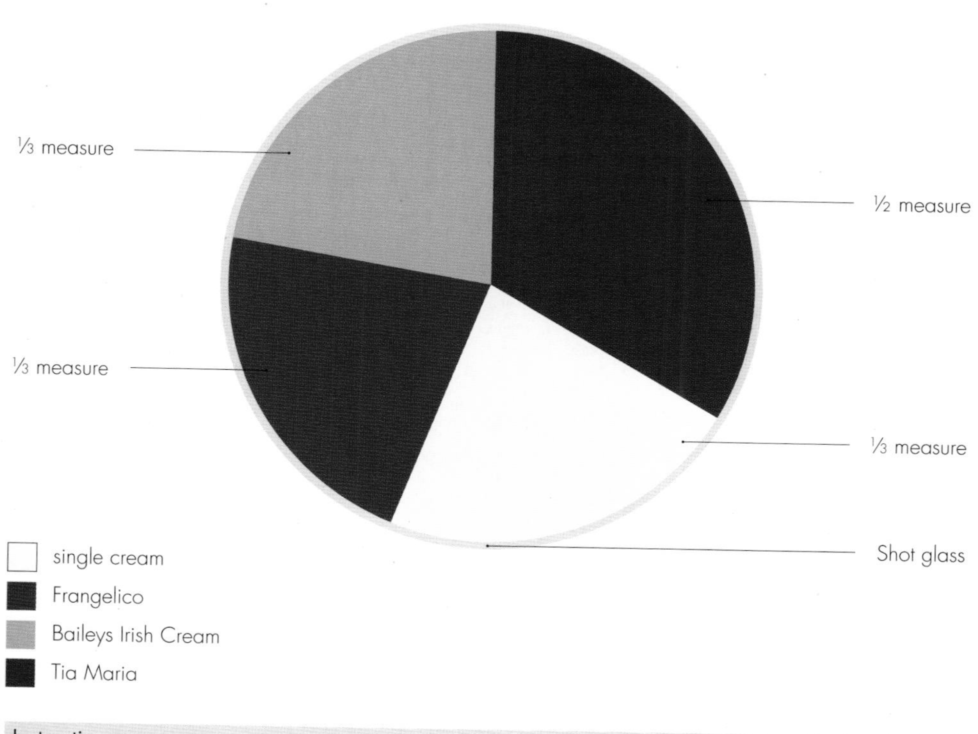
⅓ measure
½ measure
⅓ measure
⅓ measure
Shot glass
single cream
Frangelico
Baileys Irish Cream
Tia Maria

Instructions

1. In the exact order above, layer the ingredients in a shot glass and serve.

Deep Throat Shooter

½ measure
½ measure
½ measure
double cream
Grand Marnier
Kahlua
Shot glass

Instructions

1. In the exact order above, layer the ingredients in a shot glass and serve.

Sex on the Beach

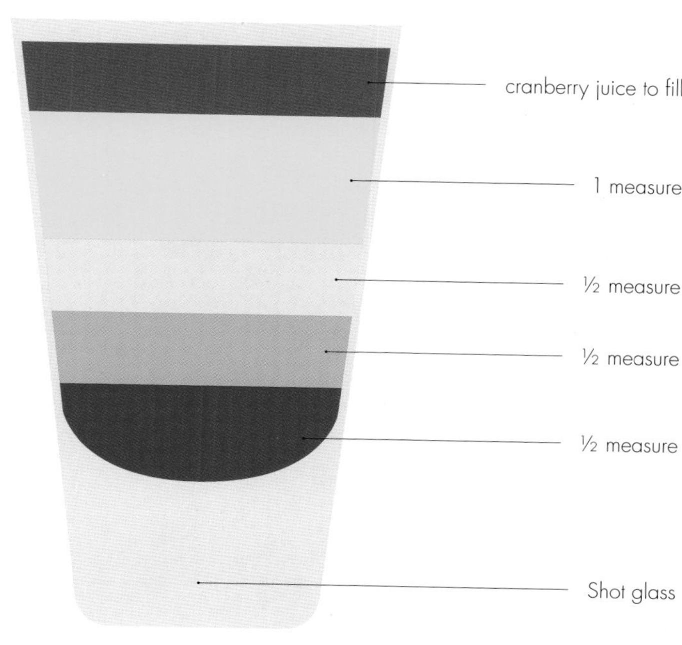

cranberry juice to fill
1 measure
½ measure
½ measure
½ measure
Shot glass

cranberry juice
pineapple juice
vodka
Midori
Chambord

Instructions

1 Stir all the ingredients together, then strain into a shot glass. 2 Top up with the cranberry juice and serve.

Slippery Nipple

⅔ measure
⅔ measure
Shot glass
Baileys Irish Cream
butterscotch schnapps

Instructions

1. Pour butterscotch schnapps into a shot glass and layer the Baileys on top.

Traffic Light

1 measure
1 measure
1 measure
Midori
Galliano
crème de noix
Shot glass

Instructions

1. Layer the ingredients in the exact order above, in a shot glass, and serve.

INDEX

Index of ingredients: for full list of cocktails see A–Z at front of book.